The Paul
C

Also by Ted Montgomery

The Beatles Through Headphones: The Quirks, Peccadilloes, Nuances and Sonic Delights of the Greatest Popular Music Ever Recorded
(McFarland, 2014)

The Paul McCartney Catalog

A Complete Annotated Discography of Solo Works, 1967–2019

Ted Montgomery

McFarland & Company, Inc., Publishers
Jefferson, North Carolina

Library of Congress Cataloguing-in-Publication Data

Names: Montgomery, Ted, 1958– author.
Title: The Paul McCartney catalog : a complete annotated discography of solo works, 1967–2019 / Ted Montgomery.
Description: Jefferson : McFarland & Company, Inc., Publishers, 2020. | Includes bibliographical references and index.
Identifiers: LCCN 2020000475 | ISBN 9781476676449 (paperback : acid free paper) ♾ | ISBN 9781476638010 (ebook)
Subjects: LCSH: McCartney, Paul—Discography. | LCGFT: Discographies.
Classification: LCC ML156.7.M34 M66 2020 | DDC 782.42166092—dc23
LC record available at https://lccn.loc.gov/2020000475

British Library cataloguing data are available

ISBN (print) 978-1-4766-7644-9
ISBN (ebook) 978-1-4766-3801-0

The front cover photograph is of Paul McCartney during the Wings over America tour in 1976 (Jim Summaria)

Printed in the United States of America

McFarland & Company, Inc., Publishers
Box 611, Jefferson, North Carolina 28640
www.mcfarlandpub.com

For my brother Dan,
who understands
the music I love

Acknowledgments

Writing a book of any magnitude requires a lot of help from family and friends. Some of the help is hands-on, but most of it comes in the form of unspoken understanding and support.

I received that and more from my family, friends and colleagues. They let me hunker down when I needed to and understood what I was doing the whole way through. Listing them all here would require several pages, so I'm trusting them to know how truly grateful I am for their support.

A few people need to be recognized by name. David Alff at McFarland believed in this project from the beginning and offered valuable and forthright advice the whole way through.

Katie McMillan was always available to listen to me talk about this project and never betrayed disinterest or boredom. The ever-resourceful Kianna Mateen conducted essential research that was key to the writing of this book. The brilliant Jessica Archer put together a social media strategy to help promote the book.

Finally, thank you to my rock 'n' roll brothers: Mark Nowlin, Bob Withrow, Will Ryan, Mark Baykian, Tom Fluent, Al Shippey, Tom Tonkin and Larry Finn. Through it all, we almost always managed to end on the same chord.

V.I.L.Y.

Table of Contents

Preface

This is a book about Paul McCartney's music in the post–Beatles period. We will examine more than 50 years of studio albums, singles, EPs, live albums, compilations, selected bootlegs, bonus tracks and various aural esoterica. A critical analysis of every album and every song he recorded is included.

Also in this analysis is a discussion of the 15 radio shows (we'd call them podcasts today, of course) he created for Westwood One in 1995. The show—*Oobu Joobu*—includes outtakes and alternative takes of familiar songs. McCartney acquitted himself well as a disc jockey, even if 90 percent of the show's content was his own music.

In the chapter about bootlegs, we will only examine just a handful, like the masterful *Cold Cuts* album. We will not parse the thousands of sound check recordings grabbed off the mixing boards during his many tours. There is very little of interest in these, and much of what is available is sonically inferior and frankly difficult to listen to.

We'll discuss the three electronica/trance albums he made with Youth as The Fireman, his forays into classical music, and the two or three oddments he released that defy easy classification.

There is a brief chapter that catalogues and critiques the many videos and DVDs McCartney produced during the past 50 years. This will not include a song-by-song review, as most of the songs on these DVDs are familiar and will have been reviewed in the discussion about the album on which they originally appeared.

A bibliography and a list of suggested reading is included.

Introduction

When Paul McCartney borrowed a Studer four-track machine from EMI in late 1969 to begin recording his first album as a solo artist, he could not have known what was in store for him in the years ahead. Still holding out at least modest hope that the Beatles would get back together in the studio, he set about making his first solo album because he needed to make music. That's just how he's built.

Now, 50 years on, he's perhaps the most famous musician on the planet, certainly in part because of his longevity, but also because he is a prodigious producer of all things musical. Now in his late 70s, he's still going strong, wowing rapt audiences around the world with marathon concerts that rely heavily on some of the best pop songs ever written.

The trajectory of his career as a solo artist and with his band Wings has certainly had its dips and upsurges, something most artists experience if they are lucky enough to have long careers. There have been times when McCartney as an artist was arguably as well-respected as the band he played in during the 1960s, just as there have been periods when his music was considered feckless, boring and startlingly inconsequential. As we will see, often he came back after a musical misstep to make some of the best music of his career. The lesson: Paul McCartney can never be counted out as a significant force in the world of music. We now have ample evidence that he will remain significant until the day he dies, and beyond.

He's made some interesting choices during his career. He was the only ex–Beatle to front another band, Wings, whose commercial success rivaled the Beatles. When Wings disbanded in 1980 (the formal dissolution was announced in 1982, but for all intents and purposes the band ceased to be when McCartney returned to England after spending nine days in a Japanese jail for possession of marijuana in January of that year), he set out on another career adventure as a one-man band who eschewed the road and basically made music for his own enjoyment.

The 1980s were definitely McCartney's fallow period. Two fine albums bookended that decade (1982's *Tug of War* and 1989's *Flowers in the Dirt*), but in between he released mostly uninspired music, teamed up with contemporary superstars like Stevie Wonder and Michael Jackson to try to jump-start his creativity, made a disastrous movie based on his own script and seemed blissfully unaware that his star had fallen. More likely, he just didn't care.

The nadir came when he wrote and produced the song and animated feature *Rupert and the Frog* in May 1984. Long excoriated as an example of McCartney's sometimes quaint songwriting tastes and only casual knowledge of what his fan base craved, *Rupert and the Frog* became the standard for mocking McCartney as a less-than-serious artist. Mick Jagger would never have done such a thing, right?

The fault lies with us. The bar of expectations for classic rock 'n' roll emanating from McCartney's creative reservoir was long ago set unattainably high. How could anyone expect McCartney to turn out "Hey Jude" or "Eleanor Rigby" every time he sat down at a piano? The truth is, McCartney wrote songs like this because he could, it interested him as an artist and, like most great artists throughout history, he wasn't always striving for mass appeal. And truth to tell, the *Rupert and the Frog* animated short is charming and clearly meant to appeal to children. Which it did.

It wasn't until he went back on the road in 1989 that he began to recapture some of the brio and energy he seemed to have lacked in that decade. Emboldened by the response and enthusiasm of concertgoers (venues routinely sold out in record time), he made an important decision that recalibrated his popularity: What if he added several Beatles songs to his set list?

He did just that, after mostly ignoring his 1960s catalogue during his 1970s tours. He discovered that his older generation of fans wanted to hear Beatles songs performed by an ex–Beatle and, more importantly, he also discovered that young fans—fans who were not alive during the 1960s but were exposed to the music by their parents—came out in droves to hear his music. Since 1989, McCartney has toured frequently and peppered his set lists with a large sampling of Beatles songs (even including some that were primarily sung by John Lennon).

He also had a habit of sometimes returning from personal or career setbacks by recording rock 'n' roll chestnuts, as if to rejuvenate by reminding himself that the core love of his life—classic rock 'n' roll—would always be there for him. As we'll see, he did this three times in his solo career, and each time he came back from the experience stronger and more self-assured.

Along the way, he has collaborated with rock 'n' roll influences (the Everly Brothers and Carl Perkins) and new pop idols (Kanye West, Dave Grohl and Rihanna). He's dabbled in poetry and painting, publishing, children's music, film, animation, electronica, jazz standards, classical music and even produced a purposefully and delightfully cheesy orchestral rendering of his *Ram* album.

Paul McCartney long ago stopped expecting hit records. The music business has changed so drastically that albums don't really sell as full units anymore. People get their music now by downloading songs and by creating playlists through streaming services like Spotify and Pandora. The days of rushing out and buying your favorite artist's newest album are long gone, and likely won't ever return.

Still, McCartney remains a force in music, and not just because of his sterling catalogue.

He can still rock when he wants to, and most of his albums contain deep cuts that are clearly songwriting descendants of "I'm Down" and "Helter Skelter." It's just that you'll never hear them unless you buy the album.

Obviously, Paul McCartney has nothing left to prove. As a songwriter, singer, instrumentalist and performer, he was enshrined long ago in the pantheon of great artists of the 20th and 21st centuries. And if along that journey he wrote more than his share of silly love songs, well, what's wrong with that?

Free as a Bird

While the Beatles successfully traded on their overall theme of love and peace, Paul McCartney as a solo artist seems to continually return to themes of freedom; freedom from oppression, authority, boredom, broken hearts and threats to the general well-being of humankind. His 1991 song "Freedom" gets right down to business with the theme in very few words. Although it's not a great song, it's a neat encapsulation of McCartney's belief that freedom is a birthright and not a privilege.

His early music explores this theme frequently ("Man We Was Lonely," "Back Seat of My Car," "Tomorrow" and "Country Dreamer," among others) and *Band on the Run* is an album specifically about freedom (the title track, "Bluebird" and "Helen Wheels"). *Tug of War, Pipes of Peace, Flowers in the Dirt, Flaming Pie* and *Driving Rain* all reference the value of freedom.

He also uses animals and other creatures often in his songs, especially birds (wrens, bluebirds, magpies, crows, pigeons, songbirds, swans, nightingales). Little wonder he settled on the name Wings for his band. Then there are lambs, rams, dragonflies, horse, sheep, dogs, cats, armadillos, squid, alligators, mice, frogs, salamanders, bears (polar and koala), moose, rabbits, geese and practically every other species gets a shout-out in McCartney's songs.

He will also occasionally use nautical themes as metaphors for love and strife. "Uncle Albert/Admiral Halsey," "Wanderlust," "Morse Moose and the Grey Goose," "Heaven on a Sunday" and "Despite Repeated Warnings," among others, come to mind.

The Bands

Following is a list of McCartney's recording and touring bands. This does not include sessions players who helped on albums or a set of players who recorded with McCartney on a single album but never toured with him.

Wings (1971): Paul McCartney, Linda McCartney, Denny Laine, Denny Seiwell.

Wings (1972–73): Paul McCartney, Linda McCartney, Denny Laine, Denny Seiwell, Henry McCullough.

Wings (1973): Paul McCartney, Linda McCartney, Denny Laine.

Wings (1974): Paul McCartney, Linda McCartney, Denny Laine, Jimmy McCulloch, Geoff Britton.

Wings (1975–77): Paul McCartney, Linda McCartney, Denny Laine, Jimmy McCulloch, Joe English.

Wings (1977–78): Paul McCartney, Linda McCartney, Denny Laine.

Wings (1978–81): Paul McCartney, Linda McCartney, Denny Laine, Laurence Juber, Steve Holly.

1989–90: Paul McCartney, Linda McCartney, Hamish Stuart, Paul Wickens, Robbie McIntosh, Chris Whitten.

1991–93: Paul McCartney, Linda McCartney, Hamish Stuart, Paul Wickens, Robbie McIntosh, Blair Cunningham.

2001–present: Paul McCartney, Paul Wickens, Rusty Anderson, Brian Ray, Abe Laboriel, Jr.

How to Use This Book

The first two chapters will examine the studio albums and singles. A track listing will proceed the discussion, along with the release date (sometimes—but not always—U.S. and U.K. release dates differ), label, catalogue number, highest chart position attained and producer. For highest chart position, we used the U.K. album and singles charts, and the U.S. Billboard album chart and Hot 100 singles charts. For the albums, there will also be a listing of the musicians who contributed.

Each song will be discussed and examined for its artistic value and general listenability.

Please note that these are the opinions of the author and I expect all readers to have widely divergent opinions of each song. That's what will make this discussion so invigorating.

The albums chapter will also include a section at the end of each entry that discusses bonus tracks added in 1993 to reissued versions of the original album. This is a common practice in the recording industry, and in many (but not all) cases brings added value to the albums.

In 1993, long before the idea of elaborately annotated and carefully curated "deluxe" and "super deluxe" reissues took hold, McCartney's recorded catalogue was re-released as *The Paul McCartney Collection. The Collection* was released on CD and cassette and was rolled out over two separate release dates. In most cases the re-releases featured bonus tracks. The release was loosely tied to McCartney and band's New World Tour.

The bonus tracks do not always align perfectly with the sessions that produced the album on which they appear. An example of this incongruity is "Sally G," the B-side of the "Junior's Farm" single released in October 1974. "Sally G" was recorded in Nashville at the beginning of the sessions for *Venus and Mars,* so that is the album the track belongs on. In *The Paul McCartney Collection,* "Sally G" shows up on *Wings at the Speed of Sound,* recorded and released more than a year later. Most of these inconsistencies have been corrected in *The Paul McCartney Archive Collection* project, which began in 2010. The ongoing *Paul McCartney Archive Collection* includes extensive collections of text, photographs, DVDs, information about the official release of the albums, and additional bonus tracks and outtakes. These will be reviewed in the entries of albums that have so far received the archival treatment.

Unless otherwise noted, every McCartney album from 1970 through 1982 was released on vinyl, cassette and 8-track tape. Manufacturers for the most part quit producing 8-tracks in 1982, although the last one appeared on the shelves as late as 1986. Later on, of course, singles also were released in cassette and CD versions. Now the trend is to release singles through streaming services like iTunes and Spotify, among others. This is partly because fewer people buy CDs, but also because it's more immediate and convenient. Most computer companies have quit including CD slots in their laptops and desktops, so it's easy to foresee the day when CDs go the way of the 8-track tape. It's already happening, in fact.

For the section about the live albums we'll list the aforementioned details but discuss only in general terms the musical merits of the work as a whole, rather than pick it apart song-by-song. Other chapters will look briefly at popular bootlegs (although bootlegs are less relevant in these days of emptying out the vaults for deluxe box sets); examine McCartney's syndicated radio program *Oobu Joobu,* a proto-podcast that was popular but short-lived; and provide a brief review of the numerous videos and DVDs. Appendices will examine one-off taped live performances, collaborations with other artists, and several other oddments that defy easy categorization. A bibliography and list of suggested readings also is included.

A Brief History of Wings

Two traumatic events bookended the 1970s for Paul McCartney. First, the Beatles officially disbanded in April 1970, an event that he spent decades processing and trying to make sense of. Then, 10 years later, he spent nine days in a Tokyo jail for smuggling marijuana into Japan in January 1980.

In each case, it would take him two years to get back on track, professionally and personally. The progress in 1980, of course, was halted by the death of John Lennon in December, officially making 1980 one of the worst years in McCartney's life.

The Japan bust also unofficially brought an end to Wings, one of the most commercially successful bands of the 1970s. That McCartney could leave the Beatles and two years later form another band that would become almost as successful (and would last one year longer than the Beatles) is an accomplishment almost unprecedented in rock 'n' roll history.

He started tentatively, jamming with his friend Denny Laine and inviting Denny Seiwell to sit in on drums. After giving Linda a quick tutorial on playing the piano, the quintet jammed for weeks at the McCartneys' Scottish farm, subsisting mostly on scotch, cigarettes and whatever quick English fry-up Linda could muster.

Once they went into the studio to record Wings' debut album—*Wings Wild Life*—they were a tight unit musically. Unfortunately, they didn't yet have a backlog of good songs and instead recorded mostly jams made up in the studio, and a couple of long and plodding ballads.

The hits would come later.

Once they added Henry McCullough to toughen up the sound Wings started to take off.

Buoyed by the smash hit "My Love" and the relative success of the album from whence it came—*Red Rose Speedway*—the band was finding its groove. McCullough and Laine were paired nicely as guitarists. Listen to "One More Kiss" and "The Mess" to see how well they complemented each other.

As far as touring went, they started out small, stopping in at 11 English universities to play at student unions, with virtually no notice at all (and, importantly, no time to publicize the concerts) in early 1972. This ramshackle tour was marred by an abject lack of stage-ready material, and by the growing pains of the band's rookie keyboard player.

Later in in 1972, they played smallish venues throughout Europe and honed their chops in front of rapt audiences who couldn't quite figure out who the other guys in the band were. In 1973, they set out on a tour of the U.K., with more nimble material and presentable stagecraft rough-hewn from nightly repetition.

Seiwell and McCullough were the first of many members of Wings to become disgruntled slowly over time. Most of their dissatisfaction resulted from issues related to compensation. There were no contracts in the band, and only the McCartneys owned the publishing to the songs (Laine obviously got a piece of the action as an occasional co-writer, and even more rarely as the sole songwriter of a handful of songs).

McCartney, sitting on what he considered a gold mine of hit songs, arranged a trip for the band to record at EMI studios in Lagos, Nigeria. Just before the band's departure, Seiwell and McCullough phoned McCartney to tell him they wouldn't be accompanying the band to Lagos.

Left with no choice but to soldier on, the McCartneys and Laine went to Nigeria and recorded their masterpiece album, *Band on the Run.*

Seiwell and McCullough were almost assuredly upset about the finances in the band. The standard tale told a million times over the years is that they both phoned McCartney to quit the band. But there is another equally plausible explanation. Perhaps neither one phoned McCartney to quit Wings; they just didn't want to go to Lagos, for a variety of reasons. They recognized that over time they could make a lot of money in a band with Paul McCartney and probably did not want to jeopardize their financial futures by resigning outright. In this scenario, McCartney would have had no choice but to turf them.

Next, Geoff Britton joined as the new drummer and Jimmy McCulloch as the new lead guitarist. Off to Nashville they went to record and jam and prepare for the next album, *Venus and Mars*. However, it became quickly apparent the two new recruits couldn't get along, so Britton was given his walking papers. Enter Joe English as the new Wings drummer.

This was the most talented and successful configuration of Wings. They embarked on a 66-date world tour that culminated in America in 1976, where McCartney captivated crowds with his charm and on-stage presence for the first time on U.S. soil since 1966. The triple live album *Wings Over America* is a great chronicle of the massively successful U.S. tour.

By 1977, when the band was putting the touches on the *London Town* album, both McCulloch and English quit. The official story had McCulloch wanting to join the reformed Small Faces (he did, briefly), and English missing his American homeland (he moved back to the States for good). But the question remained: Why couldn't McCartney keep a band together for long? The short answer: The musicians he employed either wanted a bigger slice of the pie, or more say in musical matters facing the band, or both. (Later on, McCartney would reach out to Seiwell and McCullough by sending healthy checks their way on the occasion of the release of *Wingspan.*)

In fact, leaving Wings rarely led to better things for its former members. Seiwell, Britton and English had relatively obscure musical careers after their days in Wings. Sadly, Jimmy McCulloch (1979) and Henry McCullough (2016) passed away.

Next, McCartney called on Laurence Juber (guitar) and Steve Holly (drums) to join what would become the last incarnation of Wings. They recorded *Back to the Egg* and toured the U.K. in late 1979, without much distinction. McCartney was not happy with the band's live performances and looked to the January 1980 tour of Japan with some trepidation. When the bust was made and the tour canceled, Wings were no more, at least unofficially.

Ironically, Juber and Holly were thrilled to join Wings and were the only members besides Denny Laine to never have quit the band. Instead, McCartney quit them. Bored, tired of touring and feeling musically unchallenged, he let Wings lay fallow until it became apparent the band was no more. McCartney would spend the next 10 years off the road, holed up in the studio.

In the end, Wings amassed a tremendous record of commercial success. All nine albums released by Wings topped the charts in either the U.S. or the U.K. At one time, five consecutive Wings albums made it to the top spot in the U.S. charts. The band released 23 singles and all of them reached the U.S. top 40 (six made it to No. 1). They were easily one of the most successful bands of the 1970s.

Moreover, it seemed like they were having a lot of fun. Exploratory trips to Morocco and Nashville, recording in Lagos and New Orleans, star-studded album wrap parties on yachts in Los Angeles, recording on a boat in the Virgin Islands. It all seemed very high-spirited. Then add the experience of a world tour from 1975–76, especially the American leg of the tour, and one can see that Wings were privy to the full rock 'n' roll star treatment. The miles of film taken of the band at work and at play suggests the good times far outweighed the bad.

The hidden beauty of the band's output was often overshadowed by the singles that were released. In the 1970s, radio listeners were mostly at the whim of the artist (sometimes the record label), who chose the singles to be released. McCartney knows what makes a record a hit, and most of his choices for singles bore out his hunches. You know *Wings at the Speed of Sound* mainly because of its two smash hits, "Silly Love Songs" and "Let 'Em In," but dig deeper into that album and you'll find "Beware My Love" and "Warm and Beautiful," two seriously well-constructed and recorded songs. You know *Venus and Mars* mostly from its sun-drenched hit single "Listen to What the Man Said," but check out the other tracks. "Love in Song" and "Letting Go" are standouts that still sound fresh today. And on and on.

Paul McCartney left the most famous band in the world and soon put together a rag-tag assemblage of mostly unknown but competent players in the hopes of catching lightning in a bottle once again. It worked. Paul McCartney and Wings helped define the sound of 1970s pop music and remain popular to this day.

The Albums

Studio

McCartney

Released April 17, 1970
Apple Records PCS 7102 (U.K.); 4XT-3363 (U.S.)
Highest chart position: 2 in the U.K. and 1 in the U.S.
Producer: Paul McCartney
Musicians: Paul McCartney: drums, bass, keyboards, guitars, percussion, lead and backing vocals, glasses, xylophone; Linda McCartney: backing vocals and TLC

McCartney was released to an almost unanimous chorus of disapproval; from fans, the rock press and even McCartney's former bandmates.

It's easy to see why. Released just one week after the formal announcement that the Beatles had broken up, the album is a mishmash of unrealized ideas and weird fragments of song. It's almost as if McCartney was going through the pants pockets in his laundry hamper for scraps of paper on which he had written song ideas.

He was largely regarded as the moving force being the Beatles break-up (although John Lennon went first in announcing his plans to leave the band), and the fans seemed to have expected another *Sgt. Pepper* or *Abbey Road* from him. Add to this the fact that Macca included in the press copies of the album a "self-interview" that took broad sideswipes at his former bandmates, among other sins.

Recorded mostly at home and mostly during 1969 when the Beatles were still together in name, with finishing touches added in three London studios (including Abbey Road), the album is imbued with an aura of domestic bliss, complete with sounds of slamming doors and giggling children. The fact that it is so low-fi and elemental seems to have infuriated many people whose expectations of McCartney were set very high. How could the man who co-authored the music's most revered catalogue of pop songs have exerted so little effort?

The fact is, *McCartney* has aged better than pretty much every other album he's made. Its charm is directly related to its simplicity. Since that time, of course, rock 'n' roll artists from Prince to Pete Townsend to Bruce Springsteen have made albums with a four-track machine in their living rooms. It's become *au courant* to make an album completely by oneself. McCartney pioneered this mode of recording, at least among rock 'n' rollers.

The album includes three really fine songs, a few clumsy instrumentals, and some made-up-on-the-spot ditties. It also features some really ham-fisted drumming. McCartney's drumming would improve significantly as the years went by (listen to *Band on the Run* for evidence).

The *Paul McCartney Collection* version was released on June 7, 1993 (Parlophone, 7 89239 2), with no bonus tracks. The archival package released in 2012 includes the original album remastered, seven bonus tracks, a DVD with videos of a few of the songs and a massive book of candid photos taken by Linda, Paul and photographer Donald Milne around the time of the making of *McCartney*. As with all McCartney archival packages, this one includes an interview with McCartney about the making of the album. This also includes the entire "self-interview." That alone is worth the price of this package.

The Lovely Linda: Reportedly used to test the equipment, this is 42 seconds of testament to the value and comfort of a stable marriage. Acoustic guitar, percussion and bass make up the basic track. Listen for the knowing laugh McCartney delivers as the song ends.

That Would Be Something: A bluesy workout based on a simple repetitive guitar riff. Not a lot of depth here lyrically. Lots of idiosyncratic percussion that gets augmented on every verse. McCartney's vocals are typically well-recorded. Like several songs on this album, there is a bit of a false ending.

Valentine Day: An instrumental with elemental drumming, bass, acoustic guitar, and electric guitars. It sounds like McCartney was having fun playing the electric guitar after years of principally serving as bass player in the Beatles. The song fades out with a time change.

Every Night: A seriously well-constructed song with lots of interesting acoustic guitar parts, urgent bass and a typically hummable melody. Opening with an E7 chord, followed by several chords around A, F#, F#m and Bm7, it finally resolves on the major E chord. He's even holding his own on the drums. The wordless chorus is especially memorable. This could have easily fit in on *The White Album*. It's a better version of "I Will."

Hot as Sun/Glasses: A jaunty instrumental with lots of maracas and an acoustic guitar part reminiscent of "Flying" off *Magical Mystery Tour*. Wings included this in their set list on their ill-fated 1979 British tour. As the main part of the song fades out, you can hear Mr. and Mrs. McCartney rubbing the rims of drinking glasses with varying amounts of liquid in them, to creepy effect. Then comes a few seconds of a song called "Suicide" that McCartney reportedly tried to gift to Frank Sinatra. Frank wasn't buying.

Junk: Such a sad sounding melody sung with a tone resigned to a life of loneliness. McCartney uses junk as a metaphor for "all the lonely people." The acoustic guitar is typical of his playing in this period. Finger-picked two-note chord figures with accompanying fret noise. Think "Blackbird" or "Mother Nature's Son."

Man We Was Lonely: This song offers the first hint that Linda is going to be a big part of her husband's recording output. The chorus features both singing together in a commiserative style. This is the first of McCartney's songs to have a country-and-western feel to it. Great opening and coda, with echo-y acoustic guitars.

Oo You: A nice funky guitar riff opens the song, with the artist (apparently directing himself) saying "mo' guitar." The electric guitar and the bass play the same riff. McCartney sings most of the nonsense lyrics at the top of his register. The drumming—including cowbell—is passable but hardly the work of a seasoned drummer.

Momma Miss America: The track is introduced by McCartney, in his best Monty Python voice, saying "rock and roll springtime—take one." Another instrumental, this time with piano and electric guitars with a weird shimmery effect applied. There is no discernible melody to this song, just chords pounded out over and over again. Then the original song stops abruptly, and a 12-bar workout begins with lots of lead guitar by the album's sole musician. Garage band jamming at best.

Teddy Boy: One of the few instances on this album of McCartney's vocal being double-tracked. Linda contributes some rambling oohs and aahs to the chorus. This is a strangely oedipal story line for a McCartney song, based on the premise of the title character not wanting to let his mom live her life. This song was originally slated to be included on *Let It Be*, until Lennon intentionally sabotaged it during a run-through. It's probably a good thing that it didn't make the cut.

Singalong Junk: An instrumental version of "Junk" that maintains the melancholic air of the original. This time, the acoustic guitars are doubled and a piano plays the haunting melody. During the last verse there is an annoying crash cymbal that invades the proceedings, along with a much too loud organ part. A tasteful electric guitar part augments the second half of the song. This is exactly 40 seconds longer than "Junk."

Maybe I'm Amazed: "Maybe I'm Amazed" is one McCartney's best five songs as a solo artist and is a very mature and interesting one at that. A complicated chord sequence underlays this beautiful paean to his wife. Over a strident piano part, he layered two electric guitars, organ, drums and bass. Add to the mix a vocal that is urgent and compelling, and it's not a surprise that this song was released as a single from the live *Wings Over America* triple album seven years later. Since then, it's been a staple and a highlight of McCartney's live shows.

Kreen-Akrore: McCartney has said that he recorded this track as a result of having seen a TV special on the Kreen-Akrore Indians of Brazil. This is a boring drum-dominated track, replete with heavy breathing meant to suggest that the pedestrian drumming was somehow a labor-intensive cardio workout. Unfortunately, this throwaway track is the longest on the album.

Bonus Tracks

These songs appear on the archival release from 2012 (Hear Music, HRM-32799-00).

Suicide: The full-length version of the snippet heard at the end of "Hot as Sun/Glasses," it's a clearly unfinished pastiche of meandering piano chords.

Maybe I'm Amazed: This was originally slated to appear in the film *One Hand Clapping*, made by McCartney and Wings in 1974. This version of the best song on *McCartney* features an electric piano in place of the acoustic piano used on the original version. McCartney's vocal is awash with reverb, an effect he doesn't use much on his vocal tracks. Lead guitar is played by the late Jimmy McCulloch, with Denny Laine on guitar and

Geoff Britton on drums. A few instances of screaming and general vocal histrionics close the song.

Every Night: This is a live version from Wings' 1979 British tour, featuring the last ever incarnation of that band. The main difference from the original is the inclusion of an electric guitar part (and solo) and a major slowing of the tempo.

Hot as Sun: A live version, sans "Glasses," recorded during the same 1979 tour. It's much longer than the album track and is played at a much quicker tempo. It's sounds a bit like "My Carnival," one of the bonus tracks from *Venus and Mars*. It's a really odd choice for inclusion in a live set and might even have something to do with the fact that McCartney was growing tired of carrying Wings on his back.

Maybe I'm Amazed: Also from the 1979 Wings tour. Further evidence exists here that Macca's head just wasn't fully in the game. He goes right into the second verse after the first chorus, completely bypassing the electric guitar solo and surprising his bandmates. Then, later in the song (after the second chorus) he calls for the guitar solo by saying "all right, Ivor." Guess we'll never know who Ivor is. And then, to further mash up the song's original construction, he calls for the second guitar solo after the third chorus, which is marred by some unfortunate feedback. This version is pretty messy, although it features impeccable blue-eyed soul singing from McCartney.

Don't Cry Baby/Oo You: McCartney is heard reassuring his baby daughter: "Don't cry little baby, don't cry. Daddy's going to play you a lullaby." Then, after a count-in, an instrumental version of "Oo You" commences. It's identical to the basic track on the album, except for a few extra electric guitar licks.

Woman Kind: A tongue-in-cheek ditty about the repression of women ("from the age of ten, they are chased by men") with an embarrassing exhortation to "burn your bra" included. It's clear that this was never a serious contender as a song. After he concludes the song with a series of flatulent sounding Bronx cheers, he says, "Thank you, Hank."

Ram

Released May 17, 1971 (U.S.); May 21, 1971 (U.K.)
Apple Records TC-PAS 10003 (U.K.); 4XW 3375 (U.S.)
Highest chart position: 2 in the U.S. and 1 in the U.K.

Produced by Paul and Linda McCartney

Musicians Paul McCartney: bass guitar, electric and acoustic guitars, piano, lead and backing vocals; Linda McCartney: backing vocals; Dave Spinozza: guitars; Hugh McCracken: guitars; Denny Seiwell: drums

Much like its predecessor, *Ram* was not received favorably among rock critics and former Beatles (especially Lennon, who took offense at some of the lyrics he thought were directed at him). However, the fans liked it a lot, which makes sense: Of all of McCartney's solo albums, *Ram* sounds most like the Beatles.

Recorded in New York and Los Angeles, this album was not the homemade one-man affair that *McCartney* was. The songs were more completely developed, and he employed two great session guitarists—Dave Spinozza and Hugh McCracken—plus future Wings drummer Denny Seiwell. As a result, the songs had a harder edge and seemed hookier and more steeped in the pop idiom of the day.

Although the album was recorded in the United States, many of the photos in the album packaging showed Paul and Linda on their farm in Scotland, enjoying domesticity among the sheep, dogs and kittens that roamed the homestead freely. But *Ram* does not have the homespun feel of its predecessor. Rather, it seems to be an attempt by McCartney to recapture some of the mainstream approval he squandered with the release of *McCartney*.

It also is apparent that Linda would play a pivotal role in his recording career. Here, she is heard on nearly every track, developing and honing the signature harmonies that would become such a big part of the Wings sound.

The album includes a handful of sinewy rockers, a couple of ballads, and a surprise hit that patches together three song fragments to form a cohesive whole. There is greater production, including horns and strings in places. It's also notable for how up-front McCartney's vocals are in the mix. They are brought to the fore on *Ram* as if to make a statement that he had something to say musically.

The *Paul McCartney Collection* version was released on June 7, 1993 (Parlophone 7 89139 2) with bonus tracks: "Another Day" and "Oh Woman, Oh Why." The 2012 remastered archival release features the original album in mono and stereo, eight bonus tracks, two digital download bonus tracks, the original *Thrillington* album (the orchestral version of *Ram* that will be discussed later in the book), a DVD of promo videos and a short "making of" video, plus the usual passel of candid photos and an interview with the artist.

Too Many People: A beautiful and tough rocker, with biting lyrics that John Lennon took to be a slap at him (not to mention his wife, Yoko Ono). The song opens with a plaintive acoustic guitar and some understated horns that accompany McCartney saying "piss off cake" in a voice heavily treated with echo. The guitar solo is typical of the quality performances by all the musicians on *Ram*. Lots of cowbell, acoustic guitars and whooping and hollering by McCartney.

3 Legs: A bluesy workout centered around an acoustic guitar, percussion, a galloping bass part, several electric guitars and a call-and-answer vocal that gives it an edge. McCartney's vocals during the chorus sound eerily like Lennon. The song morphs into a jazz-blues inflected lilt for the last verse. Throughout the song, McCartney interjects a handful of grunts and other vocal sounds.

Ram On: Over an intro with acoustic and electric pianos plus ukulele and finger snaps, "Ram On" is introduced by a sweet-sounding vocal and the swell of backing vocals all provided by Paul and Linda. All three verses have the same lyrics, but each adds vocal and instrumental flourishes. The backing vocals are a harbinger to the distinctive and signature sound that Wings would employ on their records. The song ends with Paul whistling the melody.

Dear Boy: This song features layered backing vocals that almost overwhelm the lead vocal. Built around a simple piano part and soaring vocals, the song was taken as another admonishment of Lennon, but it is in fact a song about Linda's first husband and how lucky her second husband was to have her as his own.

Uncle Albert/Admiral Halsey: This amalgam of several song fragments opens with a soft sounding vocal over a gently strummed acoustic guitar. Then, the sound of rain and thunder, plus strings takes it up a notch. Over a repeating two-chord progression McCartney mouths the sound of a phone being dialed before the listener is privy to the phone conversation, in which the singer apologizes to Uncle Albert for something or other. Then the song changes direction completely. Over horns and a stridently pounded piano, which introduces the "Admiral Halsey" portion of the song, the song turns into a mélange of changing time signatures and vocal sound effects. The song was a hit in America and could be heard on car radios across the country during the summer of 1971. It fades into the beginning of the next track.

Smile Away: This is a fine rocker based around a very simple chord sequence, with curiously odd lyrics. The addition of Spinozza and McCracken really toughened up the songs, and this is a prime example. McCartney's voice sounds like Elvis Presley. At one point, the singer asks the band to "smile away quietly now" and then asks them to bring it up again by imploring them to "smile away horribly now." Like many of the tracks on *Ram*, McCartney again makes a lot of weird vocal sounds during this song, especially at the fade-out where he glides into his falsetto to give the song some uplift.

Heart of the Country: This fine chunk of bluesy pseudo-country pop is distinguished by the walking pass part and McCartney's scat singing over his acoustic guitar picking. Again, the vocal is way out front in the mix. The instrumentation on this track is simple; acoustic guitar, bass, percussion and one electric guitar.

Monkberry Moon Delight: A singular song in McCartney's catalogue. He uses an affected vocal style to blast out the nonsense lyrics, with Linda doing the call-and-answer vocal. It's written in a story-telling style, but it's impossible to ascertain what it's about. Every last word in each of the verses is sung using a purposefully strangled vocal affectation. Then, during the elongated fade-out, he switches between falsetto and an echo-y vocal in his normal register. A second McCartney vocal scats throughout. A great listen, if only for the idiosyncratic singing.

Eat at Home: A fun little rocker with lots of guitar (both acoustic and electric) and harmonies from Linda. This is another example of domestic-rock, for lack of a better term. The guitar solos are ragged and unimaginative, but the tune salvages the song.

Long Haired Lady: Like on *McCartney*, the weakest track on the album is also the longest. Linda's vocal has a snooty air to it, even though the song seems to be about her, of course. Like many of the songs on this album, there are several time signature variations. The long fade-out is faintly reminiscent of "Hey Jude" and serves as a quirky diversion from the original melody.

Ram On: "Ram On" gets the reprise treatment. This version clocks in at under a minute and features a snippet of what would become "Big Barn Bed" two albums later. This is just a continuation of the original version, welded together from the fade out of the original to the fade in of this one.

Back Seat of My Car: Arguably the finest song on the album, this has so much going on in it. Reportedly written during *The White Album* sessions, it never got the full treatment. McCartney wisely resurrected it as the closing track on *Ram*. It's a smooth piano ballad with a "let's run away together" sentiment. The three-chord descending progression at the end of the song—along with the elegant strings and horn charts—turns the entire song into a mini pop opera, complete with a false ending.

Bonus Tracks

These songs appear on the archival release from 2012 (Hear Music, HRM-33452-01):

Another Day: The A-side of McCartney's first single of his solo career, this was released in February 1971, three months before the release of *Ram*. It's perfectly cheery melody belies the loneliness of the narrative in the lyrics. This has all the hallmarks of early solo McCartney; a memorable melody, shifting time signatures and cascading backing vocals.

Oh Woman, Oh Why: The B-side of the first single is a simple screamer over loud, crunchy electric guitars. Very basic instrumentation, with McCartney again occasionally slipping into his falsetto.

Little Woman Love: This song, originally a 1972 single, was included as a bonus track on the 1993 reissue of *Wild Life*. It's a fast-paced little ditty based on a piano and lots of noodling way up the neck of an acoustic guitar.

A Love for You: This song has a fascinating history, having originally been recorded during the 1971 *Ram* sessions, with overdubs added to it in 1979 by Laurence Juber (guitars) and Steve Holly (drums), two members of the final incarnation of Wings. Then, McCartney himself added a couple of overdubs in 1986. The song first saw the light of day as the opening track on the bootleg *Cold Cuts* album, and then was used in the soundtrack for the 2003 film *The In-laws* starring Michael Douglas. It's a catchy rocker based on guitars (including a 12-string acoustic) and a sinuous bass line. The original version's basic tracks were speeded up, making that version sound like a completely different song in a higher key. The soundtrack version has some vocals added to the original tracks that clearly sound like circa-1980s McCartney. This song has among the longest gestation periods of any McCartney composition.

Hey Diddle: This song is built on the kind of acoustic guitar mastery that McCartney made famous in "Blackbird" and "Junk," among many other songs. The guitar is backed by percussion, a bass, a fiddle and some steel guitar, giving it a true country feel. Linda shares the vocals and a songwriting credit with her husband. The song was first laid down during the *Ram* sessions, but overdubs were added in Nashville in 1974.

Great Cock and Seagull Race: A funky little instrumental, with some roundhouse piano and a bass line reminiscent of some of the great blues players. The piano and the guitar trade solos during the 12-bar verses. Some Christmas-y sounding bells are heard during the interlude when just an electric piano is played, quickly joined by a loud electric guitar and some more percussion, until the whole thing fades out.

Rode All Night: An improvised jam with McCartney on guitar and Denny Seiwell on drums clocking in at 8:48. The made up on the spot lyrics are rendered in the same vocal style McCartney used on "Oh Woman, Oh Why."

Sunshine Sometime: This song is as mellow as anything McCartney has ever written. It has a hypnotic feel to it and a long introduction based on acoustic guitar, with a jazz-inflected electric guitar adding various figures throughout. The song was originally an instrumental, but McCartney added vocals to it later.

Digital Download Tracks

Eat at Home/Smile Away (live): These songs were performed live during Wings' 1972 European tour. This is taken from a concert in Groningen, the Netherlands. These are obvious choices as additions to the live set list, as they are rockers, but this version is marred by a badly out of tune electric guitar playing the rhythm part. McCartney's in great voice and seems to be enjoying himself, but the band sounds plodding and unable to match his enthusiasm.

Uncle Albert Jam: This is nothing more than a vigorously strummed acoustic guitar with frenetic drumming and jazzy electric guitar playing the two opening chords to "Uncle Albert/Admiral Halsey" over and over. McCartney sings a few of the lyrics over the instruments.

In May 1971 a promotional 12-inch vinyl record called *Brung to Ewe by* (Apple SPRO 6210) was delivered to select radio stations. It consists of just under 10 minutes of nonsense chat from Paul and Linda, various animal sounds (mostly bleating) and a brief ditty apparently called "Now Hear This Song of Mine," played and sung in a variety of musical styles. Ostensibly, the cuts were made to help disc jockeys introduce songs from *Ram*, but it's so disjointed and nonsensical that it would be surprising if many jocks ever used it.

Wings Wild Life

Released November 15, 1971 (UK); December 6, 1971 (U.S.)
Apple Records TC-PCS 7142 (U.K.); 4XW 3386 (U.S.)
Highest chart position: 10 in the U.S. and 11 in the U.K.
Produced by Paul and Linda McCartney
Musicians: Paul McCartney: vocals, bass, piano, guitar, keyboards, percussion; Linda McCartney: keyboards, percussion, vocals; Denny Laine: guitars, bass, percussion, keyboards, vocals; Denny Seiwell: drums, percussion

It certainly can't be said that Paul McCartney is too conservative to take chances. Instead of choosing to build on the relative commercial appeal (if not tepid critical reception) of *Ram*, he chose instead to slap a ragtag band together and record their first album quickly and without much planning. The result—*Wings Wild Life*—was roundly criticized and, in some circles, used as proof that McCartney had completely lost the magic he brought to his former band (or worse, that his former songwriting partner had carried him in the Beatles).

But in hindsight, one can see that this was a savvy career move. McCartney sought to tear down the pedestal he'd been perched atop for the past decade and return to his live rock roots. Still intact after all the scrapes and abrasions he'd suffered on that long tumble from the top of the pop hill, he recalibrated his career by starting over with a handful of competent musicians (and his wife) and jamming with little or no real new material. He knew the rebuild would take some time, and he seems to have been comfortable with that notion. Viewed through the prism of time and context, *Wings Wild Life* is not as terrible an album as the critics made it out to be.

Denny Seiwell was a holdover from the *Ram* sessions, and former Moody Blues singer/songwriter Denny Laine (singer of the Moodies' first hit, "Go Now," a seminal piece of blue-eyed soul) was brought in to round out the first Wings lineups.

Armed with almost no material, the band jammed and recorded what they came up with. *Wild Life* consists of a couple of nonsense jams, a cover version of a 1957 Mickey and Sylvia hit, and two or three very melodic but overly long piano ballads. Unlike the first two albums, there are almost no time signature variations or other arrangement intricacies on this album.

Consisting of only eight songs, the album clocks in at just under 40 minutes. The album cover features an idyllic setting: McCartney standing in a country stream strumming an acoustic guitar, with the rest of the band sitting on a tree limb stretching over the water. The scene is not unlike the cover of Lennon's first 1970 album *Plastic Ono Band.*

The liner notes were written by one Clint Harrigan, who enthused wildly about the music the band made for this album. Of course, Harrigan and McCartney were one and the same.

Wild Life did not provide a clear indication that McCartney would go on to great success in his solo career. It didn't inspire the listening public (many of whom were very inclined to like anything McCartney released at this point) when the album's best song was its sole cover tune. He was at a crossroads very early in his career after the Beatles, and *Wild Life* was a baffling move with so much at stake. But it was the right one.

Mumbo: This is nothing more than nonsense lyrics set to a driving four-piece rock workout, complete with two very loudly mixed electric guitars. The drums, bass and organ parts add a lot to the song's sonic quality, but as a fully realized musical work, it just didn't cut it.

Bip Bop: This one showed some promise during the guitar intro, which had a certain discordant funkiness to it. When McCartney starts to sing, it's clear immediately that he still doesn't have a thing to say lyrically. The lyrics repeat themselves, and with McCartney's voice immersed in a sonic stew of echo and delay, it makes the absurd lyrics even more annoying. Also, like almost every other song on the album, it goes on way too long and still doesn't make a cogent point.

Love Is Strange: This song was written by the R&B duo Mickey Baker and Sylvia Vanderpool, and the unknown songwriter Ethel Smith, who was at the time the wife of Bo Diddley. There is a long-standing historical disagreement between Mickey and Sylvia, and Bo Diddley, about who wrote the song. It charted in 1956. In McCartney's hands it turned into a reggae-inflected, rhythm heavy pop lark. The band sounds good and McCartney's vocal shines throughout. This is arguably the best song on the entire album.

Wild Life: McCartney gets political here for the first time. Over three chords, the song blathers on for 6:40 over the singer's premise that a walk through an African park exposed political corruption that threatened wildlife—including mankind—everywhere. Again, this seems like McCartney putting his new band through an improvised jam to see what kind of chops the players had. And that's okay. But this is the first instance of many to come in which McCartney released music simply because he took the time to commit it to tape. One interesting thing about this song are the backing vocals, which showed great promise as a solid feature of Wings music to come.

Some People Never Know: Seemingly a paean to the domestic bliss he had found with Linda, this song can also be taken as a slap to those who don't share their bliss in exactly the same way. Over tasteful acoustic guitar, piano, bass and drums, a simple but elegant melody endures throughout its 6:37 time. There are touches of organ and electric guitar here and there in the mix, plus the ubiquitous backing vocals. Unfortunately, the song suffers from an overly repetitive mix of verse and middle eight alternating throughout. It fades out with wildly panned bongos taking over.

I Am Your Singer: This is the only time on record where Linda and Paul McCartney trade lines and have what could accurately be termed a duet. Lots of tremolo on the electric guitar and an interesting flute solo add to the overall cheery sound.

Bip Bop Link: Fifty-two seconds of the "Bip Bop" linked played on a heavily phased acoustic guitar. It's faster and more complicated than the song it echoes.

Tomorrow: Easily the most commercial song on the album, this could have been a hit if McCartney had decided to release it as a single. It's got a lot of the old Beatles sensibilities: Two verses, followed by a middle eight, another verse, another middle eight, and then the final verse, stretched out. The simple instrumental lineup includes piano, bass, drums and electric guitar, with McCartney singing over the basic track using his highest register. This is the only song on the album in which there is a time signature variation, mostly at the frenetic and emphatic coda.

Dear Friend: The song with the finest and most haunting melody on the album plods along at a snail's pace and clocks in at six minutes even. Again, we find the singer toiling at the top of his vocal register, singing a musical letter to a friend who can only be assumed to be John Lennon.

But as with so many of this album's tunes, it goes on way too long and there is no variation in the melody. The only flourishes are some Mellotron and horns added to the instrumental verses. He also repeats the same two verses over and over. This song would have been much better served by being pared down to half its elapsed time.

Mumbo Link: Forty-seven seconds of loud guitar and bass, with drums, reprising the album's opening track.

Bonus Tracks

"Oh Woman, Oh Why" and "Little Woman Love" were added to *Wings Wild Life* for the 1987 CD release, but oddly also appeared on the *McCartney Archive Collection* release of *Ram*. The *Paul McCartney Collection* version was released on June 7, 1993 (Parlophone 7 89237 2), with four bonus tracks.

Oh Woman, Oh Why: See discussion in the chapter on *Ram*.

Mary Had a Little Lamb: It's ironic that a song that received as much criticism as this track was also one of the best produced of McCartney's career. Lyrically complicated and filled with an astonishing complement of instruments plus a children's chorus, it is obvious that McCartney took more time and care recording and arranging this song than any song on *Wings Wild Life*. It was originally never intended for commercial release. McCartney has said with his little daughters often around as his only audience, he would sometimes write for them. This is a prime example of that.

Little Woman Love: See discussion in the chapter on *Ram*.

Mama's Little Girl: Based on a catchy acoustic guitar lick, the band adds bass, backing vocals and percussion as McCartney sings plaintively, with his voice wet with reverb. The intercession in the middle of the song is slowed down and features a haunting Mellotron part. McCartney recorded this simple song during the *Red Rose Speedway* sessions but didn't get around to doing a final mix until 1987.

Give Ireland Back to the Irish: See discussion in the Singles chapter.

On December 7, 2018, *Wings Wild Life* got the *Paul McCartney Archive Collection* treatment (Parlophone, CDPM COL 3). It came in an attractive box with lots of extras. Four discs were included:

Disc one: The original 10-song remastered album. (The album actually only includes eight songs, with "Bip Bop Link" and "Mumbo Link" consisting of snippets of those tracks.)

Disc two: Rough mixes of all eight songs from the original album.

Disc three: Bonus audio from around the time the album was being planned and recorded. Several of these "outtakes" are less than a minute long and feature acoustic guitar noodling. The first five songs were taken form a widely circulated film of Paul and Linda sitting in the Scottish countryside, singing over McCartney's acoustic guitar:

Good Rockin' Tonight: A straightforward reading of this rock chestnut, a version of which McCartney would later include on the *Unplugged* and *Paul Is Live* live albums.

Bip Bop: An acoustic version of the song that would later appear on *Wild Life.*

Hey Diddle: Working out a song that would later appear as a B-side.

She Got It Good: A simple little bluesy guitar romp that lasts exactly 44 seconds.

I Am Your Singer: A straight reading of the song that would appear on the finished album.

Outtake: A mere 29 seconds of guitar picking.

Dear Friend: A home recording of the album track, with the kids screaming in the background.

Dear Friend: More of the same.

Outtake: Thirteen seconds of guitar.

Indeed I Do: A home recording of an unreleased song which is actually pretty catchy. Pretty melody with a nice harmony from Linda.

When the Wind Is Blowing: This is a gentle acoustic guitar-based song with a hypnotic melody and some really fine acoustic guitar soloing. It's clear that a final set of lyrics hadn't been nailed down. The melody of this song was used as the instrumental hook for Kanye West's "All Day," released in 2015.

The Great Cock and Seagull Race: See discussion of this track in the analysis of *Ram.*

Outtake: Ten seconds of acoustic guitar.

Give Ireland Back to the Irish: See singles chapter for discussion.

Give Ireland Back to the Irish (version): See singles chapter for discussion.

Love Is Strange: This was an edited version of the album track that was originally planned for release as a single.

African Yeah Yeah: An ad-libbed lark in the studio. The main part of the song ends at 2:41, and with two minutes remaining a piano, percussion and a wobbly trumpet play a simple melody, with lots of chat to be heard in the background. It sounds like a limping version of "When the Saints Go Marching In." This is the only track on the bonus audio disc that was recorded in 1972, after *Wild Life* was released.

Disc four: Bonus video that includes four short films:

Scotland 1971: This is the film of Paul, Linda and child playing and singing outside at their farm in Scotland. The audio of this film is also on disc three, as noted.

The Ball: This consists of film footage of invited guests arriving at the *Wild Life* launch party at the Empire Ballroom in London on November 8, 1971. The usual suspects (Elton John, Ronnie Wood, et al.) arrive one by one. Bad haircuts abound.

ICA Rehearsals: Fragments of a rehearsal by the band that took place at the Institute of Contemporary Arts Gallery and Theatre in February 1972. Includes performances of "The Mess," "Give Ireland Back to the Irish" and "My Love."

Give Ireland Back to the Irish: A rehearsal of this song filmed in London on February 1, 1972, by ABC News.

Of all the McCartney albums that have been released as part of the *McCartney Collection Archive* so far, this one has the least interesting bonus audio and video materials. It sorely lacks the inclusion of unreleased songs and interesting outtakes.

This is partially atoned for by the inclusion of several noteworthy and wholly entertaining documents, which include a 128-page book of essays, interviews about the making of the album, photographs, newspaper clippings and other esoterica that really captures the moment of the birth of Wings as a band. It also includes a "diary" kept at the time by Linda McCartney, with set lists, chord sequences, lyrics, several random doodles and a few pages of entries by Linda during the university tour.

Also included in the package is a set of never-before-seen photographs of the band in the studio and a replica of the invitation to the launch ball the McCartneys sent out to their guest list. Finally, a card that allows the buyer of this package to download the 24bit 96kHz unlimited high resolution version of the remastered album and the bonus audio.

Red Rose Speedway

Released April 30, 1973 (U.S.); May 4, 1973 (UK)
Apple Records PCTC 251 (U.K.); SMAL-3409 (U.S.)
Highest chart position: 1 in the U.S. and 5 in the U.K.
Produced by Paul McCartney
Musicians: Paul McCartney: vocals, piano, bass, guitar, electric piano, Mellotron, celeste, Moog synthesizer; Linda McCartney: vocals, piano, organ, electric piano, electric harpsichord, percussion; Denny Laine:

vocals, guitar, bass, harmonica; Henry McCullough: guitar, backing vocals, percussion; Denny Seiwell: drums, percussion; Hugh McCracken: electric guitar (on "Little Lamb Dragonfly"); David Spinozza: electric guitar (on "Get on the Right Thing")

Red Rose Speedway was originally planned as a double album, but those plans were scrapped at the last minute. Many of the songs originally slated to appear on the album ended up as B-sides and bonus tracks.

The album provided new music that Wings could take out on the road, as they were planning their first British and European tour at the time of its making. McCartney reportedly added Henry McCullough to the lineup to toughen up the sound. It's odd, then, that *Red Rose Speedway* doesn't have much of a rock 'n' roll sound, but it is much more mainstream and radio friendly than *Wings Wild Life.*

The album cover features an astonished looking McCartney with a rose in his mouth, standing in front of what appears to be a motorcycle. The tracks include Wings' first hit single, a couple of tepid rockers, and a lot of slow-ish piano songs. Each track includes meticulous vocals (both lead and backing), a hallmark of the Wings sound to this point. And if most of the melodies are forgettable, the album did serve its purpose as a placeholder until the band could really hone their sound and work out their live chops.

The album made it to No. 1 on the U.S. Billboard charts, partly on the strength of the hit single "My Love," but mostly because Paul McCartney still had the vast fan base he had amassed as a member of the Beatles. Even he knew that he couldn't rest on those laurels forever.

Big Barn Bed: The album kicks off with this slight and repetitive rocker with typical turgid lyrics. At times the song is overwhelmed by the backing vocals, which seem to take up too much sonic space in the mix. And let's face it, rhyming "willow" with "armadillo" just shouldn't be part of the rock 'n' roll lexicon. A snippet of this song appeared at the end of the "Ram On" reprise on *Ram.*

My Love: A plaintive and lovely ballad written for Linda, "My Love" was a huge radio hit during the summer of 1973. This is easily the best track on the album and underscores the best that McCartney has to offer: a beautiful melody exquisitely rendered, interesting (but understated) instrumentation, a subtle string part and a searing guitar solo by McCullough. This became a staple of his live shows for years to come.

Get on the Right Thing: While "My Love" was the unassailable hit on the album, this track features McCartney letting his hair down and really rocking the lead vocal. It almost sounds like a live performance, with McCartney's vocal treated with just the right amount of echo and a rocking chorus supported by the backing vocals, on which Linda's voice is prominent. The lyrics don't make much sense, but the vocal performance is worth the price of admission. This was originally recorded during the sessions for *Ram*.

One More Kiss: This is the period in which the McCartneys seem almost infatuated with country-inflected pop music, and this song is yet another in that subgenre. Over two loud electric guitars and a stridently strummed acoustic guitar, McCartney delivers an apology to his "little girl." Each chorus adds a new electric guitar flourish that gives the track some extra depth. Even on the slightest songs on *Red Rose Speedway*, McCartney's vocals are impeccable.

Little Lamb Dragonfly: Guitars abound; acoustic six-strings and an acoustic 12-string, plus at least two electric guitars and the ever-present bass. The melodies are lovely in each of the three distinct sections of this song, and even if it took 6:20 and one major key modulation to get the point across, it's one of the two or three finest songs on the album. This is another song that was originally tracked during the *Ram* sessions.

Single Pigeon: A simple and brief piano-based song with surprisingly complicated vocals, "Single Pigeon" starts out with just piano, bass, acoustic guitar and lots of vocal parts, and then resolves with a full-on orchestrated coda.

When the Night: A call-and-response ballad in a slow 4/4, this song is nothing more than a showcase for the Wings sound. Lavish backing vocals over a pedestrian melody is a pretty common occurrence on this album, but the vocals keep delivering something interesting to listen to.

Loup (1st Indian on the Moon): Throughout McCartney's solo career he's had trouble resisting making self-indulgent and frankly, head-scratching decisions about including certain songs on his albums. This is a prime example. A mostly instrumental dirge with Indian sounding instrumentation and weird space age undertones, the track goes nowhere and does nothing at all to buttress the notion that McCartney was regaining his touch with melody. You might forgive his new bandmates for wondering what they might have gotten themselves into.

Medley: Hold Me Tight/Lazy Dynamite/Hands of Love/Power Cut: This album closing medley is 11:18 of mostly forgettable melodies, lazy lyrics and indifferent playing. The only nominally interesting aspect of the medley is how he weaves the melodies from each song into the basic track of "Power Cut," the last song in the medley. If anything, the closing medley gives credence to the generally lousy reviews *Red Rose Speedway* received.

Bonus Tracks

On the 1987 CD release:

I Lie Around: It's usually a bad sign when bonus tracks added on reissues are as strong or stronger than the songs on the original album, but this is the case with the *Red Rose Speedway* reissue. "I Lie Around" is an extremely intricate song, with healthy dollops of overproduction and lots of guitar. Denny Laine handles the lead vocal, with help from Paul. This and the next track continue the string of countrified ditties extolling the virtues of rural life…

Country Dreamer: …to such an extent that McCartney now wants to walk in a field, stand in a stream and climb up a hill. No doubt these types of songs were influenced by his spartan lifestyle on the farm in Scotland, but that's a tough image to sustain when you're a multimillionaire with an extremely high global profile. This is an inoffensive enough song, but it did nothing to change McCartney's reputation at the time as a country bumpkin sloshing through the mud in his knee-high waders, whistling in the breeze.

The Mess: This is a rousing rocker that would have been better than most of the other songs on the album had he held to his original idea of making a double album. Recorded live at the Hague, "The Mess" sounded like a band that was really coming together. McCartney's vocals are as good as anything he ever did on stage, and the echo on his voice gives it an earthy live sound. There are three different parts to the song. Guitar solos abound and McCartney screams throughout the end of the song. The only downer is the clichéd major seventh chord that ends the song. It deserved something a little funkier than that.

Bonus Tracks

On the 1993 *Paul McCartney Collection* (June 7, 1993; Parlophone 7 89238 2) release: "C Moon," "Hi Hi Hi," "The Mess" and "I Lie Around."

On December 7, 2018, an expanded version of *Red Rose Speedway* was released as a part of the *Paul McCartney Archive Collection* (Capitol Records, B0028658-01). The deluxe edition included three CDs, two DVDs and a Blu-Ray version of the short film *The Bruce McMouse Show*.

Disc one: The remastered nine-song version of the original album.

Disc two: The "double album" as it was originally sequenced.

Night Out: A mostly instrumental jam with very limited lyrics. It's not very inventive and seems like a weird choice for an album opening track. This one appeared years later on McCartney's abandoned *Cold Cuts* project (see the bootlegs chapter).

Get on the Right Thing

Country Dreamer

Big Barn Bed

My Love

Single Pigeon

When the Night

Seaside Woman: Co-written by Paul and Linda McCartney, this reggae-inflected song is fun and holds up pretty well today. It was released as a single in 1977 under the sobriquet Suzy and the Red Stripes.

I Lie Around

The Mess (Live at The Hague)

Best Friend (Live in Antwerp): This is a hot little rocker and one can see why Wings included it in some of their early concert set lists. There's some really nice guitar interplay between Denny Laine and Henry McCullough. McCartney is in great rock 'n' roll singing mode.

Loup (1st Indian on the Moon)

Medley: Hold Me Tight/Lazy Dynamite/Hands of Love/Power Cut

Mama's Little Girl: Nice acoustic guitar playing by McCartney, and a sweet laid-back vocal performance to boot. There's a nice busking electric guitar, joined by some percussion. The slow interlude in the middle of the song is beautiful and full of hallmark McCartney melodic flourishes.

I Would Only Smile: This Denny Laine song is full of hooks and would have been a great addition to the album. Electric guitars, acoustic guitar, bass, organ and drums give the track a solid backing. This is definitely the sound of 1970s pop music.

One More Kiss

Tragedy: The original recording of this song, by Thomas Wayne and the DeLons, went to No. 5 on the Billboard charts in 1959 and has been rerecorded by numerous artists over the years. It's tailor made for McCartney's voice because of the tricky intervals and the lovely melody. This one also later appeared on *Cold Cuts.*

Little Lamb Dragonfly

One can see why McCartney changed his mind about issuing a double album. The expanded version seems overly padded by two live songs, a cover song and three other songs cut from the same country cloth. It's reasonable to conclude that he wanted to condense the band's output to achieve a more coherent sound, and that's what the original single album does more effectively.

Disc three: Bonus audio including some of the singles that were recorded during the *Red Rose Speedway* album sessions, early mixes of some of the songs, a live track and a couple of unreleased songs. This includes the singles "Mary Had a Little Lamb," "Little Woman Love," "Hi, Hi, Hi," "C Moon" and "Live and Let Die." There are early and rough mixes of "Get on the Right Thing," "Little Lamb Dragonfly," "Little Woman Love," "Big Barn Bed" and "Mary Had a Little Lamb." There are three versions of the execrable "1882" (recordings in the studio and at home, and a live recording from Berlin). Studio versions of "The Mess," plus two unreleased songs ("Thank You Darling" and "Jazz Street") are included, as well as a "band only" version of "Live and Let Die," before George Martin scored it for an orchestra.

DVD one: Music videos of "My Love," "Hi, Hi, Hi" and "C Moon," and four videos of "Mary Had a Little Lamb," the complete *James Paul McCartney* television special that aired in America on April 7, 1973, a live performance of "Live and Let Die" in Liverpool, and an interview that Paul and Linda McCartney sat for in Newcastle on July 11, 1973, prior to a Wings performance.

DVD two: The full version of *The Bruce McMouse Show* in 5.1 surround Dolby digital sound.

Blu-ray: The full version of odd *The Bruce McMouse Show* in 5.1 surround Dolby digital sound.

It tells the story of a mouse living under the stage of a rock 'n' roll venue and how he and his wife deal with the noise and inconvenience. The film goes back and forth from a Wings concert to the animated world of Bruce McMouse. The cartoon segments are clearly from the early 1970s, as the animation is unsophisticated and the "story" doesn't amount to much. The best part of the film is seeing Wings perform live.

That's a lot to listen to and watch, but it's a much more comprehensive look at Wings than the *Wild Life* remastered archive package. Besides the discs, the *Red Rose Speedway* package also includes a book of photos taken from the band's visit to Morocco in early 1973, a book of new interviews, photos from the sessions and a behind-the-scenes look at the songs, plus some handwritten lyrics and a facsimile of a postcard of the band signed by each of its members. There are also early drawings and scripts from *The Bruce McMouse Show.* Also included is a 24bit 96kHz unlimited high resolution version of the remastered album and the bonus audio.

A limited release of a deluxe set called *Wings 1971–73* was released at the same time as the *Wild Life* and *Red Rose Speedway* sets. It combined all of the discs described above from both albums, plus a CD of a full Wings concert taken from five European venues in the summer of 1972. There are high points, but the band does sound pretty ragged at times. Most of the set list comes from *Wild Life* and *Red Rose Speedway,* with a couple of deep album gems thrown in ("Eat at Home" and "Smile Away"), a few singles and a raucous version of the concert closer "Long Tall Sally." *Wings 1971–73* sold out in three days.

Band on the Run

Released December 5, 1973 (U.S.); December 7, 1973 (U.K.)
Apple Records PAS 10007 (U.K.); 4XZ 3425 (U.S.)
Highest chart position: 1 in the U.S. and the U.K.
Produced by Paul McCartney
Musicians: Paul McCartney: vocals, acoustic, electric and bass guitars, piano, keyboards, drums and percussion; Linda McCartney: vocals, piano, keyboards; Denny Laine: vocals, acoustic, electric and bass guitars, keyboards, percussion; Howie Casey: saxophone; Ginger Baker: percussion; Remi Kabaka: percussion

Band on the Run, McCartney's last album on Apple Records, is regarded as the artist's masterpiece and remains one of the finest albums of the 1970s and one of two of the best albums ever recorded by a former Beatle.

McCartney decided to record the album at EMI's studio in Lagos, Nigeria, ostensibly to soak up the natural vibe of African music he imagined existed there. Set against a tidal wave of bad karma (last minute band member defections, terrible weather conditions, primitive recording studio amenities, an outbreak of cholera, confrontations with local musicians, health scares and armed robbery), it's amazing *Band on the Run* turn out to be such a stellar affair. Or maybe it's true that out of strife comes great art.

Denny Seiwell and Henry McCullough bailed on the band at the last minute, making Wings a trio for the first (but not the last) time. They soldiered on, with McCartney handling the drums and most of the guitar work. All songs are credited to Paul and Linda McCartney, with the exception of "No Words," which was written by Paul and Denny Laine.

This is McCartney's first solo album that does not include a bad or poorly considered song. Full of bright melodies, dramatic musical flourishes and inspired vocals, *Band on the Run* stands the test of time and still sounds exquisite, despite the sometimes annoying over-reliance on synthesizers. Although it is not a concept album in the truest sense, it does refer to common themes, established in the opening track, like escape and liberation. It also is masterfully sequenced, with the song lineup seeming to follow a logical course.

The cover photo shows the McCartneys and Laine with a crew of six celebrities of varying degrees of fame (British talk show host Michael Parkinson, singer and British TV actor Kenny Lynch, American actors James Coburn and Christopher Lee, politician Clement Freud and boxer and fellow Liverpudlian John Conteh) in black prison garb, caught by a searchlight against a brick wall. The scenario suggests a foiled prison break. This must be the band on the run.

The album struggled out of the gate, but due to some deft marketing and strategic release of key singles, it gained a foothold in the charts and made it to No. 1 in the U.S. Billboard charts on *three separate occasions* in 1973.

A quick note about the tracks. "Helen Wheels" was released as a single October 26, 1973, and was not included on the U.K. version of the album. It was included on the U.S. release of *Band on the Run*.

Band on the Run: One of McCartney's finest songs, the title track is a clever melding of three song segments. The first is sung with a world-weary voice, lamenting the isolation of the four walls the singer is stuck inside. From there, a rocking second segment finds the singer planning what he would do if he could ever escape. In the third segment, ushered in by a dramatically orchestrated few bars and the splash of bright acoustic guitars, the singer sings about the actual escape. No matter that the characters are unknown to the listener (Sailor Sam, the jailor man, the undertaker), it still sounds daring and exciting. McCartney's drumming, so thin on his first solo album, sounds as clear and confident as any drumming heard on the radio during the same time period. Plus, the vocals are rendered with a confidence absent from McCartney's first four solo albums.

Jet: Aside from the completely cheesy synthesizer solo, "Jet" is McCartney at his rocking best. Never mind that the lyrics are as obscure as can be, the strings, horns and urgent vocal propel the song forward. It does seem to lack a bottom, though; the bass is buried deep in the mix. "Jet" is still a staple of McCartney's live shows, almost 50 years on.

Bluebird: A cerebral ballad, "Bluebird" exists to show off the fully formed vocal talents of Wings. Filled with extraneous percussion, acoustic guitars and a tremendous saxophone solo by Howie Casey, the song continues the album's theme of escape and freedom. (This is the second of four "bird" songs McCartney would record. The first was "Blackbird," of course, and "Bluebird" would be followed much later by "Jenny Wren" and "Two Magpies.")

Mrs. Vandebilt: A jaunty tune with a singalong chorus, "Mrs. Vandebilt" moves back and forth from the minor key of the chorus and verses to the two bridges in a major key. As he did frequently during this period, McCartney inserted a slow instrumental interlude in the middle of the song with lead guitar, keyboards and lots of backing vocals. The song deteriorates into a chorus of giggles as the song fades out over the insistent chorus with the nonsense syllables the whole song was built around.

Let Me Roll It: One of the best songs on the album and in the Wings catalogue, "Let Me Roll It" is the simplest song on the album in terms of production and instrumentation: Two electric guitars, bass, organ and drums, playing just four chords (E major, F#, A major and F# minor) under the insistent riff, plus the absolutely gorgeous lead vocals that McCartney delivers using tasteful echo for dramatic effect. The impassioned wail that McCartney unleashes near the end of the song adds an emphatic touch that wraps the whole affair up very nicely.

Mamunia: The first song recorded for the album, "Mamunia" is an acoustic guitar-based song built around a descending chord sequence during the verses and chorus and an ascending chord sequence during the instrumental breaks at the beginning and end of the song. Lots of interesting percussion and smart lyrics make this a fun song. One nit to pick: The overbearing synthesizer rears its ugly head again during the instrumental break near the end of the song.

No Words: Written by Paul McCartney and Denny Laine, this is the shortest and simplest song on the album. The inclusion of a Fender Rhodes electric piano gives this a satisfying sound that places it smack dab in the middle of the 1970s. The strings also add a nice touch. Another example of great backing vocals with the Wings stamp firmly applied. There is also a nice electric guitar solo break that takes the song out. The middle eight features McCartney singing at the very top of his register until he inevitably slips into his falsetto.

Helen Wheels: A sort of guided driving tour from the north of England down to London, the verses and most of the choruses are sung over an A major chord before the quick insertion of an E minor chord disrupts the monotony. The electric guitar part during the last verse and the fade-out gives the song a rock 'n' roll push.

Picasso's Last Words (Drink to Me): A beautiful mélange of styles and colors, the song starts out calmly enough with the tale of Picasso's last evening spent among friends at a dinner party (with Denny Laine handling the first few lines by himself). A chiming 12-string acoustic adds nice atmosphere before an instrumental fragment that features a recorded French lesson and a clarinet intrudes. Suddenly, "Jet" is reprised over strings, electric piano and infectious and quirky percussion, and the chorus is sung in a completely different style, complete with a moving bass guitar solo! Then, the crash bam of the drums leads into a tipsy rendering of the chorus, with slurred lyrics and appropriately sloppy instrumentation. We return to the French lesson briefly, before another change in style occurs, this time a disco-ish (think "The Hustle") variation on the overall theme, with the nonsense syllables from "Mrs. Vandebilt" making a return visit. The song fades out amid vigorous shaking of pails of gravel, bass guitar and vocal interjections from the assemblage in the studio.

Nineteen Hundred and Eighty Five: The only song on the album to feature piano as its primary instrument, this is a fine example of McCartney's prowess at creating memorable piano riffs.

A typical Wings feature—a wordlessly sung slowing of the song's original tempo over organ, bass and piano—appears twice to break up the frenetic pace of the verses. The song morphs into a growing tumult of horns, clarinet, synthesizer, electric guitar, tom toms, and organ over a repeating descending three-chord sequence. Throughout, McCartney groans, wails and vocally emotes. After the dramatic cold stop, a snippet of the chorus from the title song makes a very brief appearance. This is the quintessential album closer.

Bonus Tracks

The 1993 *Paul McCartney Collection* reissue (June 7, 1993; Parlophone 7 89240 2) included the single "Helen Wheels" backed with "Country Dreamer." See the singles chapter for analysis.

The 1999 25th Anniversary Edition of *Band on the Run* (shouldn't a 25th anniversary reissue of an album made in 1973 have been released in 1998?) features some snippets of the original songs in earlier periods of gestation, but mostly it's an oral history, with McCartney, Linda (who by the time of this reissue had passed away), Denny Laine, engineer Geoff Emerick, arranger Tony Visconti, photographer Clive Arrowsmith and A&R record company guru Al Coury contributing memories of the making of the album (Capitol Records, CDP 7243 4 99176 2 0). Much of the extra disc included is devoted to a discussion of the album cover photo shoot, with all those involved weighing in with their memories. Also, Dustin Hoffman reminisces about meeting Paul in Jamaica and being present at the musical birth of "Picasso's Last Words (Drink to Me)."

Unfortunately, there is very little of interest in the music on the extra disc, mostly because brief fragments of each of the songs are included, interspersed with dialogue from the players. The only exceptions are rehearsal versions of the title track, "Jet" and "Let Me Roll It" from 1989 and 1993 with his early 1990s touring band, a set of musicians who had nothing to do with the making of the original album. That adds no value to the extras on this reissue. The packaging includes all the original photographs, plus an annotated and detailed booklet about the making of the album.

The *Paul McCartney Archive Collection* remastered version of *Band on the Run* was released in November 2010 and included lots of extras and was available on both disc and vinyl:

Disc one features the remastered U.K. version of the album (without "Helen Wheels")

Disc two features:

Helen Wheels/Country Dreamer/Bluebird [from One Hand Clapping]/Jet [from One Hand Clapping]/Let Me Roll It [from One Hand Clapping]/Band on the Run [from One Hand Clapping]/Nineteen Hundred and Eighty Five [from One Hand Clapping]/Country Dreamer [from One Hand Clapping]/Zoo Gang (see Singles section)

Disc three features:

Band on the Run video/Mamunia video/original album promo [Band on the Run, Mrs. Vandebilt, Nineteen Hundred and Eighty Five, Bluebird]/Helen Wheels video/Wings in Lagos (footage of Wings working and playing in Lagos)/Osterley Park (a brief video about the shooting of the cover) One Hand Clapping (an unreleased film featuring Wings circa late 1974 in the studio and just hanging out)

Venus and Mars

Released May 27, 1975 (U.S.); May 30, 1975 (U.K.)
Capitol Records PCTC 259 (U.K.); 4XT 11419 (U.S.)
Highest chart position: 1 in the U.S. and the U.K.
Produced by Paul McCartney
Musicians: Paul McCartney; vocals, bass guitar, piano, guitar, percussion, keyboards; Linda McCartney: backing vocals, keyboards, percussion; Denny Laine: vocals, guitar, keyboards, percussion; Jimmy McCulloch: vocals, guitar, percussion: Joe English: drums, percussion: Geoff Britton: drums on "Love in Song," "Letting Go" and "Medicine Jar"; Dave Mason: guitar on "Listen to What the Man Said"; Allen Toussaint: piano on "Rock Show"; Tom Scott: saxophone on "Listen to What the Man Said"; Kenneth Williams: congas on "Rock Show"; Gayle Levant: harp

Venus and Mars built on the theme established with *Band on the Run* but took it a couple steps further. The former album was recorded in Lagos, Nigeria, with hopes of soaking up the vibes of African music, while this one was recorded mainly in New Orleans amid the gaiety and pomp of Mardi Gras and was clearly influenced by noted Nola musicians like Fats Domino, Professor Longhair and the Meters.

McCartney had beefed up the Wings lineup by bringing on drummer Geoff Britton and guitarist Jimmy McCulloch. In June 1974, the new lineup of Wings traveled to Nashville, Tennessee, to get better acquainted and to rehearse some new songs. There, they sampled the nightlife and hobnobbed with the cream of classic country music veterans.

After a few troubled months during which Britton and McCulloch clashed incessantly, Britton was turfed and replaced by Joe English.

Three of the album's songs were recorded during an eight-day session in London in November 1974. The rest of the tracks were recorded in New

Orleans during 30 days in January and February 1975. Some overdubs were added in Los Angeles in March 1975.

It marked the first time in Paul McCartney's solo career that he followed up a great album with one that was just as good, and it also was an early harbinger that Wings planned to hit the road. The entire album seemed arena rock-friendly, and nine of the album's 13 songs made it into the *Wings Over America* set list.

The album had a weird out-of-this-world look and feel. Red and yellow pool table balls were used to represent Venus and Mars, and the photography came from a shoot in the middle of the Mojave Desert that ended up looking like Wings had managed to land on some faraway planet. Some of the songs even have an extraterrestrial vibe.

The songs are lush with acoustic six-string and 12-string guitars, an abundance of piano and other keyboards, and a beefier electric guitar sound than on previous Wings albums. But more than anything, it seemed like this was the most fun Wings had making an album. And much like *Band on the Run, Venus and Mars* does not contain a bad song in either construction or execution.

Venus and Mars: The album opens with chiming guitars playing a simple chord progression, over which the singer sets the stage of fans sitting in an arena waiting for a rock show to begin. A mere 1:19 long, the song builds tension until it blasts into the following track.

Rock Show: This thumping song employs pretty much every mid–1970s rock cliché imaginable. It even name checks several vintage rock 'n' roll palaces around the world. It weaves in and out of sinuous signature changes but always returns to the catchy verses for the call and response between the lead singer and the backing vocalists. Slide guitar and piano drive it along. After the false stop, a funky little piano riff introduces the coda, in which the singer promises to take his girlfriend to a local rock show. Could a Wings tour be in the offing?

Love in Song: The prettiest song on the album finds McCartney mining the seemingly endless mother lode of melody that he has at his ready disposal. A haunting two verses in a minor key breaks into a hummable middle eight with Indian-inflected instrumentation. The last verse is slowed down slightly, giving the cold end to the song a dramatic flourish.

You Gave Me the Answer: Here we find McCartney revisiting the 1930s–style dance hall genre he just can't seem to get enough of. This one is nicely constructed with an assortment of wind instruments and strings capturing the essence of that era. McCartney's vocal is fed through an effect that gives it a Rudy Vallee flavor.

Magneto and Titanium Man: Here we have a straightforward rocker based on comic book superheroes. McCartney's soulful singing during the middle eight is the best part of the song, along with McCulloch's brief midsong guitar solo. The backing vocals by Denny Laine and Linda (and Paul) are quintessential Wings.

Letting Go: One of McCartney's finest rockers ever, this plumbs the depths of his sometimes-latent propensity to write a scorching rock song. This one was just made for a rock show set list. The interplay between the guitar and the horns gives it a huge in-your-face sound. The lyrics, other than in the chorus, lack the punch the overall sound demands, but as a pure rocker it stands the test. McCartney would resurrect "Letting Go" at times during his live shows in 2014–18. The long fade-out gives McCulloch ample room and time to vamp on his guitar.

Venus and Mars (Reprise): This one is more straightforward. Over the same chords and very similar instrumentation, the reprise finds McCartney's voice wet with reverb and the lyrics are much spacier than the opening track. It's also almost a minute longer than its predecessor.

Spirits of Ancient Egypt: Denny Laine gets a chance to take the lead vocal spotlight on this driving, simple workout. The lyrics are hilarious during the verses, but then McCartney takes over the mike during the middle eight and sings about mystical esoterica. The song fades out over one insistent chord, with what sounds like a busy signal beeping in the background. The band sounds great.

Medicine Jar: McCulloch gets a chance to shine on this song about the evils of drugs. The sad irony in the lyrics makes the song difficult to listen to. Several years later, after McCulloch quit Wings, he was found dead in his apartment from an apparent drug overdose. McCulloch delivers a screeching guitar solo, and the McCartneys add layers of sweet backing vocals.

Call Me Back Again: Pure McCartney soul of the sort he only occasionally harnesses. Think "Oh! Darling." Over a simple arrangement of piano, guitar, bass, drums, a carnival-ish keyboard and Stax-inflected horn charts, McCartney shouts out exhortations for a return call. Well done and perfectly suited for a rock concert.

Listen to What the Man Said: This is the sound of the summer of 1975, one of the greatest summertime pop singles of all-time. The sax played by L.A. session musician Tom Scott rings out through the happy, sunshine-y vibe of the lyrics and jaunty lilt of the melody. Who cares what the song's about, or even what the man said? It's summer and Wings are in fine form. The band's complex backing vocals are prominent, and Linda sounds nearly as happy as the lead singer. The end of the song slows down considerably before it segues into…

Treat Her Gently/Lonely Old People: Another timeless melody over a simple and trite chord progression that's occasionally interrupted by a surprising diminished chord. It's certainly an interesting song (despite the dual titles, it's really one song), but its placement near the end of an album that rocks out as much as this one does seem like an odd choice.

Crossroads: This is the theme to a popular British soap opera that aired from 1964 to 1988. It was extremely popular with older viewers, so it seems likely McCartney tagged it on the end of the album as a wink, wink to the previous song's subject matter.

Bonus Tracks

On the 1993 *Paul McCartney Collection* reissue (June 7, 1993; Parlophone 7 89241 2) of *Venus and Mars* (refer to the Singles chapter for a discussion of these songs):

Zoo Gang
Lunch Box/Odd Sox
My Carnival

The *Paul McCartney Archive Collection* (Hear Music, HRM-32564-00) remastered version of *Venus and Mars* included a CD of 14 bonus tracks and a DVD with four videos. This appeared in both vinyl and digital versions in 2014.

Refer to the Singles chapter for a discussion of the first five songs on the bonus audio CD:

Junior's Farm
Sally G
Walking in the Park with Eloise
Bridge on the River Suite
My Carnival

Going to New Orleans (My Carnival): A vocal vamp by McCartney over the piano chords of "My Carnival."

Hey Diddle: This basic track was originally recorded in 1970 in New York, with Denny Seiwell and Hugh McCracken on drums and guitar, but was remixed with significant overdubs in Nashville in 1974.

Let's Love: A classic torchy piano ballad just ready made for the smoky-voiced chanteuse Peggy Lee. She recorded it as the title track for her 1974 album. McCartney produced and arranged the track.

Soily: The closest McCartney has ever come to writing and recording another "Helter Skelter," "Soily" is a big raucous noise with typically obscure lyrics and lots of interesting guitar work. This one was recorded at Abbey Road on John Lennon's 34th birthday and was featured in the unreleased film "One Hand Clapping."

Baby Face: This song was recorded in London with the Tuxedo Brass Band in November 1974, with brass overdubs added in New Orleans the following January. This sounds like a way for McCartney to indulge himself in the wash of brass instruments that are a staple of the New Orleans sound.

Lunch Box/Odd Sox: (refer to the singles chapter for a discussion of this track)

4th of July: A home demo with just a 12-string acoustic guitar and simple vocals. A very melancholy song for such a festive holiday. It goes on a bit too long and it's easy to see why it ended up on the cutting room floor.

Rock Show (old version): An unadorned version of the album track, with just bass, guitar and drums, with none of the piano or backing vocals that are so prominent on the released version.

At points, the melody strays from the final version, which makes this fun to listen to. It's obvious he hadn't yet settled on a completed set of lyrics. He also hadn't yet recorded the piano lick he tagged on at the end of the album version. In some ways this understated version is superior to the released version. McCartney's vocals shine.

Letting Go: This is an edited version of the original track, a tactic often employed in the 1970s with songs that were going to be released as singles, the idea being that radio stations wouldn't play longer songs. This truncated version is 56 seconds shorter than the album version, but in its abridged state it isn't any near as powerful as the original. Some of the great guitar work on the fade-out of the original was lopped off and ain't that a shame.

A bonus DVD consists of four short films:

The recording of the B-side single "My Carnival" (which looks like a lot of fun).

A film titled "Bon Voyageur," which shows the McCartneys and band getting down with their bad selves aboard a ship moored in New Orleans while legendary New Orleans band the Meters played a set. The film is edited from a longer film called "Voyageur" and featured some teasers segments of songs from *Venus and Mars*.

"Wings at Elstree," a film of a Wings rehearsal (to which they invited a select and very small group of audience members). Although the kinks hadn't been worked out, you can hear the beginnings of the Wings Over America set list taking place.

The TV commercial produced to promote the release of *Venus and Mars*. It's a 1:11 spot in which Wings play pool while snippets from the album's songs serve as the bed music.

Wings at the Speed of Sound

Released March 25, 1976, in the U.S.; March 26, 1976, in the U.K.
Capitol Records 8XW 11525 (U.S.); Parlophone PAS 10010 (U.K.)
Highest chart position: 1 in the U.S. and 2 in the U.K.
Produced by Paul McCartney
Musicians: Paul McCartney: vocals, acoustic, electric and bass guitars, keyboards, double bass; Linda McCartney: vocals, keyboards; Denny Laine: vocals, acoustic, electric and bass guitars, piano, harmonica; Jimmy McCulloch: vocals, acoustic, electric and bass guitars; Joe English: vocals, drums, percussion; Tony Dorsey: trombone; Thaddeus Richard: saxophone, clarinet, flute; Steve Howard: trumpet, flugelhorn; Howie Casey: saxophone; George Tidwell: trumpet

McCartney continues on with his band as a democracy philosophy on *Wings at the Speed of Sound*. Each member of the band gets a vocal spotlight (Denny Laine gets two), and it's the second consecutive album credited solely to Wings, rather than Paul McCartney and Wings.

Recorded during the preparation for Wings' first American tour, it features two massive hits that were issued as singles and a whole lot of lightweight ditties that pad the rest of the album. It seems rushed and ill-conceived. Still, it's an important work in the Wings canon, if only for the fact that "Silly Love Songs" and "Let 'Em In" were both huge chart successes in the U.S. and Europe and were received enthusiastically during concerts.

As always with McCartney, the songs are impeccably produced and recorded. No slightly out of tune guitars or off-key vocals can be heard anywhere. It's just that the songcraft seems slight. It was a problem that would dog him off and on throughout his career.

In some ways, this is Wings' last gasp. The band was about to undergo more personnel changes, and this feels like the last Wings album that Paul McCartney was fully invested in. The band had a lot to prove taking their show on the road, and he chose four of the album's best songs to include in their live set list.

The album cover has nothing but the album title on it, in orange and red capital letters.

The back of the album features a bunch of close-up head shots of the band evincing various poses, from grimaces to smiles. The album came with a small assortment of photos of the band at work in the studio.

Let 'Em In: The opening tune begins with the sound of a doorbell, then an insistent piano, bass and drums combo plays the simple backing. McCartney's sounds sufficiently laid back and he seems in his element, talking about relatives and friends coming over to the house. Everything from a single snare drum pounding out a march-like beat to a trombone solo color the repetitive arrangement. Classic Wings backing vocals, of course, make an appearance. There's an unmistakably sad element to "Let 'Em In." It has a wistful, contemplative feel to it. And for all the simplicity of the arrangement, McCartney once again delivers a memorable melody. The song goes into a live fade before ending with a two-chord flourish.

The Note You Never Wrote: This is Denny Laine's first spotlight vocal on the album, singing a song written by McCartney. It's an interesting song built around an inventive chord sequence played by an electric piano, guitar, bass and drums. McCulloch rips off a shredding guitar solo in the middle. The lyrics are typically obscure and indecipherable. Again, the melody is memorable, especially since the verses start out in a minor key, only to resolve themselves on the relative major.

She's My Baby: This is the sort of confection that McCartney writes before he brushes his teeth in the morning. Nothing to it. Catchy, with a pseudo disco beat, the lyrics are simple and repetitive. Again, the electric piano is prominent. The best part of the song comes after the false ending, when McCartney vamps over the closing chords, even inserting a purposeful crack in his voice at one point.

Beware My Love: One of the best out-and-out rockers in McCartney's catalogue begins with a dirge-like organ ushering in some acoustic guitars playing a neat little sequence. The band sings a little intro to the main event, which crashes in like a lightning bolt. Distorted guitars, keyboards, bass and drums drive the song along nicely. McCartney turns in some of his best rock 'n' roll vocals ever. It seems likely this song was written specifically for the tour. It has an undeniable drama to it that plays well on stage.

Wino Junko: This is "Medicine Jar"-light. Another song from Jimmy McCulloch warning against the evils of drugs. It seems odd that McCartney would have allowed a second consecutive anti-drug screed when he must have clearly intuited that McCulloch was battling substance abuse. The song itself is a pretty faithful rewrite of "Medicine Jar," with a similar chord sequence. The song devolves into a pretty cool jam at the fade-out, with frantically strummed acoustic guitars and a simple lead guitar part.

Silly Love Songs: Never mind that "Silly Love Songs" gave fodder to McCartney's critics who constantly chastised him for producing fluffy material; they could now say "See, he even admits they're silly love songs!" But "Silly Love Songs" is actually a pretty good song, driven by an incomparable bass part and horn chart right out of the Al Green songbook. The construction of the song, with three parts layered onto each other, is interesting and builds some drama. The horns add an inescapable tunefulness to the proceedings, and that bass just keeps chugging along. It may be about a pretty banal subject, but it's a great-sounding track.

Cook of the House: Linda steps up to the mike on this little kitchen caper. Man, I hope that's not bacon sizzling in the pan! Linda has a sort of monotone quality to her singing voice, but not much in the way of vocal ability is needed for this song. She lists ingredients she's using to concoct some dish, and there's an underlying sexual innuendo underneath the whole thing.

Time to Hide: This is Denny Laine's best song as a member of Wings. He sings it well and the instrumentation is interesting and does a good job of supporting the vocals. Lots of loud organ and inventive bass playing, plus a solid horn arrangement. McCartney supports his bandmate with urgent harmonies, and Wings sound almost like 1970s-era Jefferson Starship on this one. Great harmonica part and lead guitar break in the middle.

Must Do Something About It: Drummer Joe English shines on this McCartney-penned tune about isolation and loneliness. English delivers a clear and soulful vocal supported by acoustic guitars, bass, drums and an irritating electric guitar echoing all the lines. This could easily be mistaken for a 1970s singer-songwriter album track by Cat Stevens, Dan Fogelberg or James Taylor. The tune ends with a syncopated little bit of rhythmic horseplay.

San Ferry Anne: What an odd little song. Played in a minor key and filled with horn interjections, it's languorous and ponderous. The horns steal the spotlight.

Warm and Beautiful: The album closes with one of McCartney's best and most melodic piano ballads. Again, there's a certain sadness in the singer's delivery. The middle eight is gorgeous, and the lyrics deliver the goods. The combination of horns and electric guitar during the instrumental break is unusual but effective. The strings make their first appearance during the second middle eight. This is the work of a seriously good composer.

Bonus Tracks

The 1993 *Paul McCartney Collection* (June 7, 1993; Parlophone 7 89140 2) release featured three songs that were issued as B-sides of various singles. (See the singles chapter for a discussion of these songs.)

Walking in the Park with Eloise
Bridge on the River Suite
Sally G

The 2014 *Paul McCartney Archive* release of *Wings at the Speed of Sound* (Hear Music, HRM-35671-02) features a CD and vinyl edition of the original album, plus an audio disc of seven bonus track and a DVD with three sort features.

Silly Love Songs (demo): This is simply Paul playing the piano, singing the lyrics, with help from Linda. Lyrically, it's pretty faithful to what ended up on the album.

She's My Baby (demo): McCartney noodling on the piano while the song was still in development.

Message to Joe: A few seconds of vocal shenanigans.

Beware My Love (John Bonham version): This is an extended jam of "Beware My Love" with some different lyrics and a pretty tame drum part by Bonham, by his standards. Lots of piano and impassioned singing by McCartney. The released version of this song is better.

Must Do Something About It (Paul McCartney lead vocal): Before he decided to let Joe English take the lead vocal on this song, McCartney recorded a version of him singing it. This vocal demo, played over the backing track that supported the album version, is uninspired; it was a good call to give it to English. He made something more of it.

Let 'Em In (demo): A run-through of the album's opening track, this demo features McCartney playing piano, singing and interjecting with his voice possible drum and horn parts. The main difference is that the demo is played much faster than the version that was finally recorded.

Warm and Beautiful (instrumental demo): This is a demo on which McCartney plays the song on an electric piano. Even on this simple run-through, you can hear the majestic beauty of the melody.

The DVD consists of the original music video of "Silly Love Songs"; a short film called *Wings Over Wembley* that shows candid shots of the band on stage and backstage interspersed with crown scenes of fans getting their drinks and finding their seats (it's pretty much a run of the mill home movie); and, a short film titled *Wings in Venice*, with the band floating down a canal in a gondola while roadies set up the scaffolding and the instruments for that evening's show, with "Warm and Beautiful" serving as the soundtrack.

London Town

Released March 27, 1978 (U.S.); March 31, 1978 (U.K.)
Capitol Records 8XW-11777 ; Parlophone PAS 10012 (U.K.)
Highest chart position: 2 in the U.S. and 4 in the U.K.
Produced by Paul McCartney
Musicians: Paul McCartney: vocal, guitar, bass, keyboards, drums, percussion, violin, flageolet, recorder; Denny Laine: vocal, guitar, bass, flageolet, recorder, percussion; Linda McCartney: vocal, keyboards, percussion; Jimmy McCulloch: guitar, percussion; Joe English: vocal, drums, percussion, harmonica

London Town was recorded in London at Abbey Road studios and included a month of sessions aboard the yacht *Fair Carol* that trolled Watermelon Cay in the Virgin Islands. Its critical success paled in comparison to its predecessor *Wings at the Speed of Sound*, mainly because the songs weren't nearly as catchy or radio friendly. It's yacht rock at its limpest.

During the making of the album, Jimmy McCulloch and Joe English quit, making Wings a trio yet again. While the two now ex–Wings were credited on the album, only the McCartneys and Denny Laine were pictured on the album cover. Laine gets co-songwriting credit on five of the songs.

The first three songs are really good and hint at the promise of an excellent overall album. But it just falls apart from there. Only two other songs the rest of the way could be called good songs. It's also saddled by the lamentable "With a Little Luck," one of McCartney's worst songs ever (although, predictably, it was a hit on the pop charts).

There's a certain low-fi sound on many of the tracks, and more than ever before, McCartney is in storytelling mode. The songs don't seem as intimate and personal as some of his best music. Perhaps the atmosphere of recording on a boat surrounded by water all day dialed down the serious nature of making a good album. Whatever the reason, *London Town* makes no lasting impression on the listener, and certainly doesn't raise itself to the level of quality that McCartney had established.

Having established themselves as a potent rock 'n' roll band with the rousing success of *Wings Over America,* the band oddly reverts to pop and folk-inflected songs on *London Town.* It's light and fluffy and easily digestible, but hardly memorable rock music. There are too many unfinished lyrics and unrealized melodies to qualify *London Town* as anything more than a fair album, well below the standards of its three predecessors.

London Town: Opening with a lovely electric piano, this song has a certain majesty to it, despite the overly trite lyrics. It's a snapshot of the heart of London as McCartney sees it. There is some deep introspection in the lyrics at certain points, as if the singer himself is lost in the city in which he lives (sometimes). Beautiful harmonies and a nice melody make this one of the standout tracks on the album.

Café on the Left Bank: From London, we now go to Paris, as the singer paints a Francophile cityscape for us. This song is much more upbeat and hooky. Cafes, bars, ordinary wine, German beer and even Charles DeGaulle make appearances. An insistent percussion track propels the song along and shifts in the time signature give the song a certain listenability.

I'm Carrying: A beautiful if repetitive little ditty highlighted by acoustic guitar, synth strings and a very high lead vocal. This is the kind of memorable melody McCartney produces at least one example of per album.

Backwards Traveller: A great, gritty lead vocal with typically obscure lyrics and weird synthesizer noodling. It clocks in at just 1:09.

Cuff Link: A brief instrumental with heavily treated electric guitars and really inventive drums. Like many songs on the album, it's dominated by a synthesizer part.

Children Children: The folkiest song on the album, this one features flageolets, violin, recorders and lots of acoustic guitar. It's sung by Denny Laine, with lots of help from the McCartneys.

Girlfriend: Maybe the catchiest track on the album, "Girlfriend" is a marvel of construction, with two distinct sections. During the verses, McCartney sings in his best falsetto and then uses his lower register to deliver gutsy vocals in the other section. The middle includes a modulation and a brief guitar interlude. The song caught Michael Jackson's ear and he included his own version of it on his *Off the Wall* album.

I've Had Enough: The one true rocker on the album, "I've Had Enough" suffers from a slight melody and very repetitive lyrics. The payoff is that McCartney's vocals get grittier as the song goes on. A nice electric guitar solo appears in the middle. The cold ending fits its angry mood.

With a Little Luck: One of the worst singles ever issued by the band, "With a Little Luck" is awash in a sea of cheesy synthesizers and layer upon layer of smooth backing vocals. Still, it was a massive hit in the U.S., hitting No. 1 on the Billboard charts. Radio stations further undermined the song's appeal by creating a radio friendly edited version that clocked in well below the album's 5:47 elapsed time. Mostly, they eliminated the long instrumental break in the middle. It did little to make the song less cloying.

Famous Groupies: A snapshot of life on the road for a big rock star. One wonders what Linda must have thought about this one. McCartney comes up with the most ridiculous rhymes for the word "groupies." The chorus has a sort of sea chantey sound to it. The track is filled with weird vocal affectations and strange instrumentation.

Deliver Your Children: This song is in the same key as the previous, but the lyrics aren't nearly as silly. Denny Laine narrates the story about family values and how to properly provide for your children, but then it devolves into a classic small-town crime story. Great acoustic guitar work abounds and the vocals are strong. The McCartneys provide superb backing vocals.

Name and Address: McCartney does his best Elvis impression on this fun little rocker with a definite Sun Records vibe. Great electric guitars with just the right dose of reverb applied. McCartney plays drums and lead guitar.

Don't Let It Bring You Down: Another song in a minor key, which seems to be a bit of a motif on *London Town*. This song features a strange vocal with McCartney alternating between his lowest register and his clear high tenor. Lots of 12-string guitar and a slightly intrusive electric guitar part are main features of the backing track. This track has easily the most complicated vocal arrangement on the album.

Morse Moose and the Grey Goose: Every now and then, while parsing the McCartney oeuvre, one runs across a completely bizarre, seemingly meaningless and utterly perplexing song. This is a prime example. It seems like some sort of nautical soap opera, with a central story line about Morse Moose, and a supplemental backstory about the Grey Goose. Instrumentally, it bears an uncanny resemblance to Elton John's "Grey Seal" off his 1973 album *Goodbye, Yellow Brick Road*. Frankly, it's overly repetitive and difficult to listen to.

Bonus Tracks

The 1993 *Paul McCartney Collection* reissue (June 7, 1993; Parlophone 7 89265 2) included the single "Mull of Kintyre" and "Girls' School." See the singles chapter for analysis.

Looking ahead, it's reasonable to assume that *London Town* will get the archival treatment. We can fairly expect this to include lots of film and photos of their time aboard the *Fair Carol*, rehearsal outtakes, and perhaps a "making of 'Mull of Kintyre'" feature. Hopefully "Find a Way Somehow" will be among the bonus tracks included. It's a beautifully soulful song sung with passion by Denny Laine and could have supplanted almost any other song on the album and improved it.

Back to the Egg

Released May 24, 1979 (U.S.); June 8, 1979 (U.K.)
Columbia TC36057 (U.S.); Parlophone PCTC257 (U.K.)
Highest chart position: 8 in the U.S. and 6 in the U.K.
Produced by Paul McCartney and Chris Thomas
Musicians: Paul McCartney: vocals, guitar, bass, keyboards, piano, harpsichord, concertina; Denny Laine: vocal, guitars, backing vocals; Linda

McCartney: backing vocals, keyboard; Laurence Juber: guitars, guitar synthesizer, bass; Steve Holly: drums, percussion; Black Dyke Mills Band: horns on "Love Awake"; Dierdre Margary and Harold Margary: book readings; Rockestra line-up on "Rockestra Theme" and "So Glad to See You Here": Denny Laine, Laurence Juber, David Gilmour, Hank Marvin, Pete Townshend: guitars; Steve Holly, John Bonham, Kenney Jones: drums; Paul McCartney, John Paul Jones, Ronnie Lane, Bruce Thomas: basses; Paul McCartney, Gary Brooker, John Paul Jones: pianos; Linda McCartney, Tony Ashton: keyboards; Speedy Acquaye, Tony Carr, Ray Cooper, Morris Pert: percussion; Howie Casey, Tony Dorsey, Steve Howard, Thaddeus Richard: horns

Back to the Egg is Wings' final album and McCartney's first album for his new label, Columbia. Set against the backdrop of the new wave and punk explosion of the late 1970s, it features a tougher sound than the previous two Wings albums, aided by the recruitment of two new band members, guitarist Laurence Juber and drummer Steve Holly. Despite the tougher sound on many songs, a handful are so light and fluffy that they threaten to float away forever.

McCartney came up with an idea for the supergroup Rockestra, which is featured on two songs. Mostly comprised of English musicians with long resumes, the result was a mixed bag of overproduction and superfluous instrumentation.

The songs were recorded in four studios: Spirit of Ranachan Studios, Campbeltown; Lympne Castle, Kent; Abbey Road Studios and Replica Studio, both in London.

On the whole, the album was poorly received by critics, although "Rockestra Theme" won a Grammy for best rock instrumental performance in 1980. The album failed to live up to the sales standards of most Wings' albums, a poor result considering McCartney had just signed a very lucrative deal with Columbia Records.

The album was originally conceived as a blueprint for a concert tour, much like *Venus and Mars* four years earlier, and the band did head out on the road to support it. But McCartney seems not to have been totally enamored with this configuration of Wings and it did feel at the time like the band's tenure atop the charts was ending abruptly.

The album has an odd sort of mystical aura. The cover shows the band looking through a window in the floor at the planet Earth, and the other photos all have a sort of filmy and grainy look. Still, the album has aged better than several Wings albums, and its array of styles makes it an interesting listen.

A *Back to the Egg* television special, featuring videos of eight of the songs, aired in the U.S. in November 1979 but didn't air in the U.K. until June 1981, by which time Wings had disbanded.

Reception: This opens with the sound of a radio and turns into a rousing jam with pulsating bass and a guitar synthesizer dominating the track. There is also the sound of a man's voice and a woman speaking toward the end, and a persistent discordant chord over the whole thing.

Getting Closer: The radio dial is spun again before this track breaks through. It's a lively rocker with loud guitars and a driving bass. McCartney's voice is in great shape. Lots of typical Wings harmonies. And the drumming by Holly is hearty and vibrant. The outro features some fine rock 'n' roll shouting by McCartney.

We're Open Tonight: A quiet, hypnotic track based on a simple acoustic guitar figure, this one recalls "Love in Song" off *Venus and Mars*, right down to the odd, swirling electric guitar toward the end.

Spin It On: The finest rocker on the album, "Spin It On" references the punk explosion in 2:13 of machine gun musical attack. Complicated harmonies abound, and the lead guitar played by Juber is outstanding. This is unlike any other song McCartney has written with its grimy, raunchy feel.

Again and Again and Again: The only song on the album that is not credited solely to McCartney, co-writer Denny Laine takes the lead vocal. It's a filler, with nothing special to recommend it. It features lots of organ and frantic guitar fills.

Old Siam, Sir: Another really odd song in the McCartney catalog, this one is built around a repetitive bass and guitar riff, bolstered by piano and drums. The bridge has a different tempo with dramatic chord changes. The lyrics are typically obscure, delivered in McCartney's best rock 'n' roll vocal timbre. Unfortunately, the song meanders and doesn't really arrive at its destination, wherever that may be.

Arrow Through Me: An impossibly catchy tune, based on an electric piano and bass as its musical core, McCartney's singing is clear and effective. Weird chord changes abound, with lots of echo applied to the vocal at certain points. A nice loud horn chart punctuates the middle of the song and the outro. This proves once again that McCartney has always retained the ability to write melodic and hooky pop songs whenever he commands himself.

Rockestra Theme: A big beefy sound dominates this track played by the Rockestra supergroup, which included every member of 1979-vintage Wings. It's the memorable riff that makes this such an enjoyable song to listen to, especially since it's mostly an instrumental. The last chord is predictably held for a long time, in best rock guitar hero fashion.

To You: Over a simple chord progression, McCartney employs his gritty vocal while singing some weird lyrics. The song features a big sound with lots of power guitar chords. Unfortunately, it's really repetitive and begins to wear on the listener halfway through its 3:13 running time.

After the Ball/Million Miles: Over a plaintive piano part, McCartney sings with vigor and gives this track a definite gospel rendering. Some parts of "After the Ball" sound faintly reminiscent of "Amazing Grace." After a musical interlude complete with electric guitars, the song slides into "Million Miles." Over a simple keyboard part (which sounds like a cross between an accordion and a harmonica), McCartney sings the simple melody.

Winter Rose/Love Awake: "Winter Rose" is a lovely, haunting piano ballad in a minor key, sung with a raspy voice by McCartney. Guitars echo the melody during the instrumental interlude. "Love Awake" is the sort of acoustic guitar ballad that McCartney is known for. Lots of harmonies buttress this simple song. The Black Mills Dyke Band provides sympathetic horns to the arrangement.

The Broadcast: Over a haunting piano part, readings from t*he Sport of Kings* by Ian Hay and *The Little Man* by John Galsworthy give this short track an ethereal presence.

So Glad to See You Here: The second contribution from the Rockestra, this pulsating rocker gives McCartney a chance to let loose with his best rock voice, with lots of vocal histrionics added throughout. The song briefly reprises "We're Open Tonight" during the outro.

Baby's Request: It's just like McCartney to close his hardest edged album in years with a 1940s jazz standard send-up. This is a seriously good song, though. The whole vibe seems to authentically recall the golden age of American song, including the jazz-tinged guitar and the soulful trumpet part.

Bonus Tracks

The 1993 *Paul McCartney Collection* reissue (August 9, 1993; Parlophone 7 89136 2) included the singles "Daytime Nighttime Suffering,"

"Wonderful Christmastime" and "Rudolph the Red-Nosed Reggae." See the singles chapter for analysis.

London Town and *Back to the Egg* are the only remaining Wings albums not to have been re-released as part of the *Paul McCartney Archive Collection*. Looking ahead, it seems likely that extras included in the *Back to the Egg* re-release would include footage of the band rehearsing in several venues and a few outtakes. Hopefully, McCartney will include an audio disc of one of Wings' concerts in the U.K. toward the end of 1979, all of which had an amazingly eclectic set list.

McCartney II

Released: May 26, 1980 (U.S.); May 16, 1980 (U.K.)
Columbia (U.S.) FCA36511; Parlophone (U.K.) PCTC258
Highest chart position: 3 in the U.S. and 1 in the U.K.
Produced by Paul McCartney
Musicians: Paul McCartney: vocals, guitar, bass, keyboards, electric piano, drums, synthesizer; Linda McCartney: vocals

McCartney II was made purely for the amusement of Paul McCartney. He obviously had no commercial aspirations for the project (other than hoping people would like it), and in some ways it sounds like the work of a hobbyist down in the basement, playing with his Lionel train set.

While it was started before Wings' ill-fated tour of 1979 and before McCartney got busted in Japan in January 1980, it wasn't released until later in that year. Needing time out of the spotlight to recover from the trauma of spending nine days in a Japanese jail, McCartney revisited the tapes, made some overdubs and eventually decided to release the album.

It features an indescribably catchy single, a few requisite McCartney-esque ballads, a couple of instrumentals and lots of electronic tomfoolery. Modeled after *McCartney*, it resembles its predecessor only in its homemade qualities; this album demonstrates the confidence McCartney had gained in the 10 years since his first solo album was made.

It's interesting to note that in 1970, when *McCartney* was released, he took a lot of criticism for the DIY vibe of the album, especially after the lavish production of the Beatles' later period. By 1980, McCartney was praised for the homespun quality of this album, and it spawned lots of copycat projects.

The packaging features a head shot of McCartney looking vaguely annoyed (and astonishingly boyish), and some beautiful photos taken by Linda.

Coming Up: A great opening track with whirling guitars and lots of hooks, and McCartney's signature inventive bass part. His voice is treated with just a tad of echo, which also provides a slapback effect during the handclaps near the end. Synthesizers punctuate the proceedings with a nice salvo throughout. Here again, McCartney's drumming shows its maturity.

Temporary Secretary: What an odd chunk of electronica, replete with a passel of synthesizers and sequencers. This song would never fly during this age of #MeToo activism. Its misogyny is out of character for McCartney, and today it's almost laughably gauche. McCartney added this curio to his set list during his 2015–16 tours, much to the bemusement of the audience.

On the Way: A nice slab of bluesy guitar work, with vocals awash in echo. Uncharacteristically, there is some sloppy bass playing on this track. It's odd that he didn't fix the slip-ups. It's good to hear McCartney let loose on electric guitar after years of leaving those chores to his Wings bandmates.

Waterfalls: The quintessential McCartney ballad: strong melody, electric piano, impassioned vocal. The only problem is that about two minutes into it, the song becomes overly repetitive. There's a nice acoustic guitar interlude that pops up just a minute into the song.

Nobody Knows: A fun little rocker with the pairing of bass and drums driving the song along. It sounds almost like McCartney is making up the lyrics as he goes along. There are two lead vocals, one in each channel, with McCartney doing his best postmodern Elvis impression. The electric guitar solo is a little thin.

Front Parlour: One of two instrumentals that muddies up the momentum of the album, "Front Parlour" tries to find a suitable melody as it meanders along but doesn't quite get there. The weird electronic effect applied to the rhythm track is distracting. This doesn't even sound as if it was fun to record.

Summer's Day Song: Almost impossibly slow and plodding, the song is saved by a scintillating melody and a great triple-tracked vocal. It would have been more effective if real strings had been used instead of synthesizers, but that just wasn't on the agenda.

Frozen Jap: Another instrumental with very little to recommend it. A booming drum track underlays the wash of a bunch of synth parts. One listen will probably be enough for most listeners.

Bogey Music: Nice galloping drums and bass part propels this silly little exercise, with lots of echo-y vocals. Voice manipulation gives the song a kind of funereal aura. A simple electric guitar riff plays throughout.

Darkroom: What an odd song this is. A great vocal over insistent drums and synth noodling gives this an interesting feel. The last part of the song's tempo speeds up rapidly until the song morphs into a shuffling coda.

One of These Days: A great McCartney ballad, with just acoustic guitars and a fantastic vocal, triple-tracked during the chorus. Compared to the rest of the album this song's lyrics are as candid as McCartney gets. Sounds as if he's taking stock of his life and career on this one. The distant and slight reverb on the vocals make it sound all the more wistful.

Bonus Tracks

The *Paul McCartney Collection* 1993 reissue (August 9, 1993; Parlophone 7 89137 2) included bonus tracks "Check My Machine," "Secret Friend" and "Goodnight Tonight."

Check My Machine: This is almost six minutes of the title being repeated in a falsetto voice heavily treated with all kinds of echo. The bass and drum parts are really the only things of interest on this repetitive song. It seems likely McCartney was "checking his machines" prior to recording and thought this would be a good song title.

Secret Friend: More electronic nonsense, with the tape being sped up and slowed down throughout. You can barely understand the lyrics because they are so heavily treated with all kinds of effects. This has a sort of bossa nova feel to it. At 10:31, it tries one's patience pretty rapidly. Clearly, this is a case of McCartney amusing himself with sounds. There is really no good reason to release something like this. It's like Martin Scorsese putting out a really bad home movie.

Goodnight Tonight (refer to the singles chapter for a discussion of this song).

The 2011 *Paul McCartney Archive* reissue of *McCartney II* (Hear Music, HRM-32798-02) has so many bonus features that it's almost overwhelming trying to decide where to start. Along with the original 11-song remastered album, there are two CDs of bonus tracks and a DVD of bonus films. The DVD features a long interview with McCartney, conducted by Tim Rice in May 1980, plus videos of several songs from the album. The release comes with a coffee table size hardcover book with an astounding array of photographs and lots of information on the making of the album.

Bonus audio disc 1:

Blue Sway: A hypnotic and lengthy track that sounds almost like a soundtrack to a film. There are so many strings and horns on this production that they sometimes threaten to overwhelm the track. It has pretty vapid lyrics that don't add up to much of a coherent meaning. But there's a very 1980s-era sax part that comes in and out of the mix and a mesmerizing rhythm track that makes the song interesting to listen to.

Coming Up (Live): This is a very energetic version of the album track, taken from Wings' December 17, 1979, show at the Apollo in Glasgow, Scotland. It works better with real horns. McCartney's voice is appropriately hoarse, befitting of the vocal rigors of being on tour. He inserts alternate lyrics at certain points. This is the version that introduced American audiences to "Coming Up."

Check My Machine: A slightly edited version of the bonus track released in 1993.

Bogey Wobble: More electronic gibberish that's difficult to tolerate for very long. There's a persistent sound of bubbling water throughout.

Secret Friend: A slightly edited version of the bonus track from the 1993 reissue.

Mr. H Atom/You Know I'll Get You Baby: The first part of this medley is a poorly rendered biology lesson over an insistent beat punctuated by lots of synthesizers. This is one of the few songs on the album on which you can hear Linda's vocals. The second part is a 12-in-the-bar recitation of the title over and over again, with lots of voices and the usual synth flourishes.

Wonderful Christmastime: This is a slightly edited version of the single. Refer to the singles chapter for a discussion of this song.

All You Horse Riders/Blue Sway: The first part of this medley is an inane 12-bar bit of clip clopping percussion and McCartney urging a bunch of equestrians to jump over streams, etc. A reprise of "Blue Sway" then appears, without the over production and the original's vocal track, except for some spoken words here and there.

Bonus audio disc 2:

This disc features full length original album mixes of "Coming Up," "Front Parlour," "Frozen Jap," "Darkroom," "Check My Machine," and "Wonderful Christmastime." It also includes an instrumental only version of "Summer's Day Song" and an edited for radio version of "Waterfalls."

Tug of War

Released April 19, 1982 (U.K.); April 26, 1982 (U.S.)
Parlophone PCTC 259; Columbia TCA 37462
Highest Chart Position: 1 in the U.K. and U.S.
Produced by George Martin
Musicians: Paul McCartney: vocals, backing vocals, acoustic guitar, electric guitar, bass, piano, drums, synthesizer, percussion, vocoder; Linda McCartney: backing vocals; Denny Laine: acoustic guitar, electric guitar, guitar synthesizer, synthesizer, bass; Eric Stewart: electric guitar, backing vocals; Steve Gadd: drums, percussion; Ringo Starr: drums; George Martin: electric piano; Stanley Clarke: bass; Stevie Wonder: vocals, synthesizer, electric piano, drums; Campbell Maloney: snare drum on "Tug of War"; Adrian Brett: pan pipes on "Somebody Who Cares"; Andy Mackay: Lyricon on "What's That You're Doing?"; Jack Brymer: clarinet on "Ballroom Dancing"; Carl Perkins: vocals, electric guitar on "Get It"; Dave Mattacks: drums, percussion on "Dress Me Up as a Robber"

Tug of War is one of Paul McCartney's finest and most introspective albums. It's filled with 1980s pop conventions, beautiful arrangements and carefully constructed and rendered vocals, solo McCartney at its best.

It cannot be denied that it has a certain Beatle-y vibe to it. It was produced by George Martin, and Ringo Starr appears on one track. But more than this, it is imbued with a certain sadness owing to the tragic death of John Lennon in December 1980, the same month that McCartney started work on the album.

It was also clear by this time that Wings were no more. Although Denny Laine appears on several tracks, no other members of Wings contributed.

The album was recorded at Martin's AIR Studios in London and Monserrat. The sessions were so productive that a handful of songs recorded were held over for inclusion on the next album. The cover features a photo of a remarkably young-looking McCartney listening to a playback on headphones. Also included was a lyric sheet with a listing of the musicians on each track and a large photo of McCartney writing lyrics to a song in his cabana in Monserrat.

It includes duets with two of McCartney's heroes, Carl Perkins and Stevie Wonder, and they don't disappoint.

The album was first released on CD in February 1984. A remastered version was released as part of the *Paul McCartney Collection* without bonus tracks, a departure from the usual practice of including some B-sides on reissues. It was released again as part of the *Paul McCartney Archive* project in October 2015 with lots of bonus material.

Tug of War: A stunning album opener with a plaintive and philosophical outlook, sung over simple acoustic guitar chords and lots of orchestration. The bridge is a powerful mix of electric guitars, drums and percussion, and backing vocals. McCartney sounds reflective and frankly, a little sad. It's almost as if he's admitting that he somehow has lost an important battle.

Take It Away: There is no discernible gap between the first two songs. A heavily syncopated beat with clever bass opens this track, with McCartney's clear vocal telling the story. A catchy but simple melody drives the song along, with lots of horns and orchestration. The coda includes a burst of horns that plays the song out.

Somebody Who Cares: A simple song built around a memorable melody with Spanish flavors. McCartney plays a neat solo on a Spanish guitar. Linda McCartney and Eric Stewart help out on backing vocals.

What's That You're Doing?: A chunk o' funk that teams McCartney with Stevie Wonder in a back-and-forth romp that doesn't amount to much lyrically but is nonetheless fun because of the interplay between two pop icons. McCartney's bass playing is outstanding and he's holding his own vocally with one of the most talented and soulful singers of all time.

Here Today: This song includes the saddest and most blatantly honest set of lyrics McCartney has ever written as he remembers his friend and songwriting partner Lennon. The simple combination of acoustic guitar and strings recalls "Yesterday." This is a beautiful 2:29 of fond remembrance, tinged with regret.

Ballroom Dancing: A bouncy romp of piano and guitar-based rock 'n' roll. McCartney's vocals are exquisite and the horn chart adds a lot to the texture. The bridge features a sinewy guitar, bass and drum interplay, until it returns to its original structure.

The Pound Is Sinking: At first this seems like a simple disquisition on global monetary markets. But then it turns into a thinly veiled denial of paternity by McCartney. In 1984 McCartney summitted to a blood test after a German woman attempted to sue him for back support by claiming he fathered her grown child during his days in Hamburg. The lawsuit was eventually dismissed.

Wanderlust: This is one of those sure-footed melodies that McCartney excels at. Hummable, majestic and unforgettable. This is one of McCartney's best vocal performances ever. A brass ensemble adds some heft to the arrangement.

Get It: A jaunty rockabilly workout with the father of that genre, Carl Perkins. The song features Perkins' signature guitar solo sound and folksy vocals. The vocal interplay between Perkins and McCartney sounds natural and borne of a mutual respect and love.

Be What You See: A 34-second snippet of guitar and McCartney's vocal fed through a vocoder.

Dress Me Up as a Robber: An odd quagmire of jazz-inflected chords and synth strings, with a vocal alternating between a sweet falsetto and McCartney's normal register.

Ebony and Ivory: Another duet with Stevie Wonder, although the vocals were recorded separately. The song features a certain sentimental naivete, but as a melodic piece of work, it stands the test of time. The vocals by both singers are outstanding, especially during the long fade-out.

The Paul McCartney Collection reissue (August 9, 1993; Parlophone 7 89266 2) had no bonus tracks.

Bonus Tracks

In 2015 the album was re-issued by Hear Music/Concord Music Group as part of the *Paul McCartney Archive Collection*. It was released in multiple formats:

Standard Edition: A remixed version of the original 12-track album on the first disc, plus 11 bonus tracks on the second disc.

Deluxe Edition three-CD/one-DVD box set and a 112-page book and a 64 page-scrapbook.

Super Deluxe three-CD/one-DVD box set with the 112-page book and a 64-page scrapbook with a limited edition acrylic slipcase.

Remastered vinyl: The album was also made available in special gatefold vinyl editions.

Disc 1: remixed album. Remixed version of the original 12-track album.

Disc 2: original album (deluxe edition only). The original 12-track album.

Disc 3 includes these bonus tracks:

Stop, You Don't Know Where She Came From (demo): A barrelhouse New Orleans influenced piano workout.

Wanderlust (demo)

Ballroom Dancing (demo)

Take It Away (demo)

The Pound Is Sinking (demo)

Something That Didn't Happen (demo): A snippet of music and lyrics that was eventually incorporated into "The Pound Is Sinking."

Ebony and Ivory (demo)—1:46

Dress Me Up as a Robber/Robber Riff (demo)

Ebony and Ivory (solo version)

Rainclouds and **I'll Give You a Ring** were B-sides to singles. (See the singles chapter for a discussion of these tracks.)

Take It Away (edit version)

The DVD includes these features:

"Tug of War" video (version 1), "Tug of War" video (version 2), "Take It Away" video, "Ebony and Ivory" video, "Fly TIA"—Behind the scenes on *Take It Away* (an 18-minute documentary)

Pipes of Peace

Released October 17, 1983 (U.K.); October 17, 1983 (U.S.)
Parlophone PCTC 1652301 (U.K.); Columbia QCT 39149 (U.S.)
Highest Chart Position: 4 in the U.K. and 15 in the U.S.
Produced by George Martin

Musicians: Paul McCartney: bass, guitars, piano, keyboards, synthesizer, drums, vocals; Linda McCartney: keyboards, backing vocals; Michael Jackson: vocals on "Say Say Say" and "The Man"; Eric Stewart: guitars, backing vocals; Denny Laine: guitars, keyboards, vocals; Hughie Burns: guitar; Geoff Whitehorn: guitar; David Williams: guitar on "Say Say Say"; Stanley Clarke: bass guitar, vocals; Nathan Watts: bass on "Say Say Say"; Chris Hammer Smith: harmonica on "Say Say Say"; Bill Wolfer: keyboards on "Say Say Say"; Gavyn Wright: violin; Jerry Hey: strings, horn; Gary Herbig: flute; Andy Mackay: saxophone; Ernie Watts: saxophone; Gary Grant: horns; Ringo Starr: drums on "So Bad" and "Average Person"; Steve Gadd: drums; Dave Mattacks: drums; Ricky Lawson: drums on "Say Say Say"; James Kippen: tabla on "Pipes of Peace"; Petalozzi's Children's Choir: backing vocals on "Pipes of Peace"

Pipes of Peace is *Tug of War* lite. Although several of the songs were recorded during the *Tug of War* sessions, and there's a certain thematic similarity, the songs on *Pipes of Peace* aren't nearly as memorable. This was the first inkling that Paul McCartney might be encountering an artistic slump.

McCartney employed his usual bevy of first-rate musicians, and there is a certain sheen to the tracks, but overall the songs are weak. He teamed up with Michael Jackson on two songs, one of which was an international hit, and he once again had the benefit of George Martin's production sensibilities. The songs are played well, expertly recorded and sung with the precision for which McCartney is known. They are just not very good.

This would mark the last time McCartney would work in the studio with long-time bandmate Denny Laine. The great Stanley Clarke plays bass on the instrumental "Hey Hey" and gets a co-writing credit as well.

The album was recorded in London, Monserrat, Scotland and Los Angeles. It was made available on vinyl, cassette tape and CD.

Pipes of Peace: This track starts out with a sweet-sounding piano and simple vocal. It then devolves into a lecture on how we need to create a world in which our children are safe from the ravages of war. Who could argue with that? Then it takes another turn and attempts to save the planet. The whole thing is swathed with a children's choir urging the singer on.

Say Say Say: Nothing smacks of the 1980s music scene more than this funky little jaunt featuring two of the most famous pop stars to ever roam the planet. McCartney's vocal is clear-eyed and understated, while Jackson's is more urgent and frenetic. A nice horn chart and bluesy harmonica add to the song's dynamics. The fade-out is a danceable, club friendly mix of funky guitar, harmonica and horns, underneath the singers repeating the song's title over and over again.

The Other Me: McCartney attempts to sound reflective and contrite in this apology to a lover, but the whole thing is hamstrung by some of the worst lyrics of his solo career. The melody is strong, as usual, and the track has a certain low-fi quality to it that makes it listenable, despite the embarrassing lyrics. The song is nearly redeemed by McCartney's outstanding vocals in the outro.

Keep Under Cover: This is a continuation of the theme in the previous track. Again, the lyrics are weak and seem like they were made up on the spot in the studio. The juxtaposition of McCartney's nearly whispered vocals on the verses and his high register pleadings during the chorus is really engaging. There are some interesting guitar parts and a tasteful string chart. Nice cold ending, too.

So Bad: This seems to be a love song to both Linda and James McCartney, who was 6 at the time. McCartney uses his falsetto to great effect, and the cascade of vocals add some drama. Again, the melody is strong and the horns add a welcome dimension. Great production touches abound courtesy of Sir George Martin.

The Man: The second collaboration with Michael Jackson is dominated by a fuzzy electric guitar and shimmery acoustic guitars playing chords similar to those in "Here, There and Everywhere." The chorus is so 1980s and is indistinguishable from any Christopher Cross or Kenny Loggins offering. The difference is that McCartney and Jackson's vocals blend so well and so seamlessly, creating a wall of voices that makes this song enjoyable to listen to.

Sweetest Little Show: Great acoustic guitars gild this countrified romp with really confounding lyrics that seem to be about the pitfalls of being a public figure. There is a nice little interlude in the middle with a double-tracked acoustic guitar solo that builds some tension and morphs into a fake live environment.

Average Person: No matter how hard he tries to understand the "average person," Paul McCartney is clearly just an outside observer of the lives of the great ordinary middle and lower class. He flew that nest long ago. His personal survey of people on the street in this track seems to attempt to understand the longings of the have-nots (engine driver, waitress and a boxer).

The song is constructed well, has some interesting meter changes and the usual abundance of backing vocals and sound effects. The subject matter is so perplexing and lacks any point of view at all, reducing the song to a real head-scratcher.

Hey Hey: A jazz-electro amalgamation that features the great Stanley Clarke can never be a bad thing. This one comes complete with the soft jazz-rock center that almost lulls the listener into a hammock nap on a nice spring day before it returns to its original motif of crash-bang fusion.

Tug of Peace: The sounds of a tug of war opens this song, just as it did the song by that name on the previous album. But this is a heavily syncopated piece of call and response with lyrics from "Tug of War" and references to the pipes of peace. But again, the track suffers from a completely nebulous point of view that is almost impossible to discern.

Through Our Love: This is by far the best track on the album, and once again proves that McCartney can write a majestic and heartfelt pop opus that is equally moving and melodic. The lead vocal is epic, and the Wings-like backing vocals lend a nice counterpoint to the proceedings. George Martin's production is reminiscent of his best work with McCartney's first band. The power of love is the theme, and somehow it just works so much better than the twin themes of war and peace, especially coming from a man whose entire catalogue is limned with pro-love sentiments.

Bonus Tracks

The 1993 re-release of *Pipes of Peace* as part of the *Paul McCartney Collection* (August 9, 1993; Parlophone 89267 2) included three bonus tracks:

Twice in a Lifetime: This is an overblown ballad that was written for an obscure 1985 film of the same name starring Gene Hackman and Ann-Margret. It played over the closing credits. Weird chords and odd reverb on the lead vocal make this one of the most obscure songs in the McCartney catalog. A typical 1980s sax wails throughout.

We All Stand Together: See the singles section for a discussion of this song.

Simple as That: This song was written for The Anti-Heroin Project, which was supported by many popular artists at the time. It was McCartney's contribution to a 1986 album released to benefit The Anti-Heroin

Project and features Linda, Mary, Stella and James McCartney on backing vocals. The track has a bouncy ska feel to it.

In 2015 the album was re-issued in multiple formats by Hear Music/ Concord Music Group as part of the *Paul McCartney Archive Collection.*

Disc 1 features the original 11-track album digitally remastered.

Disc 2 features bonus tracks including "Average Person," "Keep Under Cover," "Sweetest Little Show." "It's Not On," "Simple as That," "Say Say Say," "Ode to a Koala Bear," "Twice in a Lifetime" and "Christian Bop."

The first six bonus tracks are demos; "Say Say Say" is a remix done in 2015; "Ode to a Koala Bear" was the B-side to the original "Say Say Say" single (see the singles chapter for a discussion of this song); and "Twice in a Lifetime" is the track that was also included as a bonus track in the 1993 re-release of the album. "Christian Bop" was previously unreleased and is a hypnotic piano based instrumental played in a minor key.

"It's Not On" is about as obscure as McCartney can get. Arnie Pupe, Irene E and the green woman seem to be acting out a workplace harassment scenario. A discordant woman's voice can be heard here and there.

Disc 3 is a DVD of bonus video, including the official music videos for "Pipes of Peace," "So Bad" and "Say Say Say," plus the short home movies "Hey Hey in Montserrat," "Behind the Scenes at AIR Studios" and "The Man."

Give My Regards to Broad Street

Released October 22, 1984
Parlophone EL2602781, PCTC2; Columbia CK39613
Highest chart position: 1 in the U.K. and 21 in the U.S.
Produced by George Martin
Musicians: Paul McCartney: vocals, acoustic guitar, piano, drums, electric harpsichord, bass guitar; Eric Stewart, Steve Lukather, Chris Spedding, Dave Edmunds: guitar, vocals; Linda McCartney: keyboards, vocals; David Gilmour, Eric Ford: guitar; Pat Halling, Laurie Lewis, Raymond Keenlyside, Tony Gilbert: violin; Derek Grossmith: clarinet, alto saxophone; Eddie Mordue: clarinet, tenor saxophone; Vic Ash: tenor saxophone; Ronnie Hughs, Bobby Haughey: trumpet on "Ballroom Dancing"; Chris Smith: trombone on "Ballroom Dancing"; Brass Ensemble: Philip Jones Brass Ensemble; Group Leader Philip Jones; lead trumpeter: Jimmy Watson; Jeff Bryant: French horn; Jerry Hey,

Lawrence Williams, Thomas Pergerson, Tommy Whittle: horns on "Silly Love Songs/Reprise"; George Martin: piano; Gerry Butler: keyboards; Trevor Barstow: piano; Anne Dudley: synthesizer; Russ Stableford: acoustic bass; Herbie Flowers, Louis Johnson, John Paul Jones: bass guitar; Jeff Porcaro, Dave Mattacks, Ringo Starr, Stuart Elliott, John Dean: drums; Jody Linscott: percussion

Give My Regards to Broad Street is the soundtrack album to Paul McCartney's disastrous movie of the same name, written by McCartney and also starring the McCartneys, the Starrs (Ringo and Barbara Bach) and three genuine actors: Sir Ralph Richardson, Bryan Brown and Tracy Ullman. How McCartney cajoled those three to appear in the movie remains a mystery, but it's a good bet all three regretted it soon after it was released to a wholly disinterested and bored public.

The problem with the movie and the album is simple: It relies heavily on the viewer and listener to reimagine a passel of Beatles songs as vehicles to drive the plot along, rather than as part of the soundtrack of their lives. It's an impossible task to pull off, especially since the remakes were so slick and devoid of passion that they sounded like completely different songs.

An artist should have full control of his catalog, of course, and should be able to re-record songs if he so desires, but this endeavor is so fraught with risk and a puzzling ignorance on the artist's part of what the songs mean to everyone who loves the Beatles. It's like painting over an original Picasso.

Mercifully, most of the Beatle remakes are brief and don't leave much of an impression.

Still, the album sold well, chiefly on the strength of its hit single. It was recorded in London. At 61:10, the album is longer than most single albums, so it necessitated some heavy editing on the vinyl release. Three songs from the soundtrack were held off the vinyl release, and several others were pared down considerably. Vinyl just doesn't have the bandwidth to maintain dynamic range and quality for more than an hour. This is the first McCartney album to be released on vinyl, cassette and CD at its original release.

This marked the nadir of Paul McCartney's solo career. It would take him five more years to recover fully.

No More Lonely Nights: The album starts strong with one of McCartney's superb melodic soufflés. The chorus is indelibly catchy, and

David Gilmour's electric guitar gives the tune some oomph. McCartney's in great voice, and George Martin's score creates an undercurrent of lush drama. Just a tinge of reverb on McCartney's vocal gives it some breadth. The song fades out with Gilmour's extended guitar solo, but not until a significant key modulation occurs.

Good Day Sunshine/Corridor Music: A strict reading of the original but benefitting from modern recording technology and played at a slightly faster tempo. The chorus struggles because it's missing the Beatle-y harmonies of Lennon and Harrison. Listen to McCartney say what sounds like "sheep" at 1:28 into the song, echoing Lennon's playful chatter in the original. The "Corridor Music" section features snippets of dialogue between McCartney and Starr, both stiff and seemingly uncomfortable.

Yesterday: As beautiful as ever and sung exquisitely, but why was this necessary? It doesn't advance the plot of the movie and just seems overindulgent. The strings are a little different, and there is some echo on McCartney's voice.

Here, There and Everywhere: Very lovely and haunting, but again, to what end? A horn arrangement that plays the song out adds something extra to this version.

Wanderlust: A new take on this excellent song from *Tug of War.* This seems like slightly less of a sacrilege than remaking a Beatles song, but it's still not an improvement over the original. This version has a slightly different (and busier) horn chart. There is a snippet of the "Here, There and Everywhere" melody at the close of this track.

Ballroom Dancing: Another song from *Tug of War,* this is quite a bit different than the original. First, McCartney's vocal is awash in reverb. The instrumental break in the middle features some different chords and percussion, plus a much heavier electric guitar sound. This one churns along nicely.

Silly Love Songs/Reprise: Here, McCartney takes his 1976 pop confection and turns it into a 1980s rumble filled with synthesizers and a jazz-fusion bass break but retaining the original's signature bass line. A big difference is the instrumental break modulates into a higher key and features not only the original horn chart, but an electric guitar filling in some of the breaks. "Reprise" is a few seconds of the song played in a New Age style.

Not Such a Bad Boy: Not such a bad song. This is one of only a handful of new compositions and features some hooks and bounce. The chorus is memorable and the lead guitar break is spirited. McCartney does some nice rock 'n' roll screaming at the end.

So Bad: This remake of a song from "Pipes of Peace" is almost an exact replica of the original, except for the phase shifting effect on the guitar. Again, another kind of curious choice, as the song does nothing to advance the reed-thin plot of the film.

No Values/No More Lonely Nights (Ballad Reprise): "No Values" is an electric guitar heavy song that recalls *Back to the Egg* (especially that album's "To You"). The lyrics are obscure and the song's "storyline" is hard to follow. The coda recalls one of the instrumentals on *McCartney*.

The "Ballad Reprise" is a few seconds of "No More Lonely Nights" played by a string quartet.

For No One: One of McCartney's best compositions ever gets reborn as a chamber string opus. No bass, no piano or harpsichord, just a simple acoustic guitar picking the bass notes while the strings give the saddest of all Beatle songs an extra dash of melancholy. Of all the Beatles remakes on this album, this one at least tries to reinvent itself, which is at least mildly interesting.

Eleanor Rigby/Eleanor's Dream: A note for note remake of the original, "Eleanor Rigby" offers no new insights until it morphs into the "Eleanor's Dream" section of the track. It's a mini-opus of orchestral moods and colors, all built around the style and key of the original. The ending features an incessant chirping sound over some timpani and a return of the original melody.

The Long and Winding Road: The sax-laden introduction to this one sounds like the theme song to the 1970s courtroom drama "L.A. Law." It's obvious McCartney was trying to update the sound of what is obviously one of his favorite compositions. In this he succeeds. The strings, sax and the steady 4/4 time signature turn it into just another bland mid–1980s ballad, which is the inherent objection to remaking classic Beatles songs. It tends to relegate them to the mundane category and in their original incarnations they were anything but.

No More Lonely Nights (Playout Version): This is a tuneless, meandering reworking of the album's best song, even though its disco sensibilities are about five years too late.

Goodnight Princess: McCartney channeling his dad's favorite music, this is the song that played over the closing credits in the film. It's harmless and inconsequential.

No More Lonely Nights (Extended Version): Lots of extra bits and pieces of studio trickery added to the playout version also adds 3:04 of elapsed playing time. By this time, the listener has likely had her fill of "No More Lonely Nights," in all its cute packages.

No More Lonely Night (Dance Mix): And just when you think it's over, the only entertainment value of this "dance mix" of the song is trying to imagine anyone dancing to it.

Bonus Tracks

The original album was remastered and reissued as part of the 1993 *Paul McCartney Collection* (August 9, 1993; Parolophone 7 89268 2) with the playout, extended and dance mix versions of "No More Lonely Nights" added as bonus tracks.

Press to Play

Released August 25, 1986 (U.S.); September 1, 1986 (U.K.)
Parlophone 7462692; Capitol 7462692
Highest chart position: 8 in the U.K. and 30 in the U.S.
Produced by Paul McCartney and Hugh Padgham
Musicians: Paul McCartney: lead vocals, bass guitar, acoustic guitar, electric guitar, piano, keyboards, synthesizer; Neil Jason: bass guitar: Eric Stewart: acoustic guitar, electric guitar, keyboards, backing vocals; Pete Townshend: electric guitar on "Angry"; Carlos Alomar: acoustic and electric guitars; Eddie Rayner: keyboards; Nick Glennie-Smith: keyboards; Simon Chamberlain: piano; Linda McCartney: backing vocals; Phil Collins: drums and percussion on "Angry"; Jerry Marotta: drums, percussion; John Bradbury: violin; Graham Ward: drums, percussion; Ray Cooper: percussion; Dick Morrissey: tenor saxophone; Lenny Pickett: alto saxophone, tenor saxophone; Gary Barnacle: saxophone; Gavyn Wright: violin; Kate Robbins: harmony vocals; Ruby James: harmony vocals James McCartney, Steve Jackson, Eddie Klein, John Hammel, Matt Howe: spoken word

Press to Play came out at a time when Bruce Springsteen, Michael Jackson, Madonna and Prince were dominating the pop world. Set against this landscape, the songs on *Press to Play* just couldn't compare in terms of hooks, beats and pop culture significance. McCartney's songs on this album were pop craftmanship at its finest, but the music scene at the time had little tolerance for sappy piano ballads and '70s-style rock songs made by someone who had hit his creative peak in the 1960s. There just wasn't room for McCartney's music in the pop firmament of the mid–1980s.

Still, he soldiered on and created an album that sounds better today than it did in 1986. Distanced from the context of the pop scene of 1986, it actually sounds like a decent collection of songs. He enlisted a new producer in Hugh Padgham, famous for his work with the Police and Phil Collins, and also had, among others, Collins, Pete Townsend, Carlos Alomar and Jerry Marotta along to help. Six of the songs were co-credited to Eric Stewart, formerly of 10cc, as McCartney appeared to finally acknowledge that his work might benefit from some collaboration.

McCartney's sound was definitely toughened up on *Press to Play*. Although the songs didn't approach his best work, it's clear he knew how to use the pop conventions of the day to "de–McCartney" his sound. This makes the album even more enjoyable to listen to today.

The cover of the album featured a stunning black-and-white photograph of Paul and Linda McCartney taken by George Hurrell, using the same box camera he used to take memorable photos of movie stars in the 1930s and 1940s.

Most of the album was recorded in Sussex, England, although three tracks were recorded in Scotland.

The inside of the package is really interesting. McCartney produced hand drawings of the recording mix for each of the song, which details where in the stereo picture each voice, instrument and handclap appear. This is a really fascinating look at the multi-layered creation of a song and the ultimate placement of each sound in the stereo spectrum.

Stranglehold: The best rocker on the album, complete with lots of guitars and a lively horn arrangement. The vocals are impeccably recorded, of course, and McCartney's singing is strong.

Good Times Coming/Feel the Sun: The song begins with a bunch of people singing the title in what sounds like a singalong around a bonfire at the beach. Then the hyper-syncopated main song begins, with all the prerequisite 1980s recording frills: electronic percussion, synthesizers and weird vocal effects. Great guitar solo by Carlos Alomar, known for his studio work with David Bowie. McCartney's bass work shines throughout. The "Feel the Sun" part crashes in over a simple chord structure and lots of guitar and synths before it comes to a faded end.

Talk More Talk: Weird spoken parts usher in this miasma of percussion heavy gobbledygook. The chord sequence is interesting, but the lyrics are virtually indecipherable. There's a lovely little vocal break in the middle where McCartney triple-tracks some vocal gymnastics. The song pauses toward the end with varied speeds of spoken word phrases that, of course, make no sense at all. It fades with some electronic drums trying hard to drown out more spoken words.

Footprints: This Latin-inflected acoustic guitar ballad played in a minor key tells the tale of an old man who prefers to be outside in the snow. As each verse starts, new musical enhancements are added, including pipes, clavinet, congas and electric guitars. McCartney plays a nice Spanish guitar figure to take the song out.

Only Love Remains: A typical McCartney love ballad, played on piano and larded by a bevy of musical embellishments, including strings, synthesizers and marimbas. The melody is strong and McCartney delivers a memorable vocal. The song comes to an overly dramatic end that features over-the-top orchestration.

Press: "Press" is unlike any other song in the McCartney catalog and is such a product of its time. Over a huge drum sound and biting electric guitars, McCartney delivers an echo-laden vocal extolling the virtues of a good massage. A funky guitar solo by Alomar toughens the sound. A bass sequencer is used and lots of white noise invades the entire track. The main feature, however, is the galactic drum sound. It just explodes out of your speakers.

Pretty Little Head: This track would have fit nicely on any of The Fireman albums. Its hypnotic backing track and the machismo of the half-spoken vocal, along with the weird lyrics, give the song an unearthly sound. Again, the song relies heavily on the bass, synth and drums combination that was so prevalent at the time.

Move Over Busker: An old-time rocker (with even older time lyrics) built around a catchy guitar riff and still more loud drums morphs into a randy tale of Nell Gwynn, Mae West and Errol Flynn and a pubescent youth waiting for his first shot at sexual adventure. The electric guitars flesh out the sound nicely, and McCartney slips in a subtle key modulation in time for the last verse, which gives the entire track some lift.

Angry: McCartney, Townsend and Collins get down to it with a nice three-piece rocker that careens down the aural highway. Anger is not usually a topic McCartney explores in his songs, but this is a fun little romp. Townsend delivers a typical Who-like guitar solo. A trio of saxes augment the song on the last chorus until it ends in one last angry burst.

However Absurd: Based on the nonsensical writing of W.H. Auden, this slow piano ballad uses the same technique, although the title of the track at least acknowledges the absurdity of the words. The chords are similar during the verse to George Harrison's "Isn't It a Pity." The best part of the song by far is the epic middle eight, in which McCartney briefly resurrects his "Monkberry Moon Delight" vocal style. The ending features a frenetic chorus emboldened by a military-style drum part and lots of synthesizer.

Bonus Tracks

The CD release of *Press to Play* included three bonus tracks:

Write Away: A jazzy percussion-heavy basic track supports this catchy tune that also feature a lively piano solo. Lots of percussive accents, a saxophone and reverb-laden vocals bring the song to a cold ending.

It's Not True: There's nothing too memorable about this simple tune, but it's a great workout for McCartney's vocal. Lots of echo, another big drum sound, and a sinewy sax solo over electric piano and an inventive bass part fill out the middle of the song. The guitar dominated fade-out features lots of echo-y vocals by McCartney and a false ending. A different (and slightly tamer) version of "It's Not True" appeared on the B-side of the "Press" single.

Tough on a Tightrope: A mini-opera about the trials of love features lots of interesting instrumentation. Hammond organ, fuzz guitar, a full orchestra, flute and congas all round out the big sound. McCartney can't help himself; even his slightest compositions drip with melody.

The 1993 re-release of *Press to Play* as part of the *Paul McCartney Collection* (August 9, 1993; Parlophone 7 89269 2) included "Spies Like Us" and "Once Upon a Long Ago." See the singles chapter for a discussion of these songs.

Flowers in the Dirt

Released June 5, 1989
Parlophone CDPCSD 106; Capitol CDP 7916532
Highest chart position: 1 in the U.K. and 21 in the U.S.

Produced by Paul McCartney, Mitchell Froom, Neil Dorfsman, Elvis Costello, Trevor Horn, Steve Lipson, Chris Hughes, Russ Cullum, David Foster and Phil Ramone (CD reissue tracks only)

Musicians: Paul McCartney: vocals, bass guitar, 12-string guitar, electric and acoustic guitars, synth, drum overdubs, percussion, celeste, piano, keyboards, Mellotron, flugelhorn, wood saw; Linda McCartney: Minimoog, background vocals; Robbie McIntosh: acoustic and electric guitars; Hamish Stuart: bass guitar, electric and acoustic guitars, percussion, backing vocals; Paul Wickens: keyboards; Chris Whitten: drums and synth drums, percussion; Elvis Costello: vocals, keyboards; Dave Mattacks: drums; David Gilmour: electric guitar on "We Got Married"; David Foster: keyboards; Steve Lipson: computer and drum programming, electric and bass guitar, keyboards; Peter Henderson: computer programming; Guy Barker: trumpet; Trevor Horn: keyboards; Nicky Hopkins: piano; Mitchell Fromm: keyboards; Judd Lander: harmonica; Chris Davis: saxophone; Chris White: saxophone; Dave Bishop: saxophone; John Taylor: cornet; Tony Goodard: cornet; David Rhodes: ebow guitar; Ian Peters: euphonium; Ian Harper: tenor horn; Jah Bunny: "tongue styley"; Eddie Klein: computer programming

Flowers in the Dirt is the best "comeback" album Paul McCartney ever recorded. After two disastrous albums in a row, McCartney enlisted the help of a bevy of producers and the largest collection of session musicians he's ever used on an album. And the songs were a lot better: more cohesive, with stronger melodies expertly played and sung.

This had something to do with McCartney's decision to collaborate with Elvis Costello (Declan MacManus), at the writing table and in the studio. There were four McCartney-MacManus songs on the album, a whole mess of them still in the tape boxes, and enough left over to include on the next album. McCartney also collaborated with Costello on the latter's 1989 album *Spike,* including a co-writing credit on the top 20 hit "Veronica."

During the recording of *Flowers in the Dirt,* McCartney also recruited a touring band for his first tour in 10 years. Hamish Stuart, Robbie McIntosh, Paul "Wix" Wickens and Chris Whitten were all veterans of other well-known bands and had lots of road and studio experience. They would commence on a massive world tour starting in September 1989, during which the set list featured songs from the new album plus a heavy complement of Beatles songs.

This album marks a major turning point in Paul McCartney's career. From here on out he would never be off the road for long stretches, and his public persona as a galactically talented live performer seemed to burnish his reputation as a musician and songwriter. The following 20 years saw McCartney's work being praised by even his harshest critics and in those 20 years he would never again release an album that was widely excoriated (like *Give My Regards to Broad Street* and *Press to Play*).

Flowers in the Dirt included the hit single "My Brave Face," which peaked at 18 in the British charts and 25 in the U.S. charts.

My Brave Face: Over multiple harmonies, the songs busts out with an a cappella burst of joyous vocals. The melody is strong, and some of the lyrics are surely from the pen of one Declan MacManus. His trademark of fitting a lot of words into small musical spaces is evident. Electric and acoustic guitars abound all over the mix, and a bubbly bass part frames the whole backing track. More importantly, McCartney sounds assured and confident. It's the perfect opening track for a comeback album and one of McCartney's most underappreciated songs.

Rough Ride: Over some snaky guitars and an electronic drum kit, McCartney lets it all hang out on his lead vocal. The bouncy melody is supported by synthesizers and a nifty horn chart, with McCartney vamping over the blare of the horns. The song is lyrically thin, but the groove is strong.

You Want Her Too: This might be the best of all the McCartney-Costello collaborations. It's got a slightly discordant sound with incredibly soulful vocals featuring a call-and-response musical "argument" between McCartney and Costello. Lyrically, it's a much more mature and less tongue-in-cheek version of "The Girl Is Mine." The fade-out coda features the surprise appearance of a full orchestra that sounds like it's playing the stage exit riff for Frank Sinatra.

Distractions: This is just the sort of soft and lovely song McCartney has always been able to come up with. This one forgoes the gooey sentimentality of some of his loveliest songs and seems so much more philosophical and inward-looking than usual. He sings the entire song in a sort of quasi-whisper in his lower register, but during the last verse he lets loose in his higher register. He plays a moving acoustic guitar solo that has some Latin undertones. The cold ending is effective.

We Got Married: This retelling of the McCartney wedding and marriage is the weakest song on the album, but it has some interesting time signature changes and features a scathing electric guitar played by David Gilmour. The song has a multi-layered structure, and meanders back and forth between the verses and the bridge. Except for the synths and the trumpet, the basic track sounds a little like Wings. The song fades with McCartney repeating his advice for a successful marriage.

Put It There: A beautiful and brief acoustic guitar workout with McCartney recalling one of his dad's favorite expressions. McCartney adds some percussion by slapping his thighs and harmonizes with himself throughout.

Figure of Eight: A great rocker with McCartney's lead vocal soaked with echo. This served as a very effective opening number in the setlist during the world tour (listen to the version on *Tripping the Live Fantastic* to hear how powerful it sounds live). This is one of the best and catchiest songs on the album.

This One: An interesting, meditative song with a strong message. Chiming acoustic guitars, joined by a big bass and drums combo propel the song along. Like all songs on this album, McCartney's vocals are strong and clear. The middle eight continues the theme of missed opportunities. A funky little coda takes the song out. Another underappreciated McCartney gem.

Don't Be Careless Love: McCartney, accompanied by a trio of voices, starts this quasi-gospel song singing in his highest non-falsetto voice. Handclaps and an electric piano underpin the verses. Some of the lyrics are pretty dark, pointing again to the collaboration with Elvis Costello.

That Day Is Done: Another gospel-tinged song with a powerful vocal by McCartney, imbued with regret and contrition. The verses are in a major key, but the chorus shifts into the relative minor, amping up the drama of the track. The best part of this song is the bridge, which McCartney kills with his larynx-shredding vocal.

How Many People: A reggae-inflected song with more lyrics about negative consequences. An interesting production decision is made: During the first two verses and chorus, McCartney's voice is treated with reasonable amounts of reverb. During the third verse, his vocal is completely dry. The contrast is stark and effective.

Motor of Love: This sounds so much like the Cars' "Drive" that it's impossible to overlook the similarities. A wash of harmony vocals with a healthy dollop of computer drum programming and keyboards dominate the overall sound. There is a certain religious undertone in the lyrics.

This features another strong vocal by McCartney.

Ou Est Le Soleil: This song appeared on the CD and cassette versions of the album only. It's pretty much a throwaway track, with the lyrics consisting of an eight-word phrase repeated over and over. There is a certain trance-like quality to the basic track. This would not have been out of place on one of The Fireman albums.

Bonus Tracks

The 1993 reissue of *Flowers in the Dirt* as part of the *Paul McCartney Collection* (August 9, 1993; Parlophone 7 89138 2) included three bonus tracks. See the singles chapter for a discussion of these songs.

Back on My Feet
Flying to My Home
Loveliest Thing

The 2017 remastered version of *Flowers in the Dirt* (Capitol Records, B0026450-02) included a special edition with the original 13-song album plus nine bonus tracks, which consisted of McCartney-Costello originals in demo form.

The Lovers That Never Were: A soulful reading of this song that would appear on McCartney's next album, with just piano, acoustic guitar and two vocals.

Tommy's Coming Home: Two acoustic guitars and two amazing harmonizing vocals frame this interesting story song. The lyrics are complex and dense.

Twenty Fine Fingers: This one includes a guide drum track plus two acoustic guitars and two vocals. The lyrics are spit out rapid-fire and the tempo is upbeat. It would've been fun to hear a fully produced version of this fun song.

So Like Candy: A contemplative, quietly strummed acoustic guitar-based song, with McCartney and Costello harmonizing throughout.

You Want Her Too: This is pretty faithful to the finished version, with the call and response vocals.

That Day Is Done: A gospel-tinged piano ballad with both McCartney and Costello singing the lyrics, with clever harmonizing in places.

Don't Be Careless Love: This is more tender and slower than the finished version. It has some complicated harmonies that never showed up in the finished version.

My Brave Face: A pretty straightforward acoustic version of the album's first single. It's clear McCartney and Costello are still learning this one. It's also quite a bit shorter than the album version.

Playboy to a Man: A great rousing rocker with McCartney taking the lead vocal. It has a similar musical structure to "My Brave Face."

The Lovers That Never Were (mixed by Geoff Emerick): This mix features more spirited vocals from McCartney and a more prominent piano part.

A disc included in the deluxe edition has the first nine songs listed above in slightly different demo configurations, recorded in 1988.

The deluxe edition included three CDs (the original album, 18 bonus tracks, three previously unheard cassette demos, a 32-page notebook of handwritten lyrics, a catalogue from Linda McCartney's *Flowers in the Dirt* photo exhibition, a photobook, and a 112-page book recounting the making of the album through interviews with McCartney, Costello and others).

The DVD includes music videos of several of the album's songs, plus three short films ("Paul and Elvis," "Buds in the Studio" and "The Making of 'This One.'") It also includes the 65-minute long video "Put It There," which includes performances of many of the album's songs, plus some Beatles songs and a handful of oldies covers. A special limited edition "World Tour Pack" numbered individually was also released to coincide with the 1989–90 tour. The 12 × 12 cardboard package resembled an equipment box. This included the original album, plus a 3-inch CD of "Party Party." It also included a tour poster, family tree, bumper sticker, six postcards and a tour itinerary.

The cassette demos include:

I Don't Want to Confess: It's easy to see why this one ended up on the cutting room floor. The lyrics are odd and there isn't much in the way of melody.

Shallow Grave: A funky little ditty that would have fit the style of the original Elvis. This is a playful version that sounds like it was fun to make.

Mistress and Maid: A slower and more contemplative version than the version that showed up on *Off the Ground*. It's also played and sung in a lower key.

A digital download only collection includes many of the songs on *Flowers in the Dirt* (including four versions of "Ou Est Le Soleil") and a few B-sides. Demo versions of "Distractions," "This One" and "Back on

My Feet" were made available by digital download exclusively through paulmccartney.com. Those four B-sides will be discussed in the singles chapter.

Party Party: A jazzy jam that is credited to the entire touring band. It's mostly an ad-libbed jam session, with some prominent percussion and a sax solo moving in and out of the mix.

Off the Ground

Released February 2, 1993
Parlophone PCSD 125; Capitol CDP 0777 7 80362 2 7
Highest Chart Position: 5 in the U.K. and 17 in the U.S.
Produced by Paul McCartney and Julian Mendelsohn
Musicians: Paul McCartney: vocals, bass, keyboards, electric and acoustic guitars, Spanish guitars, ocarina, percussion, congas, sitar, congas, drums; Linda McCartney: vocals, keyboards, percussion, train whistle; Hamish Stuart: vocals, electric and acoustic guitars, 12-string guitar, bass, percussion, piano; Robbie McIntosh: electric and acoustic guitars, Spanish guitars, slide guitar, mandolin, backing vocals; Paul Wickens: keyboards, piano, organ, clavinet, synthesizer, accordion, LinnDrum, drum programming, percussion, backing vocals; Blair Cunningham: drums, congas, percussion, backing vocals

Off the Ground is a studio album made with McCartney's touring band at the time, with Blair Cunningham taking over for Chris Whitten on drums. As a follow-up to the astounding *Flowers in the Dirt*, it fails to match the intensity and the songcraft of its predecessor. Whereas the latter was chock full of great melodies, skilled musicianship and an overall theme of love and peace (sound familiar?), *Off the Ground* too often resorts to tired sloganeering and vapid jingoism. McCartney has certainly earned the right to opine about animal rights and the environment, but here he just doesn't pull it off with any sort of aplomb. A handful of songs were preachy and scolding, and another set of songs were just plain uninteresting.

The album was recorded between September 1991 and June 1992 in Sussex and London. Unlike most studio albums, this one had very few overdubs. Most of it was recorded live in the studio, with the necessary tweaks and punch-ins added later. The album included two songs left over from the previous album's collaboration with Elvis Costello. This is the album that the 1993 New World Tour promoted (see the review of *Paul Is Live* in the live album section). Six of the 22 stops on the North American leg of the tour failed to sell out, an almost unheard-of occurrence on other McCartney tours. It would be nine years before McCartney would go back out on tour, with many of those years spent dealing with the breast cancer that eventually cost Linda McCartney her life.

The 2007 iTunes release of *Off the Ground* contained a bonus track called "I Can't Imagine." A companion two-CD set called *Off the Ground: The Complete Works* included the original album, plus 12 unreleased songs and B-sides. This was released only in Germany and the Netherlands and is now out of print and not available for sale. (The B-sides will be discussed in the singles chapter.)

Off the Ground: The title track has a heavy sound to it, dominated by electric guitars and a busy drum part. The lead vocal, in contrast, is rendered with a certain sweetness that belies the heavy rock sound of the backing track. Robbie McIntosh plays a nice little slide guitar solo. Lots of nicely delivered backing and harmony vocals augment the lead singer's vocal. Nice little outro to a cold ending.

Looking for Changes: Another heavy sounding rocker, but this one is bogged down by the kind of hand-wringing angst that sounds too preachy and unimaginative. Most of us who value animals agree that we could treat our fellow creatures with more kindness, and changes in how we treat them is a great idea. But this song offers no solutions to the problem. It just rants.

Hope of Deliverance: This is one of McCartney's best songs of the 1990s, and its sentiments are timeless. Over vigorously strummed acoustic guitars and a poppy and percussive drum track, the lyrics are hopeful and uplifting. McCartney and McIntosh play a nice harmony acoustic guitar solo that gives the song a special gravitas.

Mistress and Maid: A McCartney-Costello leftover from the *Flowers in the Dirt* sessions. Ponderous lyrics and a choppy time signature are its main features. A memorable chord sequence moves the chorus along nicely.

I Owe It All to You: This song boasts the best melody on the album. The verses are played in a minor key, and then are resolved during the chorus, which is in a major key. Interesting musical flourishes abound. McCartney, obviously addressing Linda, harmonizes with himself on the choruses. He sounds clear and contented. Over the ascending/descending chords of the verse, the song draws to a slow close with a subtle guitar figure and lots of vocal calisthenics.

Biker Like an Icon: There are just some songs McCartney assigns titles to simply because he likes how the phrase sounds. This is one of those. It's not much of a song, with a murky story repeating the title ad nauseum. The best part is the guitar solo by McIntosh in the middle, and the zippy rock steady sound of the backing track.

Peace in the Neighborhood: The intro is pretty catchy, with lots of guitars and piano, and some effective stops and starts, all over a bed of two repeating chords. McCartney stretches his vocal chops throughout, hurdling lots of tricky intervals. Some Wings-like backing vocals move in and out of the mix. A lengthy vamp plays the song out.

Golden Earth Girl: A very characteristic piano ballad with lots of melody and dream-like lyrics. Bass, guitars and a simple drum part join in starting with the second verse. The whole song has an odd time signature.

The Lovers That Never Were: This is by far the better of the two McCartney-Costello collaborations on this album. It opens with a dramatic piano intro, framed by lyrics that really scan like many of Costello's best songs. Lots of loud percussion is added during the bridge. McCartney effectively harmonizes with himself throughout, taking the part Costello took on the early demos.

Get Out of My Way: By far the best rocker on the album, augmented by exquisite lead guitar work from McIntosh. McCartney has just the right amount of reverb on his vocal to give the whole track a big wide sound. The band played this song on a few early dates during the 1993 tour, but quickly dropped it from the set list. A false ending ushers in a guitar and horn heavy cold ending.

Winedark Open Sea: A really nice and simple melody underpins this pop ballad with a nice mix of acoustic and electric guitars, and a cool sounding electric piano. Most of the song is built around two chords. The song stops with two minutes left in its running time, then resumes with an electric guitar riffing over the two same chords. There is a certain elegant serenity to this song.

C'mon People: Not matter how hard he tried to make this into a "we, the people" anthem of epic proportions, with concert crowds waving their raised arms slowly back and forth in rhythm with the song, McCartney fails to deliver a memorable melody. His intentions were pure, to be sure, but the song just isn't very good. It's endless repeating of a two-word phrase made famous by the Beatles—"oh, yeah"—bogs the whole thing down instead of giving it the affirmation he probably intended. This is one of the songs on the 1993 tour during which people got up to get a drink or use the restroom.

Cosmically Conscious: A snippet McCartney reportedly wrote in India in 1968. It's got a "Give Peace a Chance" vibe to it.

Bonus Tracks

From the 2007 iTunes release:

I Can't Imagine: This starts out as a simple acoustic guitar ballad, then drums and a trio of guitars enter the mix and round out the overall sound. There are some very complicated harmonies during the chorus, giving this song a really catchy sound. This one could have replaced three or four of the lesser songs on *Off the Ground* without much of a net loss.

Bonus tracks from *Off the Ground: The Complete Works*:

Long Leather Coat See singles section.

Keep Coming Back to Love: A jazzy riff is played first on an acoustic piano, and then an electric piano, before guitars, bass and drums come in. McCartney harmonizes with himself on the verses. It's a bit repetitive and has a very 1980s sound to it.

Sweet Sweet Memories: A jaunty rocker with walls of Wings-like backing vocals. McCartney slips effortlessly in and out of his falsetto at times. Again, it's repetitive and gets old after about two minutes. The long fade-out features a slow phrase of four chords played over and over.

Things We Said Today: This is a completely acoustic work-up of the old Beatles song that was recorded for the *Unplugged* album but not included on the official release.

Midnight Special: Likewise, this is a cover of a chestnut that didn't make the *Unplugged* official release.

Style: A guitar-heavy paean to a woman with style. Could dad be singing about Stella McCartney? This track has the production values of the songs on *Flowers in the Dirt*. A really good but brief electric guitar solo is played during the instrumental break.

I Can't Imagine: See above 2007 iTunes bonus track discussion.

Cosmically Conscious: This is the full version of the snippet that was tagged on the end of *Off the Ground*. Lots of weird sound effects and a heavy drum beat are the main musical features. This would have fit right in on *Magical Mystery Tour*. It morphs into a snippet of "Down to the River" (see below).

Kicked Around No More: See singles section.

Big Boys Bickering: See singles section.

Down to the River: This sounds like a classic Creedence Clearwater Revival song, with the harmonica, acoustic guitars, rhythm and subject matter. Very thin lyrically, but interesting in that McCartney doesn't usually dabble in this style.

Soggy Noodle: Twenty-eight seconds of electric guitar noodling. Get it?

Flaming Pie

Released May 5, 1997

Parlophone 7243 8 56500 2 4, CDPCSD 171; Capitol CDP 7243 8 56500 2 4

Highest Chart Position: 2 in the U.K. and the U.S.

Produced by Paul McCartney, Jeff Lynne and George Martin

Musicians: Paul McCartney: vocals, electric and acoustic guitars, 12-string guitar, bass guitar, double bass, drums, piano percussion, harmonium, organ, electric piano, harpsichord, vibraphone, Mellotron; Linda McCartney: backing vocals; Jeff Lynne: harmony vocal, electric guitar, acoustic guitar, keyboards, backing vocals, spinet, harpsichord; Steve Miller: lead vocal on "Used to Be Bad," harmony vocal, electric guitar, acoustic guitar, backing vocal, rhythm guitar; James McCartney: electric guitar; Ringo Starr: drums, backing vocals, percussion; and a multitude of classical musicians on "Some Days" and "Beautiful Night"

Flaming Pie is the album on which Paul McCartney starts the long process of taking an unflinching look at his past. From here on out, each subsequent McCartney album would include some stock-taking and retrospection.

It makes sense that this trend started in earnest on *Flaming Pie.* He had just come off several years of working on *The Beatles Anthology* project (film, CDs and book), so that must have roused a few ghosts for him. More importantly, by this time he was aware that Linda's cancer had spread and that she likely didn't have much time left.

As he always has done in the midst of strife, he soldiered on and made a beautiful album, full of wistful longings, joyous gratitude and musings slightly more elegiac and plaintive than is his normal custom.

The band that he had worked with since 1988 and toured with in 1989–90 and 1993 was no longer a going concern. Instead, McCartney relied on a simpler studio formula by enlisting former ELO leader Jeff Lynne, and the ever-faithful George Martin was on hand to lend some familiarity and gentleness to the proceedings. Most of the songs were recorded in three studios in England, and one ("Young Boy") was recorded at Steve Miller's ranch in Idaho. Two songs ("Calico Skies" and "Great Day") were recorded in September 1992; the rest were recorded sporadically in 1995 and 1997.

Flaming Pie refers to the made-up-on-the-spot response John Lennon once gave to a reporter when asked how the group came up with the name "Beatles." Lennon replied that a man on a flaming pie came to them in a vision and declared that from then on they were "Beatles with an 'a.'"

Ten other songs were recorded and were considered for inclusion on the album but ended up as B-sides or received debut airings on McCartney's 1995 radio streaming program *Oobu Joobu*. More about this later.

Flaming Pie received generally excellent reviews and charted at No. 2 in both England and the U.S. It was McCartney's first studio album in four years, and the last time Linda McCartney appeared on one of her husband's albums.

The Song We Were Singing: Over an acoustic guitar picked in slow 3/4 time, McCartney remembers days sitting knee to knee with John Lennon, smoking a pipe and drinking wine in his dad's living room as they nurtured their nascent songwriting partnership. The chorus has a bigger sound, with electric guitars, drums, bass and lots of backing vocals.

The World Tonight: This is one of McCartney's catchiest singles of the 1990s, with a menacing backing track, clever lyrics, and McCartney singing both a high and low vocal part. It's catchy and infectious. Lots of crunchy electric guitars and a funky electric piano part add a meaty grit to the song. The bridge offers an interesting interlude where McCartney's voice is filtered through some effects. This would have worked well on just about any Wings album.

If You Wanna: This is mostly just a made-up jam featuring McCartney on a multitude of electric guitars, bass and drums, and Steve Miller playing electric and acoustic guitars, in a particularly menacing minor key.

Somedays: This is a beautiful mediation on McCartney's life with Linda. Other than the orchestra, McCartney plays all the instruments. The arrangement by George Martin recalls "Eleanor Rigby." A nice guitar solo, with an acoustic guitar echoing the Spanish guitar lead, fills out the middle nicely.

Young Boy: Recorded at Steve Miller's home in Idaho, this is by far the most Beatles-like song on the album. McCartney and Miller handle all the instruments and vocals, with Miller playing an especially scorching guitar solo. The cool Hammond organ dominated slowdown toward the end is a highlight. This marked the first time the two had collaborated since May 1969 when McCartney, under the pseudonym Paul Ramon, played drums on Miller's "My Dark Hour."

Calico Skies: A complicated acoustic guitar part underpins the moving vocal, which McCartney wrote after being caught in the aftermath of Hurricane Bob, which knocked out the power in the house he was staying at in Long Island. McCartney added this to the *Back in the World* tour set list and it went over really well.

Flaming Pie: A potboiler with nonsense lyrics, this one is also reminiscent of 1968-era Beatles. The rollicking piano part that appears twice in the song is a nice addition to the straight 4/4 of the verses.

Heaven on a Sunday: A jazzy meditation on the joys of leisurely Sundays, inspired by a peaceful sailing excursion McCartney had recently been on. James McCartney, 19 at the time, adds the simple but effective electric guitar solo, trading licks with his old man.

Used to Be Bad: A totally ad-libbed jam by McCartney and Miller, with both men singing into the same microphone. McCartney plays drums and bass and Miller plays the snaky electric guitar. They take turns singing lines on the verses. Miller rattles off a really powerful guitar solo.

Souvenir: By far the most soulful song on the album, "Souvenir" is a great example of McCartney's ability to conjure blue-eyed soul. Over piano and guitars amid various stops and starts, McCartney delivers a vocal that is memorable and moving. This is one of the best songs in his entire catalogue.

Little Willow: This song was written for the children of Maureen Starkey, Ringo Starr's former wife, who had recently died of cancer. It's of course very moving, especially when you consider that McCartney could have just as well been singing to his own children, who would endure a similar loss in April 1998. Here he sings with clear eyes and a strong resolve to withstand any of life's tragedies.

Really Love You: The band: McCartney, Lynne and Starr. That adds up to a tight little rock 'n' roll trio playing a simple bluesy workout, with simple lyrics. Starr's in the pocket, as usual, and McCartney's bass reminds us that they once made up one of the greatest rhythm sections in all of rock 'n' roll. The song evolves into an echo-laden falsetto shout-athon, with a call and response vocal.

Beautiful Night: This song was originally recorded during a time in 1986–87 when McCartney was working with producer Phil Ramone in New York. It sat on the shelf for a decade before McCartney dusted it off, rerecorded parts of it, and invited Starr to come and play drums on it (and add some backing vocals). As usual, the melody is strong, and George Martin's orchestral arrangement enhances the song. The final 1:36 of the song is a long and fast fade-out with beefy horns and lots of guitars. McCartney harmonizes till the song ends with lots of studio chat.

Great Day: This is a song McCartney had lying around for 25 years. It sounds like a *McCartney* outtake. Only Paul and Linda appear. It stands as a beautiful coda to the album, and to the long collaboration and marriage the McCartneys shared.

Driving Rain

Released November 12, 2001
Parlophone 7243 5 35510 2 5; Capitol 7243 5 35510 2 5
Highest chart position: 46 in the U.K.; 26 in the U.S.
Produced by David Kahne
Musicians: Paul McCartney: vocals, bass guitar, acoustic, electric and Spanish guitars, piano; Rusty Anderson: guitars and backing vocals; Abe Laboriel, Jr.: drums, percussion and backing vocals; Gabe Dixon: keyboards and backing vocals; David Kahne: programming, orchestral samples, synth and guitar; James McCartney: percussion on "Spinning on an Axis" and guitar on "Back in the Sunshine Again"; Eric Clapton: guitar on "Freedom" (hidden track)

Flush with the giddiness of new love, *Driving Rain* is an extended love letter to Heather Mills, McCartney's new girlfriend at the time and soon-to-be second wife. At least five of the songs on this album were inspired by Mills, and the generally upbeat vibe of this set can be at least partially attributed to McCartney's enthusiasm for his new paramour.

Studio

The album was recorded in Los Angeles under the direction of David Kahne, a prolific producer of a wide range of acts, a soundtrack composer and a designer. Kahne recommended Rusty Anderson and Abe Laboriel Jr., and they helped toughen up the sound with their guitars and drums, respectively. They also became part of McCartney's touring band, which has now been together longer than both the Beatles and Wings. The 2002 U.S. tour included three songs from *Driving Rain* in the set list.

Three months after the album was finished (but two months before it was released), the terrorist attacks on New York (and in Washington, D.C., and Pennsylvania) occurred on September 11. McCartney was stuck on an airplane in New York City when the attacks occurred and, like everyone, was saddened and moved by the tragic events of that day. He organized the Concert for New York City, which was held on October 20 at Madison Square Garden. The 60+ performers donated their time and contributed autographed merchandise to be auctioned off for charity, primarily to honor the victims and the first responders to the attack, many of whom also lost their lives. McCartney closed the show by performing six songs, debuting "Freedom," which was included as the last track on *Driving Rain.* Because the album's artwork had already been finalized the song is not listed on the CD but appears as a "hidden track."

Driving Rain is a good album and has a lot of interesting moments on it, but it does not stand alongside the best of McCartney's work. It's overly long, clocking in at 67:21, and indeed the vinyl release was a double album. It could have been improved with a little strategic editing.

Still, it formed the basis for the almost continual touring McCartney has done since the album's release and introduced him to two key members of the band he's held together since 2001.

Lonely Road: One of the best rock 'n' roll songs McCartney has written and recorded, "Lonely Road" starts out with a lone ominous bass line, and builds intensity through tough, sinewy guitars and a lively drum part. McCartney's vocals sound assured and enthusiastic. The song gallops along, aided by McCartney's looping bass and rough-hewn vocal. This is the only one of three songs from the album that went down well during his 2002 tour.

From a Lover to a Friend: Seemingly a simple and pedestrian piano ballad (think "Pipes of Peace"), "From a Lover to a Friend" has an interesting choppy syncopation, and some of the vocal stylings seem ad-libbed. Lots of introspective questions in the lyrics. This seems like a mediation on the wisdom of loving again after losing one's life partner.

She's Given Up Talking: A plaintive acoustic guitar and vocal in a minor key open this odd song. Lots of vocal effects and heavily treated electric guitars limn the mix, with Paul playing the drums. The phased lead vocal is a little wearisome after a couple of minutes.

Driving Rain: The title track to the album gets off to a rough start with the trite counting: "five" rhyming with "drive" and "10" rhyming with "again." The song is in a major seventh key and is a mostly boring treatise on driving in the rain. Overly repetitive and slightly corny. But hey, there's usually one of these on McCartney albums.

I Do: A really interesting song with earnest lyrics and vocals rotating between McCartney's low and high registers. It's also notable for its use of diminished chords, something that McCartney rarely employs (unlike his former bandmate George Harrison, who used diminished chords so often in his solo career that it became somewhat of a musical trademark). This song resembles "Somedays" from *Flaming Pie.*

Tiny Bubble: This songs starts out with much promise, with a funky bluesy minor key intro reminiscent of Al Green, but the chorus eventually cancels out that excitement. It reverts to a trite bromide sung repeatedly over major chords. Rusty Anderson plays a tasty guitar solo in the middle.

Magic: A fond recollection of the night Paul met Linda in the Bag o' Nails club in London. Adding to the drama is the fact that it's the most Beatle-esque on the entire album. Lots of acoustic and electric guitars and a driving bass part propel the song along nicely. Understandably, there is a definite undercurrent of wistfulness in the singer's voice. A false ending and some random jamming close the song.

Your Way: A clever bouncy acoustic guitar song that could have easily fit in on the *McCartney* and *Ram* albums. It's a combination of "Man We Was Lonely" and "Heart of the Country." Again, McCartney switches between his low and high register. He also namechecks *Venus and Mars* in the lyrics.

Spinning on an Axis: It's at this point that *Driving Rain* seemingly veers into "bonus track" territory. Most of the remaining seven tracks on the album seem worthy of being B-sides, but not strong enough to be album tracks, even deep ones. This one, in particular, seems poorly thought out and it almost sounds as if McCartney is making up the words live in the studio. It's also the second-longest song on the album, adding to the listener's ennui.

About You: This seems like an outtake from *Back to the Egg.* Lots of loud electric guitars and keyboards, based around two minor chords, give this one a 1970s sound.

Heather: This is mostly a simple piano ballad with very few lyrics. Sounds like a fun little jam for the boys in the band. The spare vocal doesn't appear until 2:31.

Back in the Sunshine Again: Lots of reverb on McCartney's vocal, which is sung over two repeating chords during the verses. James McCartney plays an interesting electric guitar solo in the middle that kind of gets lost in the mix. Despite the tedious repetition, there is a certain bluesy vibe to this track.

Your Loving Flame: Heather Mills-McCartney's big moment in the sun. Here she has the best pop songwriter of the century writing one of his signature piano ballads in tribute to her, and she still blew the gig. This is a sister companion piece to "From a Lover to a Friend" in construction and instrumentation. It's a strong enough song to still be performed live in concert if not for its subject matter.

Riding into Jaipur: This mostly instrumental track trades on the sound of Indian rhythms and instruments, with only 17 words sung. At least McCartney imbued it with some interesting bass playing. Otherwise, it's like being stuck in an elevator with "Love You Too" on a continuous loop.

Rinse the Raindrops: The real star of this song is Rusty Anderson, who plays two scorching electric guitars throughout the song's 10:08 time. Although interesting, this is clearly a jam based around four repeating chords and interspersed with an oddly syncopated break between verses. At 2:42, the song morphs into a steady jam reminiscent of the Doors, except considerably less indulgent. At 8:49 in, the song reverts to its original form, but this time with different sound effects applied to the entire mix.

Freedom: I guarantee you this song was written in about 10 minutes, so trite are the chords and the melody. This is the bonus track taken from the Concert for New York City, with Eric Clapton on electric guitar. As hard as it tries, its pseudo-anthem aspirations fall flat. It almost seems opportunistic to construct such a stale and uninspiring song at such a terrible time. McCartney eventually dropped it from his tour set list, and eventually added "Give Peace a Chance," which works much better precisely because of the absence of the patriotic jingoism of "Freedom."

Bonus Track

When iTunes added McCartney's catalogue in 2007, it included on *Driving Rain* David Kahne's remix of "From a Lover to a Friend," which was the B-side of the "Freedom" single. See the singles chapter for a discussion of the remix.

Chaos and Creation in the Backyard

Released September 13, 2005
Parlophone 00946 337959 2 1; Capitol CDP 0946 3 38759 2 0
Highest chart position: 10 in the U.K. and 6 in the U.S.
Produced by Nigel Godrich

Musicians: Paul McCartney: piano, electric pianos, bass guitar, acoustic and electric guitars, drums, violin, percussion, lead and backing vocals, flugelhorn, guiro, cello, vibes, organ, classical and 12-string guitar, melodica, recorder, autoharp, harmonium, tubular bells, glockenspiel synthesizer; Nigel Godrich: piano and acoustic guitar loops; Jason Falkner: electric and classical guitars; James Gadson: drums; Joey Waronker: bass drum, shaker, bongos; Pedro Eustache: duduk; Rusty Anderson: acoustic guitar; Brian Ray: acoustic guitar; Abe Laboriel, Jr.: percussion, block, tambourine; the Los Angeles Music Players: strings; Millenia Ensemble: strings, brass

If *Driving Rain* rings with the rosy optimism of a brand-new love, *Chaos and Creation in the Backyard* foretells the storm clouds gathering on the horizon. At least five of the songs sound like laments about unrequited love, persnickety behavior and the unreliability of someone who should be firmly by your side as a life partner. It seems all was not well in the McCartney-Mills union. Future events would bear this out.

But on this album, McCartney marshals his discontent and creates a cohesive, simple and elegant album, filled with memorable melodies, strong musicianship and a stiff upper lip. Instead of running from his personal problems, here he seems to own them. It makes for a unique, incisive recitation of Paul McCartney in the moment, staring bravely into the dimly lit abyss of a failed marriage. This isn't the same McCartney we usually get to see, and because of that the album stands out as a fully formed piece of artistic chutzpah.

The album was produced by long-time Beck and Radiohead producer Nigel Godrich, who did not abide any wanderings into cliched McCartney territory: The rule in the studio was no musical pastiches and no weak and unformed songs allowed to pad out the album. Godrich also wanted

McCartney to play all of the instruments, rather than use his successful touring band in the studio. Thus, Rusty Anderson, Brian Ray and Abe Laboriel, Jr., only appeared on one track ("Follow Me").

To say that Godrich and McCartney locked horns is an understatement. It's telling that McCartney, despite the success of *Chaos and Creation,* quickly moved on to a familiar producer for his next album, rather than trying to establish a template for making successful McCartney albums moving forward.

The album was recorded at two London studios and in Los Angeles and was nearly two years in the making. It was the first album since *Give My Regards to Broad Street* in 1984 on which McCartney was not involved in the production duties.

The cover photo was shot in the backyard of McCartney's boyhood Liverpool home by his brother, Michael; Paul is a young man playing his guitar under the morning wash.

"Jenny Wren" won a Grammy for best pop vocal performance in 2007 (after it was released as a single), and the album was nominated for album of the year and best pop vocal album in 2006.

Six additional songs which were recorded but not included on the album appeared as B-sides of singles and on alternative pressings. Additionally, an hour-long live concert was released on video as *Chaos and Creation at Abbey Road.* It aired on PBS in the U.S. on February 27, 2006, as part of the *Great Performances* series. It features 12 songs played and sung by McCartney in front of a small but lively studio audience, but only three of the songs are from *Chaos and Creation in the Backyard.*

Fine Line: A fine piano rocker with a simple chord progression, "Fine Line" is a good album opener: upbeat, optimistic and simple. McCartney's in fine voice and sings with a brio that effectively presages the vibe of the rest of the songs on the album.

How Kind of You: Starting out with a swirl of keyboards and synths, this track is slow and contemplative. There is a certain hypnotic feel to the backing track, and McCartney alternates singing in both his low and high registers.

Jenny Wren: Revisiting "Blackbird" land, "Jenny Wren" tells the story of a bird flying off to find her own freedom amid the chaos of our world. The tricky acoustic guitar is miked so loudly that it threatens to dominate the vocals, and the finger movements on the frets can clearly be heard. McCartney sings in a sort of lilting whisper throughout. The use of the

Armenian double reed duduk gives the instrumental break a unique sound. Expertly constructed and played by McCartney, this is one of the finest songs on the album.

At the Mercy: Another slow piano ballad with very reflective lyrics that seem to be referring to the gut-wrenching choices we sometimes are forced to make about love. Two electric guitars back up the piano, bass and drums.

Friends to Go: Over a couple of acoustic guitars earnestly strumming along, McCartney seems to be singing about hiding out in the bedroom while his wife entertains friends he doesn't want to mingle with. One of the most obtuse sets of lyrics McCartney has ever written.

English Tea: It seems weird that Godrich let McCartney record this one. It has all of the hallmark McCartney touches: cheesy lyrics, chamber music flourishes and a complete inattention to the style of music popular in 2005. Nice strings and piano, and some fine harmonies abound.

Too Much Rain: Using the same basic musical formula (piano, bass, acoustic guitars, drums) that much of the album employs, the singer seems to be consoling someone who has had too much tragedy in his life. The middle-eights have a definite Beatle sound, with slick harmonies and a pounding piano part.

A Certain Softness: A Latin-inflected musical backing track, dominated by guitars and piano, is the foundation over which McCartney adds his memorable vocals. This song recalls "Somebody Who Cares" off *Tug of War* and "Distractions" off *Flowers in the Dirt.*

Riding to Vanity Fair: This track sounds like nothing McCartney has ever produced before, with its sullen, plodding rhythm, and lyrics dripping with venom. The man sounds downright pissed off. A sultry interplay between an electric guitar and electric piano adds a sense of extra drama to the instrumental break. The song stops and starts several times. The last time it stops it begins with some strings and glissandos underpinning the guitar and piano, all dressed up in a downcast minor key.

Follow Me: The first song recorded for the album, it's a simple acoustic guitar-based celebration of support and love. When McCartney toured in support of the album in 2005, hundreds of signs flashed by audience members had the song's title emblazoned on them.

Promise to You Girl: One of the catchiest songs on the album, "Promise to You Girl" starts out slow before a funky piano lick ushers in the Beatle-esque romp that includes drums, bass, piano and electric guitar. The slow interludes are filled with four-part harmonies recalling the Beach Boys. This song has a definite 1960s feel.

This Never Happened Before: A haunting piano, backed with bass, drums and lovely strings, provides the bedrock for McCartney's stirring vocal performance. The melody is strong and very evocative of some of the best piano ballads McCartney has written.

Anyway: By far the best song on the album, "Anyway" has a superb melody, first played on the piano, and then echoed by McCartney's vocals, which sometimes strain when he is forced to sing at the top of his register. When the second verse comes in drums, electric and acoustic guitars and brass augment the piano and bass. The strings add lift to the last several measures. He seems to be singing about the frustration of not being able to get in touch with a lover, despite his frantic pleading for her to get in touch with him. It is impossible not to draw some conclusions about the state of the McCartneys' marriage after listening to this album, and especially this song.

I've Only Got Two Hands: Twenty-one seconds after the end of "Anyway," a hidden track titled "I've Only Got Two Hands" bursts out of your speakers. Then 54 seconds in, the song morphs from a straight rock jam into a piano dominated rave-up, before finally settling into a slow and bluesy jam filled with what sounds like car horns, and finally marinating in a miasma of weird sound effects. This track would have fit in well on one of The Fireman albums.

Memory Almost Full

Released June 4, 2007 (U.K.); June 5, 2007 (U.S.)
Hear Music HMCD-30348 (U.S.); HMLP-30348 (U.K.)
Highest chart position: 5 in the U.K. and 3 in the U.S.
Produced by David Kahne
Musicians: Paul McCartney: vocals, backing vocals, piano, keyboards, bass, acoustic and electric guitars, mandolin, drums, percussion, synthesizers, flugelhorn, organ, Mellotron; Rusty Anderson: electric guitar, backing vocals; Brian Ray: electric guitar, backing vocals; Paul Wickens: piano, keyboards, synthesizer, backing vocals; Abe Laboriel, Jr.: drums, backing vocals

Memory Almost Full finds Paul McCartney looking back through the mists of time with clear eyes and an uncommon sense of how he got to this point of his life and career. Reflections on his childhood, his Beatles days, his marriages to Linda and Heather, and the eventual end of the ride are all rendered with a sort of bonhomie and philosophical self-knowledge that make most of the songs on this album fun to listen to.

The album is McCartney's first on Starbucks' Hear Me label, a move he made chiefly because he had grown tired of the long gestation periods of promotional plans devised by major label marketing teams. Recording of the album first commenced in 2003, then was temporarily shelved as he started work on *Chaos and Creation in the Backyard*. He then returned to work on *Memory Almost Full* in 2006, using five studios in London, Sussex, Los Angeles and New York to complete the album.

The album was promoted on the day of its U.S. release with a listening event that involved 10,000 Starbucks stores playing it all day long. Two days later, McCartney and his band played a live show at the Electric Ballroom in Los Angeles to promote the album.

McCartney played all of the instruments on 10 of the 16 songs eventually released on CD, with his touring band playing on the other six. Only two of the songs on *Memory Almost Full* would be included in future tour set lists.

The album was nominated for four Grammys and is the first Paul McCartney album to be made available via digital download.

In some ways, *Memory Almost Full* occupies a curious place in the McCartney catalogue. It did not include a major hit song and the critical reaction to it was positive, but not overwhelmingly so. Still, it's a significant stepping stone from the darkly introspective *Chaos and Creation* to the sunny optimism of *New* and *Egypt Station*.

Dance Tonight: Over an insistent drum part and a vigorously strummed mandolin, McCartney sings simple lyrics during the opening verse, and then whistles part of the melody. Then, he totally Beatles it up with an astounding middle eight instrumental break that includes ascending minor chords, electric guitar and various keyboards. The cold faded ending is effective.

Ever Present Past: Easily the catchiest song on the album, this one finds the singer ruminating about how time moves faster as you get older. The chorus is memorable and tuneful. The electric guitars are prominent and twin with various keyboards to give the basic track a powerful drive.

See Your Sunshine: This one would have fit in well on *Chaos and Creation*, and in fact was started during the making of that album. It's another exhortation to Heather to assert herself so she wouldn't get overwhelmed by the global celebrity of her then-husband. The middle eights are chock full of Beatley musical flourishes, and the bass is busy and inventive.

Only Mama Knows: Maybe only mama knows what this curiosity of a song is about. Over a chunky guitar-driven basic track, the lyrics tell the story of a mother who takes her child away to some unsavory outpost away from his father. It begins and ends with a haunting string part.

You Tell Me: One of the best songs on the album, "You Tell Me" is a languorous acoustic guitar-dominated ballad. McCartney sings at the top of his register throughout, with some great backing vocals and a hot electric guitar played by Rusty Anderson.

Mr. Bellamy: Over a tricky piano part, McCartney crafts a perfectly obtuse story song that includes everything from a harpsichord, strings, electric guitars and lots of vocals with heavy effects. The song closes with a completely different melody built around piano, bass, drums, strings and synths.

Gratitude: This fairly repetitive song is very similar to the sublime "Souvenir" off *Flaming Pie*. More reflections of his time with Heather, but this time delivered with a primal vocal that seems to attempt to exorcise the memories of their time together.

Vintage Clothes: This kicks off a five-song medley with a very Beatlesque basic track filled with acoustic guitars, piano, bass, drums and lots of harmony vocals. This would not have sounded out of place on *Magical Mystery Tour*.

That Was Me: A great acoustic guitar and bass driven rocker that namechecks several parts of McCartney's life. McCartney sings the first two verses in his normal register, but really rips it up on the last verse. One of the catchiest songs on the album, this one should have found its rightful home on a tour set list.

Feet in the Clouds: A little trip back through McCartney's schooldays and early childhood. A nice little Beach Boys tribute occurs toward the end, as McCartney layers several harmony vocals into a nice take on the melodic brilliance of his friend Brian Wilson.

House of Wax: Lots of reverb on McCartney's vocal as he sings about the pitfalls of worldwide fame. This track has a certain majesty in its structure, chord sequence and full-out production values. Strings, loud guitars, pounding piano and a heavy drum sound build to a crescendo featuring a final scorching electric guitar solo.

The End of the End: This is a simple valediction on the inevitably of death. It features many common McCartney musical trademarks: a piano ballad larded by a string arrangement played in two keys. This is McCartney's musical last will and testament.

Nod Your Head: This is a catchy rocker with McCartney screaming the simple lyrics, all delivered in less than two minutes. A persistent distorted electric guitar plays throughout.

The bonus CD of *Memory Almost Full* included the following tracks:

In Private: A percussion heavy instrumental with crunchy electric guitars, supported by keyboards, bass and acoustic guitars.

Why So Blue: Based on a simple acoustic guitar part accompanied by strings, the chorus adds piano, electric guitars, bass and drums to fill out the sound. This definitely sounds like a leftover from the *Chaos and Creation* sessions.

222: Mix in a little samba, with a Schroeder-like piano part, add a xylophone and nonsense lyrics and you get this appealing little confection. It probably won't be played as an example of McCartney's genius at "the end of the end" but it showcases his facility with different rhythms and styles, and his exquisite competence on a variety of instruments.

An expanded deluxe version of *Memory Almost Full* was released on November 6, 2007, and included the 16 songs discussed above, plus a DVD that included five of the tracks played at the Electric Ballroom show and music videos of "Dance Tonight" and "Ever Present Past."

NEW

Released October 14, 2013, in the U.K: October 15, 2013, in the U.S.
Virgin EMI (U.K.) 888072348486
Hear Music (U.S.) HRM 34837-02
Highest chart position: 3 in both the U.K. and U.S.
Produced by Giles Martin, Paul Epworth, Ethan Johns and Mark Ronson
Musicians: Paul McCartney: vocals, guitars, bass, piano, keyboards, drums, percussion, synthesizer, glockenspiel, celeste, harmonium, harpsichord, bouzouki, Mellotron; Rusty Anderson: guitars, bouzouki, backing vocals; Brian Ray: guitars, backing vocals, dulcimer, congas; Paul Wickens: keyboards, piano, organ, guitar, accordion, backing vocals; Abe Laboriel, Jr.: drums, backing vocals, djembe; Ethan Johns: drums, percussion, guitar; Paul Epworth: drums; Eliza Marshall and Anna Noakes: flute; Cathy Thompson, Nina Foster, Patrick Kiernan and Laura Melhuish: violin; Rachel Robson and Peter Lale: viola; Richard Pryce

and Steve McManus: double bass; Caroline Dale, Katherine Jenkinson and Chris Worsey: cello; Dave Bishop: baritone saxophone; Jamie Talbot: tenor saxophone; Toby Pitman: keyboards, programming; Steve Sidwell: trumpet; McCartney family chorus on "Everybody Out There."

NEW was Paul McCartney's first album of original compositions since 2007's *Memory Almost Full.* It was recorded in Los Angeles, New York, London and East Sussex and the production duties went to four producers, all of whom McCartney admired for their recent work with contemporary artists.

While on the surface the overall vibe of *NEW* is sunny and optimistic, there are some dark turns if you listen hard enough. McCartney continues on the retrospective walkabout he began on *Flaming Pie,* with new and less veiled references to his past life and career.

Producer Paul Epworth received co-writing credit with McCartney on "Save Us," "Queenie Eye" and "Road," the three songs on the album that McCartney admitted were mostly made up on the spot in the studio. Giles Martin produced six of the tracks, with Ethan Johns and Mark Ronson producing two tracks each. With four producers on board, one might expect the album to sound disjointed, but there is a certain cohesiveness to the sound that belies the too many cooks theory.

McCartney himself seemed especially proud of this album. It's the first album of originals that really bore the full influence of his new marriage to Nancy Shevell. Four of the songs on *NEW* were included in most of the set lists during McCartney's tours in 2013–2017.

By now, McCartney and his team were dab hands at using new media to promote the album. They made use of iTunes, SoundCloud, Instagram, Twitter and Yahoo as they rolled out the new album. They played brief live shows in Times Square, Queens, and on *Jimmy Kimmel Live* and *Late Night with Jimmy Fallon.*

Save Us: The opening song bursts out of the gate with an energetic push of guitar and drums. A rapid-fire delivery of the lyrics lays on top of the backing track which also includes piano, bass, synthesizers and mellifluous backing vocals. McCartney is in fine voice.

Alligator: Chiming acoustic guitars, flutes, electric guitars and an unusual chord sequence make this one of the most eccentric tracks on the album. For the second song in a row, McCartney sings about "saving." At 1:25 into the track, a Mellotron plays simple chords as McCartney sings in his highest register, his vocal larded with some reverb. This same interlude pops up again toward the end of the song.

On My Way to Work: This song finds McCartney recalling his boyhood trips to work as an assistant at Speedy Prompt Delivery in Liverpool. This song has a daydream-y feel to it. Lots of minor chords give this musical reminiscence a slightly ominous tone. Although he's looking back, he was also thinking ahead to a time when he would finally meet and get to write with John Lennon.

Queenie Eye: A lovely little keyboard intro ushers in this piano-banging rocker. Wild vocal intervals are handled adeptly by McCartney. The chorus features a call-and-response. This has been a staple of McCartney's live shows since 2013. A contemplative bridge with echo-y keyboards interrupts the intense backing track, until the chorus makes its reappearance.

Early Days: McCartney picks a folky acoustic guitar while he sings about the pain and laughter in those early days of the Beatles. He reminisces about he and Lennon canvassing the record shops in Liverpool and trying to get someone important to listen to their songs. He also uses this opportunity to slap down the hangers-on and biographers who continually rewrite the history books as they related to the Lennon and McCartney songwriting partnership. Hey, he has the microphone.

New: This song belongs on *Magical Mystery Tour*, right alongside "Penny Lane" and "Hello Goodbye." All the ingredients are there: A bouncy piano, lively vocals and harmonies, a sweet melody and lots of different piece parts that make up the whole. It's almost overwhelmed by its obvious Beatle DNA. The last 30 seconds feature a several-part harmony vocal romp reminiscent of the Beach Boys.

Appreciate: This is the bluesiest track on the album, and one of its best. Simple drumming and a galloping bass part hold down the rhythm section, while synthesizers and guitars fill out the sound. McCartney's lead vocal is heavy with effects as he delivers lyrics that urge appreciation of life, both the good times and the bad. A funky guitar solo plays over the faded outro.

Everybody Out There: This acoustic guitar-heavy anthem is a call for action to everybody to do some good during their time on earth. The second chorus features McCartney's voice heavily filtered by effects. This is a well-intentioned sentiment that McCartney has delivered more effectively in some of his past work.

Hosanna: The oldest song on the album is also one of the most hypnotic. Over an acoustic guitar, synths, bass and drums, the singer seems to be asking a lover for more time and attention. Backwards guitars and more keyboards appeared between verses and at the end of the track. The song has one of the most inventive bass parts on the album.

I Can Bet: This throwaway track seems to be mining some of the same lyrical territory that has been explored at length in many of the other tracks on the album. It's repetitive, doesn't have much in the way of melody, and features a brief but cheesy 1980s-style synthesizer solo.

Looking at Her: This catchy little charmer is McCartney at his playful best. The chorus is melodic, clever and weaves in and out between verses, although in a different key. A beautiful little acoustic guitar solo appears in the middle. Lots of acoustic and electric guitars, a vigorous drum part and synths make up the majority of the backing track.

Road: A story-song about the early days of McCartney and Shevell's relationship, as they navigated the twists and turns on the road to true love. Lots of subtle keyboards round out the sound of the basic track, which also features guitar, bass, drums and lots of smooth backing vocals. This is a modern-day update of "Back Seat of My Car."

Scared: This hidden track is not listed on the CD, but it's one of the best on the album. Over a plaintive piano, McCartney expresses his reluctance to give himself totally to a new relationship. The honest lyrics and poignant delivery by the singer make this a gem of a deep album cut.

Bonus Tracks

The deluxe version of the *NEW* CD included these two bonus tracks:

Turned Out: This a hybrid of "My Brave Face" and "The World Tonight," with the frequent chord changes, and its slow musical interlude halfway through the track. A pounding beat supports several acoustic and electric guitars. The intro and outro sound very much like something George Harrison might have written.

Get Me Out of Here: A bluesy lament whose primary instrument is an acoustic guitar, supported by percussion, drums and great backing vocals by McCartney. It has the same homemade vibe as the *McCartney* album.

The collector's edition of the album included a two CD/DVD reissue package, released in 2014. One CD includes clips from shows, the promotional campaign for the album, a "making of" video and clips from talk show appearances. The other CD features three bonus tracks recorded during the sessions for *NEW,* plus live versions of "Save Us," "New," "Queenie Eye" and "Everybody Out There" recorded at a concert in Tokyo in November 2013.

Struggle: This keyboard and synthesizer-heavy track is distinguished by the hypnotic lead vocal superbly rendered by McCartney. This might be the creepiest song McCartney has ever recorded. The evident randiness of the singer presages the outright horniness he would sing about unabashedly on his next album.

Hell to Pay: It's difficult to figure out exactly who is the recipient of this diatribe, but safe money says it's Heather Mills. McCartney doesn't do angry very often in his songs, but this one ranks right up there. Lively drums and a strident piano underscore the venom in the lyrics.

Demons Dance: This begins like a fun little piano ditty from the 1975-era Wings. See "Struggle" for more on the same topic treated here. But this one seems unfinished and less polished. Uncharacteristically, McCartney struggles with pitch issues here and there.

The DVD includes a documentary called "Something New" which includes footage from around the world, plus music videos of four of the album's songs.

On May 18, 2018, *NEW* was released on vinyl for the first time. Both black and pink vinyl versions were made available and both included a 180-gram vinyl LP with download card and 12 × 12" insert.

Egypt Station

Released September 7, 2018
Capitol 00602557696509 (U.K.); B002873602 (U.S.)
Highest chart position: 1 in the U.S. and 3 in the U.K.
Produced by Greg Kurstin, Paul McCartney; Ryan Tedder and Zach Skelton co-produced "Fuh You"
Musicians: Paul McCartney: lead and backing vocals, electric acoustic and bass guitars, keyboards, drums, percussion, harmonica; Greg Kurstin: keyboards, percussion, backing vocals, Mellotron, electric guitar, marimba, vibraphone; Rusty Anderson: electric and acoustic guitars, backing vocals; Brian Ray: electric, acoustic and bass guitars, backing vocals; Paul Wickens: keyboards; Abe Laboriel, Jr.: drums, per-

cussion, backing vocals; Greg Phillinganes: piano; Tim Loo, Vanessa Freebairn-Smith and Jodi Burnett: cello; Rob Millet: cimbalom; Pedro Eustache: flute, duduk; Ryan Tedder: backing vocals on "Fuh You"; Inara George, Alex Pasco, Matt Tuggle, Collin Kadlec and Julian Burg: backing vocals on "People Want Peace"; Caroline Le'gene and Roy Bennett: backing vocals on "Caesar Rock"

Egypt Station is a remarkable album that finds Paul McCartney at the top of his form at all levels: composing, playing, singing and just having a damn good time. It's melodic, playful and also contains some of McCartney's finest songs in years. It's his best album since 2005's *Chaos and Creation in the Backyard,* and critical reaction to the album was almost unanimously positive.

It became McCartney's first album to debut at No. 1 on the Billboard charts, and his first No. 1 album since 1982's *Tug of War,* a span of 36 years between No. 1 albums. In all, McCartney has had eight No. 1 albums.

It was recorded over two years in studios in Sussex, London and Los Angeles. "Back in Brazil" was recorded in Sao Paulo. Most of the album was produced by Greg Kurstin, best known for his work with Adele, Pink and Foo Fighters, among others. Ryan Tedder, a songwriter, producer and member of the band OneRepublic, produced "Fuh You" and the bonus track "Nothing for Free."

But make no mistake about it, McCartney's the star on *Egypt Station.* He turns in some of his most fully formed songs on this album, and the sound is tough and modern. Evergreen subjects like peace and love, of course, abound, but McCartney also takes a scathing swipe at U.S. President Donald Trump and reveals a sort of schoolboy randiness that most 76-year-olds can only faintly recall. That vegetarian diet must keep the blood flowing to all the right areas.

The album was announced on June 20, 2018, the same day that the two A-side single, "Come on to Me"/"I Don't Know" was released. A third single, "Fuh You," was released on August 15.

Other important events helped *Egypt Station* get off to a running start. On July 3, McCartney announced that he and his band were going out on the "Freshen Up" tour, which would commence in Canada in September. More significantly, McCartney appeared in a segment of "Carpool Karaoke" with James Corden of *The Late Late Show* that was at once hilarious, moving and easily the finest (and most popular) "Carpool Karaoke" segment that Corden has produced. The segment aired the week of June 17 and helped to promote the first single.

The cover art features a painting McCartney did in 1988. The rest of the package is fairly standard, with liner notes and lyrics.

That McCartney produced one of his finest albums at this late stage in his career is testament to his otherworldly talent, his work ethic, and his pure love of writing and recording songs. *Egypt Station* is built to stand the test of time.

Opening Station: This is 42 seconds of a heavenly choir over sounds from a train station that morphs beautifully into…

I Don't Know: This starts out with a haunting piano playing a simple melody joined by a strummed acoustic guitar. The lyrics find McCartney wondering what he's doing wrong, a far cry from his habit of opening albums with an upbeat and positive song. It seems to be about all the demands on his time and energy. It's refreshing to hear McCartney being introspective; we all have insecurities and fears, even rich, globally famous superstars.

Come on to Me: The lyrics seem to recall a flirtatious moment between the singer and a secret someone. Over an insistent beat, piano and electric guitars propel the song along. Although very repetitive, the first single from the album is infectious and lingers in one's mind. The horn interlude halfway through the song toughens up the song and provides a brief respite from the repetitive chorus. The fake ending is a riot.

Happy with You: This beautiful little acoustic workout would have fit in nicely on *The White Album*, at least musically. The confessional nature of the lyrics never would have found a place in a McCartney song circa 1968. The acoustic guitar picking recalls "Blackbird" and "Mother Nature's Son." McCartney sounds content in his marriage and his life on this track. The honest lyrics make this one of the album's most interesting songs.

Who Cares: A fine little rocker that finds McCartney railing against bullying. A mélange of electric guitars, acoustic guitars, organ, drums and bass make this one of the toughest sounding songs on the album. In December 2018, McCartney released a video of this song in which he plays a counselor to a patient played by Emma Stone.

Fuh You: Although catchy, "Fuh You" seems unbecoming of Sir Paul in terms of its bluntness and obvious sexual connotation. It has a big sound during the chorus and some interesting string parts woven throughout, but it's the least interesting song on the entire album.

Confidante: Acoustic guitars provide the framework for another trip to the confessional. A chiming acoustic guitar solo appears halfway through and is echoed by a keyboard during its second go-round. It's unclear who McCartney is singing about: John Lennon? Heather Mills? Former PR director Geoff Baker? I guess we'll never know. A great, simple ballad.

People Want Peace: How many times can McCartney put a different spin on a song calling for peace? Here he does it with grace and aplomb. Pianos, bass, drums, acoustic and electric guitars round out the backing track, along with some effective backing vocals, especially the chant-like vocals that take the song out.

Hand in Hand: A typical McCartney piano ballad about love and togetherness. The instrumentation is spare and effective. The Armenian wind instrument the duduk makes its second appearance on a McCartney song, after first appearing on "Jenny Wren."

Dominoes: This features a great vocal performance by McCartney, with a really fine set of lyrics. It seems to be about reconciliation and new beginnings, and also about the constant requests to play out or for interviews. Lots of acoustic and electric guitars play over the constant 4/4 beat. A nice little Beatlesque backwards guitar appears toward the end.

Back in Brazil: A nice little story song, actually recorded in Brazil. A samba-like beat is accompanied by keyboards, synths, bass and various percussion, plus a flute. McCartney's voice is triple-tracked at times. The ending is almost whispered over completely different chords.

Do It Now: This is by far the most Beatle-like song on the album. The combination of piano and harpsichord recalls "For No One." The melody is starkly simple, but elegant. The complicated vocal parts and strings turn the song into a philosophical manifesto with an anthemic vibe. The message: Don't wait to accomplish what you want.

Caesar Rock: A sloppy intro turns into a battle cry of love over stridently strummed acoustic guitars. Despite the song's title, it appears the singer is singing "she's a rock" throughout. Lots of echo on McCartney's voice gives the vocal track a faraway sound. The funky little musical connections between the verses add a lot of flavor to the song.

Despite Repeated Warnings: This is a medley of sorts. It has three distinct parts. It starts with a simple piano ballad introducing the captain, who is obviously modeled after Trump. Using the metaphor of a ship's crew and captain, the song then turns into a lyrical discussion of mutiny over a driving beat, with lots of guitars and horns. The third part is a galloping horn-driven imperative to overthrow the captain, before it eventually returns to the original ballad style that opened the medley. This is McCartney at his most political and actually turns out to be quite prophetic.

Station II: Continuing with the theme of the opening track, this one also features an angelic choir over more sounds from a trains station, before you hear the guitar lick that opens…

Hunt You Down/Naked/C-Link: This fun melding of three songs starts out with a very 1970s sounding guitar-based song complete with tons of cowbell. Complicated guitar lines end this part and usher in "Naked." A choppy piano part supports the vocal and some interesting backing vocals move in and out of the mix. "C-Link" is not much more than a slow, bluesy jam in a minor key, with a guitar part that recalls the instrumentals on *McCartney*, thus seemingly bringing everything full circle.

Bonus Tracks

A version of *Egypt Station* that was only available at Walmart contained two bonus tracks.

Nothing for Free: This is a really catchy song with lots of hooks, a driving bass part and a cool chord sequence. McCartney's vocals sound great, especially when triple-tracked, with a dollop of echo applied. McCartney is clearly in touch with modern sounds and what resonates with today's listener, even if he's just dabbling.

Get Started: A typically sunny and buoyant McCartney guitar-based song built on a descending chord sequence during the verses. This could have fit in well on *Flowers in the Dirt* or *NEW*.

On May 10, 2019, McCartney released a new "Traveller's Edition" (sometimes referred to as "Explorer's Edition") of *Egypt Station*. It's a deluxe edition limited to 3,000 pressings. It contains unreleased tracks, a jigsaw puzzle, playing cards, travel ticket facsimiles, luggage stickers, a map, lyrics handwritten by McCartney, a vintage *Egypt Station* artwork suitcase, a handwritten note from McCartney, and much more. It's an embarrassment of riches and frilly artifacts. For audiophiles, the best part of the package are the exclusive tracks.

"Get Enough" is included as a bonus track added to the original album. The other exclusive bonus tracks are:

Frank Sinatra's Party: A curious chunk of faux reggae about hanging out with Frank and his Rat Pack. Heavily processed electric guitars and lots of synths fill out the backing track, and McCartney's voice is wet with echo.

Sixty Second Street: Fingered acoustic guitar figures get augmented by electric guitars and repetitive bass and drum parts round out the sound. Time signature changes abound.

Who Cares (longer version): A really interesting longer version of what was already the best song on the album, this features a much longer introduction, and lots of added acoustic guitars, plus a slightly different lead vocal in spots.

Come on to Me (live at Abbey Road Studios): This song works better live, with a plethora of interesting touches, like a better vocal, an organ part, and great guitars. The band adds frenetic backing vocals. This version was recorded at Abbey Road Studios on July 23, 2018, as part of McCartney's five-show secret gig tour in London, Liverpool and New York City.

Fuh You (live at the Cavern Club): This song is nearly redeemed by the live treatment at the Cavern Club. But not quite.

Confidante (live at the Liverpool Institute of Performing Arts): This live version of a sweet song features chiming acoustic guitars and accordion, plus some interesting (and challenging) backing vocals.

Who Cares (live at Grand Central Station): A moving and beefy version of McCartney's anti-bullying anthem. Crunchy guitars, a great rhythm section and a sprightly vocal all give this a dramatic patina.

Live

Wings Over America

Released December 10, 1976
Highest chart position: 1 in the U.S. and 8 in the U.K.
Capital Records SWCO-11593
Produced by Paul McCartney
Musicians: Paul McCartney: lead and backing vocals, bass, acoustic guitar, piano, keyboards; Linda McCartney: piano, keyboards, backing

vocals, percussion; Denny Laine: electric and acoustic guitars, bass, backing vocals, piano, keyboards, percussion, harmonica, lead vocals; Jimmy McCulloch: electric and acoustic guitars, bass, backing vocals, lead vocals; Joe English: drums, percussion, backing vocals; Tony Dorsey: trombone, percussion; Howie Casey: saxophone, percussion; Steve Howard: trumpet, flugelhorn, percussion; Thaddeus Richard: saxophone, clarinet, flute, percussion

Venus and Mars/Rock Show /Jet/Let Me Roll It/Spirits of Ancient Egypt/Medicine Jar/Maybe I'm Amazed/Call Me Back Again/Lady Madonna/The Long and Winding Road/Live and Let Die/Picasso's Last Words (Drink to Me)/Richard Cory/Bluebird/I've Just Seen a Face/Blackbird/Yesterday/You Gave Me the Answer/Magneto and Titanium Man/Go Now/My Love/Listen to What the Man Said/Let 'Em In/Time to Hide/Silly Love Songs/Beware My Love/Letting Go/Band on the Run/Hi Hi Hi/Soily

Wings Over America is the definitive soundtrack of Wings at its peak moment and captures perfectly the musical maturity and inventiveness this configuration of the band had achieved by the time they began their first American tour in May 1976. Recorded at a variety of indoor venues in May and June 1976, the triple (vinyl) album is a strict reading of their set list, with all the songs in order as they played them every night on the road.

The set list draws heavily from *Band on the Run* (five songs) and *Venus and Mars* (nine songs), and samples the newly released *Wings at the Speed of Sound* (four songs). It borrows sparingly from the Beatles songbook, and the five songs chosen from that vast catalogue are unmistakably songs McCartney wrote without the help of Lennon. He even switched their names in the writing credits (McCartney-Lennon) in the LP's liner notes.

The best of this set is when McCartney conjures his innate rock 'n' roll vocal instincts ("Let Me Roll It," "Maybe I'm Amazed," "Call Me Back Again," "Beware My Love," "Letting Go" and "Hi Hi Hi"). In fact, this entire set finds him in remarkably great voice, and it can fairly be said that the he was at the apogee of his vocal abilities during this period.

The lesser moments occur when McCartney lets his sense of band democracy (limited though it might have been) creep in to the proceedings ("Spirits of Ancient Egypt," "Medicine Jar," and "Richard Cory"). Also, some of the instruments chosen seem odd. All of the acoustic guitars are Ovation 6- and 12-strings, not the Martins and Gibsons favored by most acoustic guitarists at the time. Moreover, the electric guitars are engulfed by some sort of weird effect (applied either on stage live or during mixing of the album) that shifts between a phase and mild distortion. The bass is high in the mix, which is appropriate given that the instrument is a huge part of the overall sound of these songs.

Overdubs were done in London in October and November 1976; most of the overdubs were to fix backing vocals that occasionally fell apart during the live performances.

The 2013 *Paul McCartney Archive* release featured the original LP on two discs; eight tracks taken from a show at San Francisco's Cow Palace; a DVD of the rarely seen *Wings Over the World* television special; lots of tour mementos, including a 112-page book featuring interviews and tour photography; a 60-page book of Linda's photos chronicling life on the road; a 136-page tour book; and an 80-page book of drawings by artist Humphrey Ocean. The eight bonus tracks are versions of songs that appeared on the released album. None of them are remarkably different, and they were obviously not originally intended for release because they weren't mastered with the same care as the songs on the official release.

The album was released on colored vinyl and CD on July 12, 2019.

Tripping the Live Fantastic

Released: November 5, 1990 (UK & U.S.)
Parlophone CATC-PCSD 114 (UK); Capitol Records C4-95379 (U.S.)
Highest Chart Position: 17 in the (UK) and 26 (U.S.)
Produced by Paul McCartney, Bob Clearmountain, and Peter Henderson
Musicians: Paul McCartney: bass, electric and acoustic guitars, piano, keyboards, vocals; Linda McCartney: keyboards, percussion, backing vocals; Hamish Stuart: acoustic and electric guitars, bass, backing vocals; Robbie McIntosh: electric guitars, backing vocals; Paul Wickens: keyboards, acoustic guitar, percussion, backing vocals; Chris Whitten: drums, percussion

Showtime/Figure of Eight/Jet/Rough Ride/Got to Get You Into My Life/ Band on the Run/Birthday/We Got Married/Ebony and Ivory/ Inner City Madness/Maybe I'm Amazed/The Long and Winding Road/ Crackin' Up/The Fool on the Hill/Sgt. Pepper's Lonely Hearts Club

Band/Can't Buy Me Love/Matchbox/Put it There/Together/Things We Said Today/Eleanor Rigby/This One/My Brave Face/Back in the U.S.S.R./I Saw Her Standing There/Twenty Flight Rock/Coming Up/ Sally/Let It Be/Ain't That a Shame/Live and Let Die/If I Were Not Upon the Stage/Hey Jude/Yesterday/Get Back/Golden Slumbers/ Carry That Weight/The End/Don't Let the Sun Catch You Crying

The Paul McCartney World Tour, which *Tripping the Live Fantastic* documents, was a major turning point in McCartney's career. It established him as a showman of exquisite taste, energy and class, and finally unburdened him of the Beatles albatross, something he carried around with him for nearly two decades.

No longer reticent to play some of his most famous songs, he peppered the set list with 16 Beatle classics, much to the delight of the throngs of concertgoers who shelled out top dollar to see this living legend. He also included six new songs from the 1989 album *Flowers in the Dirt*. More telling, he played rock chestnuts "Twenty Fight Rock" (the song he taught Lennon to play on the day they met) and "Ain't That a Shame" as a nod to his musical influences and to prove that he could still rock out at 48 years of age.

Beginning on September 26, 1989, the band played 103 shows in North and South America, Europe and Asia, before the final show at Soldier Field in Chicago on July 29, 1990.

Backed by a new and talented band, the songs crackled with energy and brio and, unlike most marathon rock concerts, this one did not have a slow segment where everyone went to get a beer. People were riveted to their seats throughout the two-and-a-half-hour show. No one wanted to miss a thing.

There were songs on which McCartney's voice faltered, and he had a stretch in the U.S. leg of the tour during which he had a mild case of pneumonia, but by and large he sang the old songs in their original keys. The onstage banter was friendly and funny, and he seemed totally in his element as storyteller and rock 'n' roll performer.

The album included every song played during the U.S. leg, except for "Good Day Sunshine," which was later released as a single. Interspersed with the concert set list was a handful of sound check run-throughs ("Inner City Madness," "Together," "Crackin' Up," "Matchbox," "Sally" and a soulful version of "Don't Let the Sun Catch You Crying," written by Joe Greene and made famous by Ray Charles). There was also the fake-out start to "Hey Jude," called "If I Were Not Upon the Stage."

But make no mistake about it, the stars of the show were the Beatles songs. The majesty of "The Fool on the Hill," the crunchy rock of "Can't Buy Me Love" and "Sgt. Pepper's Lonely Hearts Club Band," the dramatically beautiful segue between "Things We Said Today" and "Eleanor Rigby," and the utter emotional surge of "Let It Be," "Hey Jude" and "Yesterday" all served to enthrall the crowd and energize the band. The show was top-notch from beginning to end, and this stands as one of the best live albums McCartney has released.

The mixing of the live tapes, mostly done by Bob Clearmountain, was done with great care, making sure the listener had a real sense of being at a legendary rock 'n' roll show. The vocals were in your face, and the guitars and keyboards were all tastefully sympathetic to the songs. The album was released as a triple vinyl LP, a double cassette and a double CD. The packaging included astounding photos of the band on stage.

Also in 1990, a truncated version of *Tripping the Live Fantastic* called *Tripping the Live Fantastic: Highlights*! was released. This contained only 17 tracks, 13 of which were Beatles songs, and did not include the sound check numbers. The U.S. version featured "Put It There," but the U.K. version replaced that with "All My Trials," a traditional gospel song that McCartney turned into a soulful plea for equality for all people (and only performed six times). *Highlights!* didn't chart in the U.K. but made it to 141 in the Billboard 200 and eventually went platinum.

Henceforth, McCartney would not stay off the concert stage for long periods. He correctly realized that his legacy was a thick songbook of classic pop and rock 'n' roll that millions of people worldwide clamored to witness in person.

Unplugged—The Official Bootleg

Released May 13, 1991 (U.K.); June 4, 1991 (U.S.)
Highest chart position: 7 in the U.K.; 14 in the U.S.
Parlophone PCSD116
Producer: Joe Gallen (for MTV)
Musicians: Paul McCartney: acoustic guitar, vocals, drums on "Ain't No Sunshine"; Linda McCartney: harmonium, percussion, harmony vocals on "And I Love Her"; Hamish Stuart: acoustic bass guitar, acoustic guitar and lead vocals on "And I Love Her" and "Ain't No Sunshine"; Robbie McIntosh: acoustic guitars, Dobro, vocals, piano on "Ain't No

Sunshine"; Paul Wickens: piano, keyboards, accordion, percussion, vocals, acoustic bass on "Ain't No Sunshine"; Blair Cunningham: drums, percussions, vocals

Be-Bop-A-Lula/I Lost My Little Girl/Here, There and Everywhere/Blue Moon of Kentucky/We Can Work It Out/ San Francisco Bay Blues/I've Just Seen a Face/ Every Night/She's a Woman/Hi-Hell Sneakers/And I Lover Her/That Would Be Something/Blackbird/ Ain't No Sunshine/Good Rockin' Tonight/Singing the Blues/Junk

Fresh off a stunning world tour, McCartney and band (with new drummer Blair Cunningham) scaled back for an episode of MTV's new series, *Unplugged.* Recorded in London on January 25, 1991, before an intimate audience, the band powered through golden oldies from rock's nascent period, Beatles and solo McCartney material (although no Wings songs) and a cover of a Bill Withers hit.

Despite his mastery of the recording studio, Paul McCartney is at his best when he's entertaining an audience with faithful readings of classic tunes and between-song banter which, in this case, gives the proceedings a live in the living room feel.

Seventeen songs were released on the "bootleg," but the band also treated the live audience to five songs that didn't make the CD: "Matchbox," "Mean Woman Blues," "Midnight Special," "The Fool" and "Things We Said Today." Three songs from the CD were not aired on the *Unplugged* episode: "San Francisco Bay Blues," "Hi-Heel Sneakers" and "Ain't No Sunshine."

McCartney did not originally plan to release an album of this performance but reconsidered after hearing the tapes and realizing they were outstanding. Only 25,000 copies were pressed in the original run, making this a rare addition to the McCartney catalogue. The album was released in vinyl, CD and cassette formats.

Many people attribute this concert as the event that made MTV's *Unplugged* program so popular. Many other notable artists (Bob Dylan, Neil Young, Eric Clapton, Tony Bennett and a host of others) released *Unplugged* albums after McCartney's.

Highlights of this set include a slow-burning, soulful "And I Love Her," rollicking rock chestnuts "Be-Bop-A-Lula" and "Good Rockin' Tonight" and seminal renderings of "Every Night" and "That Would Be Something" from McCartney's first solo album. Perhaps the set's highlight was "Ain't No Sunshine," on which all the band members played instruments they didn't normally play. McCartney played drums and the very underrated Hamish Stuart delivered the exquisite lead vocal.

Paul Is Live

Released November 8, 1993 (U.K.); November 16, 1993 (U.S.)
Highest chart position: 78 in the U.S.; 34 in the U.K.
Parlophone PCSD147 (U.K.); Capitol Records CDP7243827704428 (U.S.)
Produced by Paul McCartney
Musicians: Paul McCartney: vocals, bass, electric and acoustic guitars, piano; Linda McCartney: vocals, keyboards; Hamish Stuart: vocals, electric and acoustic guitars, bass; Robbie McIntosh: electric and acoustic guitars, vocals; Paul Wickens: keyboards, vocals; Blair Cunningham: drums, percussion

Drive My Car/Let Me Roll It/Looking for Changes/ Peace in the Neighborhood/ All My Loving/ Robbie's Bit/Good Rocking Tonight/We Can Work It Out/Hope of Deliverance/ Michelle/Biker Like an Icon/Here There and Everywhere/My Love/Magical Mystery Tour/C'mon People/Lady Madonna/Paperback Writer/Penny Lane/ Live and Let Die/Kansas City/Welcome to Soundcheck/Hotel in Benidorm/I Wanna Be Your Man/A Fine Day

Going out on tour to support a new album is a noble and necessary endeavor, but only if the album is any good. Unfortunately, *Paul Is Live* is only a snapshot of the New World Tour's setlist, padded by unexciting sound check jams, all supporting the mediocre studio album *Off the Ground*. By contrast, *Tripping the Live Fantastic* supported the far superior *Flowers in the Dirt* album and as a result is a better and more cohesive chronicle of a McCartney tour.

No doubt part of the problem was that the band played in some terrible venues, especially during the spring/summer U.S. leg of the tour. Venues like the Pontiac Silverdome near Detroit and Exhibition Stadium in Toronto just didn't lend themselves to an invigorating live showcase. On occasion, the sound was poor, and there were far more bad seats than good ones in these cavernous old edifices.

The setlist on most nights of the tour included "Coming Up," "Jet," "Off the Ground," "Can't Buy Me Love," "And I Love Her," "Every Night,"

"Let It Be," "Sgt. Pepper's Lonely Hearts Club Band," "Another Day," "Fixing a Hole," "Band on the Run," "The Long and Winding Road," "Yesterday," "I Saw Her Standing There," "Hey Jude" and occasionally "Back in the U.S.S.R." While most of these songs can be heard on other McCartney live albums, at least a few of them ("Another Day" and "Fixing a Hole," notably) would have been great replacements for dreck like "Biker Like an Icon" and "Looking for Changes." In fact, of the six songs from *Off the Ground* in the setlist, only the majestic "Hope of Deliverance" was worthy of inclusion.

It's possible McCartney was just trying to create a thumbnail sketch of where the band was at the time, while trying to avoid releasing live versions of songs that were on *Tripping*. Still, the sequencing underscores the fact that the set list is rickety without the omissions mentioned.

There were some highlights. McCartney dusted off "Let Me Roll It" and turned it into a guitar-blazing fireball with scorching vocals. "All My Loving" was sung in its original key and proved to be a big crowd-pleaser. "Good Rocking Tonight" chugged along even more urgently than the version on *Unplugged* and featured a great acoustic guitar solo played by Robbie McIntosh. "Kansas City" had a certain raucous appeal, mostly because an unrehearsed version was played in front of a partisan crowd at Arrowhead Stadium in Kansas City on May 31, 1993, the only time the band played this song on the tour.

Still, *Paul Is Live* is a strangely tepid live album and was not received well by critics or fans. It remains McCartney's worst-selling live album.

The album was released on vinyl, cassette and CD and features a cover that has McCartney reenacting the famous *Abbey Road* cover and a poster full of tour photographs. In 1994, McCartney released a DVD called *Paul Is Live in Concert on The New World Tour*, a video replica of the live album. The album was released on colored vinyl and CD on July 12, 2019.

Back in the U.S.

Released November 11, 2002
Capitol (U.S.; no U.K. release) CDP724354231827
Highest chart position: 8 in the U.S.
Produced by David Kahne
Musicians: Paul McCartney: vocals, bass, piano, electric and acoustic guitars, ukulele; Paul Wickens: keyboards, synthesizer, acoustic guitar,

accordion, backing vocals; Rusty Anderson: acoustic and electric guitars, backing vocals; Brian Ray: acoustic and electric guitars, bass, backing vocals; Abe Laboriel, Jr.: drums, percussion, backing vocals

Hello Goodbye/Jet/All My Loving/Getting Better/Coming Up/Let Me Roll It/Lonely Road/Driving Rain/Your Loving Flame/Blackbird/Every Night/We Can Work It Out/Mother Nature's Son/Vanilla Sky/Carry That Weight/The Fool on the Hill/Here Today/Something/Eleanor Rigby/Here, There and Everywhere/Band on the Run/Back in the U.S.S.R./Maybe I'm Amazed/C Moon/My Love/Can't Buy Me Love/Freedom/Live and Let Die/Let It Be/Hey Jude/The Long and Winding Road/Lady Madonna/I Saw Her Standing There/Yesterday/Sgt. Pepper's Lonely Hearts Club Band (reprise)/The End

Back in the U.S. is the finest McCartney live album among the six he has released. It has the most joyous and uplifting set list, he's in great voice, and he's backed by the best band he's had since the 1960s. Twenty-one of the 35 songs on the set are Beatles songs, and most of them were sung and played in the original key.

This was the tour that began on April 1, 2002, to promote the *Driving Rain* album, a good but not great album. McCartney wisely chose to include just three of the songs from that album, so as not to disrupt the pure, high-energy of the rest of the set. That said, one of those songs—"Lonely Road"—stands as one of the finest late-period McCartney rockers.

The opening salvo of the first six songs (three Beatles songs, two Wings songs, and one solo McCartney song) set the tone for the rest of the show. The sellout crowds were enthralled throughout the U.S. leg of the tour, and their enthusiasm was expertly captured on this album. You can feel the emotion during McCartney's tributes to his former bandmates: A moving "Here Today" for John Lennon, and a beautifully rendered "Something" for George Harrison, played here on Harrison's favorite instrument, the ukulele.

One quibble: Several of the songs are played at a breakneck pace, much faster than the originals. This happens a lot in live shows, but here "Band on the Run," "The Long and Winding Road" and "Hey Jude" don't benefit from the rush treatment. Also, unlike *Tripping the Live Fantastic*, there is virtually no stage banter by McCartney included between tracks on this set.

This CD was not released in the U.K. and is McCartney's first album not available on vinyl. A companion DVD was released with very moving concert footage of 32 of the 35 songs, including a soundcheck version of "Matchbox."

This is the best document of Paul McCartney as the quintessential performer of some of the finest pop songs ever written.

Back in the World

Released March 17, 2003
Parlophone (U.K.) 58300529
Highest chart position: 5 in the U.K.
Produced by Paul McCartney and David Kahne
Musicians: Same as *Back in the U.S.*

Back in the World was released four months after *Back in the U.S.* and chronicles the tour as it meandered through other parts of the globe. The only differences between this and its predecessor are that "Vanilla Sky," "C Moon" and "Freedom" have been dropped, replaced by the songs McCartney added for the rest of the tour: "Let 'Em In," "She's Leaving Home," "Michelle" and the exquisite "Calico Skies."

Also, the version of "Hey Jude" on this album was recorded in Mexico City, while the version of "Hey Jude" on *Back in the U.S.* was recorded in New York City.

Amoeba's Secret

Released: November 13, 2007
Hear Music HRM-31306-02
Highest chart position: 81 in the U.K. and 119 in the U.S.
Musicians: Paul McCartney: vocals, bass, piano, electric and acoustic guitars, mandolin; Rusty Anderson: acoustic and electric guitars, backing vocals; Brian Ray: acoustic and electric guitars, bass, backing vocals; Abe Laboriel Jr.: drums, percussion, backing vocals; David Arch: Keyboards, synthesizer, accordion/

A sampler of songs ("Only Mama Knows," "C Moon," "That Was Me," "I Saw Her Standing There") performed at a surprise show at the mega-record store Amoeba Music in Hollywood on June 27, 2007. It was released initially as a 12-inch limited edition vinyl EP. Culled from a set list of 21 songs, these four each stand out for different reasons. The best by far is "That Was Me" from *Memory Almost Full,* here rendered in a cheekier and more bombastic styling. In fact, McCartney received a 2008 Grammy nomination for Best Male Pop Vocal Performance for the song. Paul Wickens, long-time McCartney keyboard player and musical director, was unavailable so English composer and pianist David Arch sat in with the band for this gig.

Good Evening New York City

Released November 17, 2009 (U.S.) and December 4, 2009, in Europe
Hear Music HRM-31926-00
Highest chart position: 16 in the U.S. and 28 in the U.K.
Produced by Paul McCartney
Musicians: Paul McCartney: vocals, bass, piano, electric and acoustic guitars, mandolin, ukulele; Paul Wickens: keyboards, synthesizer, electric guitar, accordion, percussion, harmonica, backing vocals; Rusty Anderson: acoustic and electric guitars, backing vocals; Brian Ray: acoustic and electric guitars, bass, backing vocals; Abe Laboriel, Jr.: drums, percussion, backing vocals; Billy Joel: vocals and piano on "I Saw Her Standing There"

Drive My Car/Jet/Only Mama Knows/Flaming Pie/Got to Get You Into My Life/Let Me Roll It/Highway/The Long and Winding Road/ My Love/Blackbird/Here Today/Dance Tonight/Calico Skies/Mrs. Vandebilt/Eleanor Rigby/Sing the Changes/Band on the Run/Back in the U.S.S.R./I'm Down/Something/I've Got a Feeling/Paperback Writer/A Day in the Life/Give Peace a Chance/Let It Be/Live and Let Die/Hey Jude/Day Tripper/Lady Madonna/I Saw Her Standing There/ Yesterday/Helter Skelter/Get Back/Sgt. Pepper's Lonely Hearts Club Band (reprise)/The End

Good Evening New York City had the perfect chance to be a monumental hit and a ground-breaking moment in the long history of live albums by rock icons. Recorded over three nights at Citi Field, just a short stroll from the site of Shea Stadium, where the Beatles played their most memorable outdoor concert 44 years earlier, the entire proceedings were filled with an air of nostalgia, excitement and the realization that one of popular music's true legends was still rocking. And for those in attendance on those three nights, it *was* perfect.

Not so for listeners of this album. McCartney's voice fails him on half a dozen songs, most notably "Blackbird," "My Love" and "Back in the U.S.S.R.," and on a couple of others he muffs the lyrics. The band is as strong as ever and the playing is in the pocket, but the lead singer sometimes falters at crucial moments in the set.

The album also has this weird faraway feel to it. Perhaps the producer and engineers wanted to replicate the abrasive white noise that drowned out the Beatles' concert in Shea Stadium so they potted up the crowd sounds in the mix, but there are several occasions when the crowd is louder than the singer.

Still, any set that includes "I'm Down" and "Day Tripper" counts as something good. The inclusion of two songs from 2008's *Electric Arguments* by The Fireman ("Sing the Changes" and "Highway"), and two songs from 2007's *Memory Almost Full* ("Only Mama Knows" and "Dance Tonight") helped to freshen up a set list that was threatening to become stale. Billy Joel's cameo on piano and vocals on "I Saw Her Standing There" added a certain Gotham-inflected touch.

But if you want to hear a live recording of Paul McCartney at his best, stick with *Tripping the Live Fantastic* or *Back in the U.S.* Both are far superior to *Good Evening New York City.*

The CD was released in two versions, standard and deluxe. The standard version includes two CDs of the concert, and a DVD with concert footage. The deluxe version adds a seven-song set McCartney and band played on top of the marquee of the *Late Night with David Letterman Show* on July 15, 2009, plus a short documentary film titled *Good Evening People* and concert footage of "I'm Down."

(As an aside while we are discussing McCartney live albums, it might be interesting if he went through all of his recorded concerts and chose 25 or so of the lesser known live performances and released them as a live album. "Jet," "Yesterday," "Hey Jude" and "Live and Let Die" populate most of his live albums [obviously, it'd be hard for McCartney not to play these songs in concert], but there are songs he's played live in the 2000s that would make a fabulous compilation of lesser known live cuts. "For No One," "Fixing a Hole," "She Came in Through the Bathroom Window," "Ram On," "Too Many People," "I Want to Come Home," "Mull of Kintyre," "Listen to What the Man Said," "I'll Get You," "Please Please Me," "Lovely Rita," "I'll Follow the Sun," "She's a Woman," "Letting Go" and "Junior's

Farm" come immediately to mind. Also, there is a beautiful rendition of "Here, There and Everywhere" with just McCartney playing the piano and singing that reinvents the pure loveliness of that song.)

Amoeba Gig

Released: July 12, 2019
Capitol Records B0029496-02
Musicians: Paul McCartney: vocals, bass, piano, electric and acoustic guitars, mandolin; Rusty Anderson: acoustic and electric guitars, backing vocals; Brian Ray: acoustic and electric guitars, bass, backing vocals; Abe Laboriel, Jr.: drums, percussion, backing vocals; David Arch: keyboards, synthesizer, accordion.

Drive My Car/Only Mama Knows/Dance Tonight/C Moon/The Long and Winding Road/I'll Follow the Sun/Calico Skies/That Was Me/Blackbird/Here Today/Back in the U.S.S.R./Nod Your Head/House of Wax/I've Got a Feeling/Matchbox/Get Back/Baby Face/Hey Jude/Let It Be/Lady Madonna/I Saw Her Standing There/Coming Up (soundcheck version only available on vinyl)

This greatly expanded version of *Amoeba's Secret* easily ranks among McCartney's best live albums. Devoid of the magnitude and distance inherent in stadium and arena live shows, this set is awash in an intimacy not usually felt at performances by rock icons. The band is in fine form and the set includes some nice surprises. The many highlights include a raucous opener with "Drive My Car," an intimate reading of "Dance Tonight," a playful "C Moon," a moving version of "Calico Skies" and a heart-rending rendition of "Here Today," during which McCartney gets a little weepy. But by far the highlights are the back-to-back versions of "I've Got a Feeling" and "Matchbox." The guitars (especially McCartney's) are loud and crunchy and the vocals are fervent and energetic. The ad-libbed coda to "I've Got a Feeling" provides an opportunity for McCartney to turn up his Les Paul and rock out with abandon. It's interesting to hear him play the initial licks before realizing that he failed to deploy the foot pedal that turned on the distortion. Once he did that, everything got dirtier and funkier.

Paul McCartney is at his best when he's got a crowd (no matter how large or small) just a few feet away from the stage, and when he lards his set with a combination of new songs, rock chestnuts and familiar Beatles tunes. *Amoeba Gig* is a shining testament to this, and it's a far better live album than *Paul Is Live* and *Good Evening, New York City.*

Covers

Choba B CCCP

Released October 31, 1988 (Russia only; released in other markets in 1991)
Melodiya (Russia) A60 00415 006
Parlophone CDP 7976152; Capitol CDP 7976152
Highest chart position: 63 in the U.K. and 109 in the U.S.
Produced by Paul McCartney
Musicians: Paul McCartney: bass guitar, guitar, vocals; Mike Green: guitar; Mick Gallagher: piano, keyboards; Chris Whitten: drums; Nick Garvey: bass guitar, backing vocals; Henry Spinetti: drums

Kansas City/Twenty Flight Rock/ Lawdy, Miss Clawdy/I'm in Love Again/Bring It on Home to Me/Lucille/Don't Get Around Much Anymore/I'm Gonna Be a Wheel Someday/That's All Right Mama/ Summertime/Ain't That a Shame/Crackin' Up/Just Because/Midnight Special

Paul McCartney holed up for two consecutive days in July 1987 to record some of his favorite rock oldies with a group of talented session musicians for an album he planned to release only in Russia. In all, 20 songs were recorded, although only 14 made it onto the album ("I'm in Love Again" was not included on the original release but was added to the 1991 CD release).

On the first day, McCartney played only the bass guitar and sang the lead vocals. On the second day, he switched to electric guitar and sang vocals. For the most part, all the songs were recorded live, without the benefit of overdubbing.

The album title's English rendering is roughly *Back in the U.S.S.R.* McCartney at first wanted to release the album in the United Kingdom through non-traditional distribution channels, making it seem like it was smuggled out of Russia, but his record company nixed that idea. A record deal, brokered with the noble intention of promoting peace, was made with Soviet-run record label Melodiya, which pressed 400,000 copies. After bootlegs fetching hundreds of dollars began to appear elsewhere, the album was released in Europe and the United States in 1991.

The album is a lot of fun. McCartney sings with a brio he hadn't brought to his vocals during the preceding several years, when he was recording less than inspired studio albums. This project seemed like just the tonic McCartney needed to rediscover his spark.

The album is filled with rock 'n' roll chestnuts that McCartney was familiar with, having sung many of them during the Beatles days on stage in Hamburg. He chose songs from his musical forefathers, including Eddie Cochran, Lloyd Price, Fats Domino, Sam Cooke and Little Richard, among others. He even reached deeper into the American musical grab-bag to cover songs by George Gershwin and Duke Ellington.

The sound is tough and cocky, with crunchy electric guitars, classic rock 'n' roll piano, and simple bass and drum parts holding down the rhythm section. He added two of these songs to his 1989–90 world tour, and they are two of the strongest tracks on this album: "Twenty Flight Rock" and "Ain't That a Shame." He also played "Crackin' Up" during soundchecks on that tour.

Highlights of this set include a rousing "Kansas City," a bawdy "Lawdy, Miss Clawdy," a Sun Records workout on "That's All Right Mama" and a Mersey Beat version of the jazz standard "Don't Get Around Much Anymore."

But the best song by far is the shining jewel of a B-side from Bo Diddley called "Crackin' Up." A busy syncopated beat with funky organ and dampened guitar chords playing the same four chords over and over, makes the listener want to dance to this track on the veranda of some tropical resort at dusk.

One can see how this project could inspire McCartney to consider touring again. Paul McCartney is at his best when he is performing songs he loves (whether or not he wrote them himself) and *Choba B CCCP* is testament to his abiding love and respect for classic rock 'n' roll.

The album was released on colored vinyl and CD on July 12, 2019.

Run Devil Run

Released October 4, 1999 (U.K.); October 5, 1999 (U.S.)
Parlophone 7243 5 22351 2 4; Capitol CDP 7243 5 22351 2 4
Highest chart position: 12 in the U.K. and 27 in the U.S.
Produced by Paul McCartney and Chris Thomas
Musicians: Paul McCartney: vocals, electric and acoustic guitars, bass guitar, percussion; David Gilmour: electric guitar, steel guitar, backing vocals; Mick Green: electric guitar; Ian Paice: drums, percussion; Dave Mattacks: drums, percussion; Pete Wingfield: keyboards, organ, piano; Geraint Watkins: piano; Chris Hall: accordion

Blue Jean Bop/She Said Yeah/All Shook Up/Run Devil Run/No Other Baby/Lonesome Town/Tray Not to Cry/Movie Magg/Brown Eyed Handsome Man/What It Is/Coquette/I Got Stung/Honey Hush/Shake a Hand/Party/Fabulous (iTunes exclusive track added when McCartney's catalogue became available on iTunes in 2007)

Run Devil Run is the first rock album McCartney made after Linda's death in 1998. Apparently, Linda had been urging him to make another covers album of some of their favorite songs. In that way, it's a bit of a tribute album.

And what a tribute album it is. Fresh from the most agonizing period of grief in his life, McCartney demonstrates compellingly that good music can be an antidote for even the most heart-wrenching pain. He uses the studio to pull the Band-Aid off his wounds in one swift motion, confident all along that all he needs as an anodyne is a dose of good old rock 'n' roll. And it succeeds. He sounds gritty, committed to the music he recorded and certainly ready to return to the only thing he knows how to do to quell the grief.

It includes 13 mostly lesser known classics and three outstanding McCartney originals. The band is tight and really supports the lead singer well. McCartney mines the usual trove of classic rock songs made by some of his favorite artists: Gene Vincent, Elvis Presley, Carl Perkins, Rick Nelson, Chuck Berry and Fats Domino, among others.

Of the covers, a sinuous "Blue Jean Bop," a ZZ-Top–like guitar powered "All Shook Up," a wistful and understated "No Other Baby," a rueful "Lonesome Town" and a celebratory and echo-laden "Shake a Hand" stand out as the best tracks in this set.

The cover features a photo of the storefront of Miller's Rexall Drugstore in Atlanta, a store that features herbal medicine and other wellness arcana. McCartney composed the title track after seeing the store.

Run Devil Run: This original sounds the most like classic rock, with a rapid-fire delivery of the Chuck Berry-esque lyrics and fits in well with the rest of the songs. McCartney's bass lopes along nicely and the guitar solo and piano trade frenetic solos. The drums are bashed with wild abandon.

Try Not to Cry: The second original has an insistent beat, and some really fine guitar figures. The verses are sung with McCartney harmonizing with himself. For a song with such poignant lyrics, it rocks outs as much as any other song on the album. McCartney's vocals throughout the album conjure memories of his early career larynx-shredding outings on "Long Tall Sally" and "I'm Down."

What It Is: This is the most commercial and bluesy song among the three originals on the album. Nice little guitar figures fit in between lines in the verses. Quick and numerous chord changes underpin the rollicking backing track. Again, McCartney harmonizes with himself in spots. There's a certain delectable snarl in his vocal. This is 2:23 worth of the choicest classic rock, even though it was originally written in 1999.

A limited edition of *Run Devil Run* featured a bonus disc of a McCartney interview about the making of the album. Another limited edition included the original artists of four of the songs McCartney covered on the album.

On December 14, 1999, McCartney returned to the Cavern Club and performed several of the album's songs, using some of the musicians who played on *Run Devil Run*. This performance was filmed and released on video in June 2001 (see the video/DVD chapter for a discussion).

Kisses on the Bottom

Released February 6, 2012, in the U.K. and February 7, 2012, in the U.S.

Hear Music HRM-33598-01 (U.K) and HRM-33369-02 (U.S.)

Highest chart position: 3 in both the U.K. and U.S.

Produced by Tommy LiPuma

Musicians: Paul McCartney: vocals and acoustic guitar; Diana Krall: piano; Tamir Hendelman: piano on "Only Our Hearts"; Stevie Wonder: harmonica on "Only Our Hearts"; John Pizzarelli: guitar; Anthony Wilson:

guitar; Eric Clapton: guitar on "My Valentine" and "Get Yourself Another Fool"; Bucky Pizzarelli: guitar; John Chiodini: guitar; Robert Hurst, John Clayton, Christian McBride and Chuck Berghofer: double bass; Vinnie Colaiuta, Karriem Riggins and Jeff Hamilton: drums; Mike Mainieri: vibraphone; Ira Nepus: trombone; London Symphony Orchestra; children's choir

I'm Gonna Sit Right Down and Write Myself a Letter/Home (Where Shadows Fall)/It's Only a Paper Moon/More I Cannot Wish You/The Glory of Love/We Three (My Echo, My Shadow and Me)/ Ac-Cent-Tchu-Ate the Positive/My Valentine/Always/My Very Good Friend the Milkman/Bye Bye Blackbird/Get Yourself Another Fool/ The Inch Worm/Only Our Hearts

Countless rock and pop stars have made cover albums exploring the great American songbook since the beginning of the rock 'n' roll era. Harry Nilsson, Linda Ronstadt, Bryan Ferry and Rod Stewart and many others have interpreted the best compositions written by the finest 20th century American songsmiths. But no one has ever tackled this massive task with the class and genuine love of the material than Paul McCartney on *Kisses on the Bottom.*

Here, he interprets songs he remembers his dad playing during his childhood during family parties and pub singalongs. While many of the songs are familiar to all, there are four or five "deep tracks" that don't jump to mind when you think about the most popular songs in history. And that's definitely part of the fun.

In fact, "Home (When Shadows Fall)," "We Three (My Echo, My Shadow and Me)," "Get Yourself Another Fool" and especially "My Very Good Friend the Milkman" have a baked in feel of humor and romantic sensibilities, a hallmark trait of the best songwriters of the 1930s and '40s.

McCartney surrounded himself with crack jazz musicians and the famed jazz producer Tommy LiPuma to produce a sound almost indistinguishable from the original recordings. Diana Krall adds tasteful piano, and McCartney's contemporaries Stevie Wonder and Eric Clapton pitch in on a couple of songs. McCartney was there to choose the songs and sing them; his only instrumental contribution was playing the acoustic guitar on two tracks. McCartney caresses the lyrics with his sweet, albeit weathered, tenor and during the instrumental breaks one can almost smell the cigarette smoke and gin.

The album was recorded in Los Angeles, New York and London

over a year's time, beginning in early 2010. On February 9, 2012, iTunes streamed a live performance by McCartney and the team assembled for the album as he sang 13 songs live in Capitol Studios in Los Angeles. The performance was recorded and released as *Paul McCartney's Live Kisses* and later aired on the PBS series *Great Performances.*

Two of the songs on this album were original compositions. One—"My Valentine"—is cut from the same musical cloth as all of the others and has been a staple of McCartney's live shows since 2012.

My Valentine: Moody and dark, this paean of love written for McCartney's wife is as melodically dense and rich as any other song on this album. It's just astounding how a pop music icon from a later era can conjure the mood and vibe of a bygone time so effortlessly.

Only Our Hearts: This original composition is steeped in the Nat King Cole tradition of producing a performance with a slow and sad introduction featuring only strings, before the whole band comes in to back the singer as he carries that smoldering torch through to the song's conclusion. Throw in several bars of a trademark Stevie Wonder harmonica solo and this one is a definite winner.

The deluxe version of *Kisses on the Bottom* included two bonus tracks ("Baby's Request" and "My One and Only Love"). "Baby's Request" is an original McCartney composition that first appeared on 1979's *Back to the Egg.* This version is more buoyant and features a finger-snappin' instrumental outro.

Kisses on the Bottom—Complete Kisses was an expanded version of the original album, released exclusively on iTunes in November 2012. It featured the original 14-track album, four bonus tracks (including a rendition of "The Christmas Song," better known as "Chestnuts Roasting on an Open Fire") and the complete *Live from Capitol Studios* performance.

Compilations and Greatest Hits

Wings Greatest

Released December 1, 1978 (U.K.); November 22, 1978 (U.S.)
Parlophone PCTC256; Capitol SOO-11905

Highest Chart Position: 5 in the U.K. and 29 in the U.S.
Produced by Paul McCartney

Another Day/Silly Love Songs/Live and Let Die/ Junior's Farm/ With a Little Luck/Band on the Run/Uncle Albert/Admiral Halsey/Hi Hi Hi/Let 'Em In/My Love/Jet/Mull of Kintyre

Wings Greatest was Paul McCartney's first compilation of greatest hits during his solo career. It's a fair representation of the band's best songs to this date, except that both "Another Day" and "Uncle Albert/Admiral Halsey" were written and recorded in McCartney's pre–Wings days.

This seems like a quibble given that both songs were massive hits, but their inclusion squeezed out "Listen to What the Man Said," one of Wings' finest singles and a No. 1 hit in the U.S. Making this omission even more regrettable is the inclusion of "With a Little Luck," by far the slightest and most annoying of the songs on *Wings Greatest.*

The album did well and acted as sales placeholder until Wings released their final album six months later.

The album was available on vinyl, cassette and 8-track tape, and was issued in CD format in 1986. The Paul McCartney Collection version (August 9, 1993; Parlophone 7 89317 2) had no bonus tracks. In May 2018, it was re-released in three formats: a CD digipak, 180 gram black vinyl, and a limited edition 180 gram blue vinyl format.

All the Best

Released November 2, 1987
Parlophone CDPMTV1; Capitol CDP7482872
Highest chart position: 2 in the U.K. and 36 in the U.S.
Produced by Paul McCartney and George Martin

The Japanese, Canadian, Australian and U.K. versions featured this track listing:

Jet/Band on the Run/Coming Up/Ebony and Ivory/Listen to What the Man Said/No More Lonely Nights/Silly Love Songs/Let 'Em In/C Moon/Pipes of Peace/Live and Let Die/Another Day/Maybe I'm Amazed/Goodnight Tonight/Once Upon a Long Ago/Say Say Say/ With a Little Luck/My Love/We All Stand Together/Mull of Kintyre

The U.S. release differed slightly, principally to capitalize on those songs that were more popular in the States than in England:

Band on the Run/Jet/Ebony and Ivory/Listen to What the Man Said/No More Lonely Nights/Silly Love Songs/Let 'Em In/ Say Say Say/Live and Let Die/Another Day/C Moon/Junior's Farm/Uncle Albert/Admiral Halsey/Coming Up /Goodnight Tonight/With a Little Luck (edit)/My Love

All the Best is an expanded version of *Wings Greatest,* padded out by McCartney's most popular songs from 1980–87.

The most interesting songs are two minor curiosities, both found only on the U.K. release: "We All Stand Together" and a new composition called "Once Upon a Long Ago." Both songs will be discussed in the singles chapter.

The vinyl version in the U.K., Canada, Australia and Japan included 20 tracks. The CD version includes 17 tracks, omitting "Maybe I'm Amazed," "Goodnight Tonight" and "With a Little Luck."

To this point in time, this was a good snapshot of Paul McCartney's post–Beatles career. He would release two more compilations that would be much more comprehensive versions of his body of work.

Wingspan: Hits and History

Released May 7, 2001
Parlophone 724353287627; Capitol CDP724353294625
Highest chart position: 2 in the U.S. and 5 in the U.K.
Executive producer: Paul McCartney
Co-producers on various tracks: Linda McCartney, George Martin and Chris Thomas

Hits disc: Listen to What the Man Said/Band on the Run/Another Day/Live and Let Die/Jet/My Love/Silly Love Songs/Pipes of Peace/C Moon/Hi Hi Hi/Let 'Em In/Goodnight Tonight/Junior's Farm (DJ edit)/Mull of Kintyre/Uncle Albert/Admiral Halsey/With a Little Luck (DJ edit)/Coming Up (live version from the Glasgow Apollo Theatre)/No More Lonely Nights

History disc: Let Me Roll It/The Lovely Linda/Daytime Nighttime Suffering/Maybe I'm Amazed/Helen Wheels/Bluebird/Heart of

the Country/Every Night/Take It Away/Junk/Man We Was Lonely/ Venus and Mars/Rockshow (edit)/The Back Seat of My Car/Rockestra Theme/Girlfriend/Waterfalls (DJ edit)/Tomorrow/Too Many People/ Call Me Back Again/Tug of War/Bip Bop/Hey Diddle/No More Lonely Nights (playout version)

Wingspan is far better than the two previous hits compilations McCartney released. It's more comprehensive and the history disc digs deeper into the music than most greatest hits packages do.

However, it's impossible not to notice that fully 16 of the 41 tracks compiled are not Wings songs: "Another Day," "Pipes of Peace," "Uncle Albert/Admiral Halsey," "No More Lonely Nights," "The Lovely Linda," "Maybe I'm Amazed," "Heart of the Country," "Every Night," "Take It Away," "Junk," "Man We Was Lonely," "Back Seat of My Car," "Waterfalls," "Too Many People," "Tug of War" and the playout version of "No More Lonely Nights" were all written and recorded either before Wings formed over after they broke up. I'm not sure how any of these songs advance the Wings story at all.

I can easily think of 16 true Wings songs that would have fit nicely into this set, among them "Letting Go," "Nineteen Hundred and Eighty Five," "London Town," "Getting Closer," "Beware My Love" and "Love in Song." The list goes on.

Because we've heard the hits so often, the history disc of this two-disc set is much more interesting. "Let Me Roll It," "Daytime Nightime Suffering," "Every Night," "Call Me Back Again" and "Girlfriend" are all melodic pop gems from McCartney that deserved a wider listen.

The album release coincided roughly with a TV documentary by the same name that featured Mary McCartney interviewing her dad about the Wings era, complete with home movies, never before seen photos taken by Linda, and keen insights by the bandleader himself. An oral history book of the same name was also released, with lots of great photos and insights that followed the contour of the TV documentary closely.

What's missing from both, obviously, are insights from anyone else involved in the band. Only Paul and Linda McCartney contribute comments, which means that Denny Seiwell, Denny Laine, Joe English, Laurence Juber, Steve Holly and many others couldn't weigh in on the historic artistic arc of Wings. That seems like a missed opportunity, because we can safely assume that all would have provided fresh looks.

Pure McCartney

Released June 10, 2016
Hear Music (U.K.) HRM-386699-02666999387197
Concord Music Group (U.S.)
Highest chart position: 3 in the U.K. and 15 in the U.S.
Producers: Paul McCartney, Linda McCartney, Youth, Nigel Godrich, Paul Epworth, George Martin, Chris Thomas

Maybe I'm Amazed/Heart of the Country/Jet/Warm and Beautiful/Listen to What the Man Said/Dear Boy/Silly Love Songs/The Song We Were Singing/Uncle Albert/Admiral Halsey/Early Days/Big Barn Bed/Another Day/Flaming Pie/Jenny Wren/Too Many People/Let Me Roll It/New/Live and Let Die/English Tea/Mull of Kintyre/Save Us/ My Love/Bip Bop/Let 'Em In/Nineteen Hundred and Eighty Five/Calico Skies/Hi Hi Hi/Waterfalls/Band on the Run/Appreciate/Sing the Changes/Arrow Through Me/Every Night/Junior's Farm/Mrs. Vandebilt/Say Say Say/My Valentine/Pipes of Peace/The World Tonight/ Souvenir/Dance Tonight/Ebony and Ivory/Fine Line/Here Today/ Press/Wanderlust/Winedark Open Sea/Beautiful Night/Girlfriend/ Queenie Eye/We All Stand Together/Coming Up/Too Much Rain/ Good Times Coming/Feel the Sun/Goodnight Tonight/Baby's Request/With a Little Luck/Little Willow/Only Mama Knows/Don't Let it Bring You Down/The Back Seat of My Car/No More Lonely Nights/ Great Day/Venus and Mars/Rock Show/Temporary Secretary/Hope for the Future/Junk

Pure McCartney is the ultimate solo McCartney jukebox. Two versions were released; a two-disc set with 39 songs, and a deluxe edition with the 67 songs listed above. This version is a perfect thumbnail of McCartney's solo career and would work well as an introduction to his music to somebody who somehow had never heard him.

Sure, you have to suffer through "With a Little Luck" and "Ebony and Ivory," but the deep album tracks included on this set make the whole endeavor worth it. The gentle beauty of "Warm and Beautiful"; the raw soul of "Souvenir"; the cascading lilt of "Winedark Open Sea"; the sunny optimism of "Sing the Changes" and even the quirky weirdness of "Temporary Secretary" display all of McCartney's musical and melodic attributes.

Another advantage of listening to *Pure McCartney* is that there is absolutely no rhyme nor reason to the sequencing of the songs. They are not sequenced in chronological order, so it's even more interesting when you hear, say, "Girlfriend" (1978) followed by "Queenie Eye" (2013), two very distinct and wildly different periods of the man's career. It's like listening to the entire McCartney catalogue on shuffle on your digital music device.

It's nice that the whole set begins and ends with two of the best songs from his first solo album. There is a certain artistic symmetry to that.

Electronica, Trance and Mash-Up

Strawberries Oceans Ships Forest

Released November 14, 1993 (U.S.); November 15, 1993 (U.K.)
Capitol Records C2-27167; Parlophone PCSD145
Highest chart position: Did not chart
Produced by The Fireman
Musicians: Paul McCartney: flute, upright bass, banjo: Youth: various instruments

Paul McCartney's first foray into ambient/trance music was a collaboration with the producer Youth (Martin Glover), well known for his extensive and complicated remixes for a variety of artists. McCartney had dabbled with the newest digital sampling and remixing equipment and had come up with remixes of a couple of songs off *Back to the Egg* and much of his most recent studio album *Off the Ground.* He took these remixes to Youth, who gave them the full-on treatment.

The album is credited to The Fireman, with no mention of McCartney. But by listening to the samples from some of his songs and the record label it was released on it's easy to draw some conclusions. The result was a fully formed if oddly conceptualized album of trance music which, in its way, is captivating. That McCartney, creator of so many enduring three-minute pop songs, would embark on such a project speaks to his abiding love of creating new sounds, a craft he learned well during his years as a Beatle.

The album was not meant to be a chart-topper and had no pretensions as such. But as a curio in McCartney's catalogue, unlike anything he had ever done before, it's valuable. It's not an album you'd throw on while having Sunday brunch, but it certainly is interesting.

Most of the songs are based on the same musical motif and a similar beat. It's unclear how much hands-on work McCartney did to create this album, other than providing samples of some of his previous songs. It seems likely Youth carried the water on this project.

Transpiritual Stomp: Loud and boisterous, this repetitive stomp features lots of deeply buried snippets from the spoken word passages off *Back to the Egg.*

Trans Lunar Rising: This is a slightly mellower version of the previous track, with spoken word passages that are easier to discern. The long fadeout features a pared down instrumental backing with some eerie sound effects and spoken words with a multitude of effects applied to them, then a nice and brief string arrangement.

Transcrystaline: It's about at this point where you might need to take a break from listening. This is the third track in a row that is based on the same beat, with different variations of the vocals interspersed in the previous two tracks. Once again, the long fade-out includes a quieter and rather surreal coda.

Pure Trance: This is an apt title for this track. It's trancelike throughout its 8:42 running time. One can easily imagine being disoriented on the dance club floor, with flashing lights and this track playing. Once again, it grows quieter and less frenetic toward the end.

Arizona Light: The variation on this track is the plethora of percussion instruments that dominate. It gives it a slightly different feel from the previous tracks, even though it hews closely to the overall musical theme.

Celtic Stomp: This track is almost identical to "Transpiritual Stomp." It uses the same backing tracks, except for the inclusion of some loud organ parts.

Strawberries, Oceans, Ships, Forest: More variations on the theme, with lots of synths and extra percussion. It's a reworking of "Trans Lunar Rising."

4-4-4: This starts with a more complicated beat playing over the same musical motif. What makes this track slightly more interesting is the inclusion of some interludes of simple percussion just beneath the spoken word passages, put through a heavy phase effect.

Sunrise Mix: The final track marries all the musical themes heard throughout the album, with some interesting vocal interjections dropped in. It fades out with the eerie two-chord progression that is the hallmark of all the songs.

Rushes

Released: October 20, 1998 (U.S.); September 21, 1998 (U.K.)
Hydra 4970551
Highest chart position: Did not chart
Produced by Paul McCartney and Youth
All songs performed and composed by The Fireman

Rushes, the second album produced through collaboration between Paul McCartney and Youth, is much more accessible and easier to listen to than *Strawberries Oceans Ships Forest.*

It relies much less on sampling other songs and does not have as much as a unifying musical theme than the first album.

This album was released on the Parlophone subsidiary Hydra, which was established solely for the purpose of releasing *Rushes*. It was also McCartney's first work since the death of Linda in April 1998.

Watercolour Guitars: This is the perfect title. A guitar, played way up on the fretboard, repeats a hypnotic riff, with the rest of the mix awash with underwater sounds and dissonant synth noodling.

Palo Verde: "Palo Verde" revisits the motif of the previous track, but adds some twists, most notably some echo-y, faraway spoken voices and drums and percussion. A swampy electric keyboard echoes the riff in parts. Some lyrics included on this track and sung by McCartney were taken from "Let Me Love You Always," recorded in 1995 and unreleased.

Auraveda: This swirling track features a prominent sitar and Indian inflected percussion, plus some brief backwards instrumentation, making it sound like a latter-day *Revolver* outtake. McCartney's voice, wet with echo, is sampled here and there. At 7:25 into the track, it quiets down into a gentle morass of synths and percussion.

Fluid: This is the first appearance of a track with an acoustic piano as the main instrument. It repeats a simple melody while the sound of water and weather rages in the background. Spoken words intrude every once in a while, and synths, percussion and a guitar join the mix eventually. After the piano fades out halfway through, a beautiful guitar lick is repeated over the sound of someone really enjoying himself. Then a woman's voice seems to recall a strange experience she had.

Appletree Cinnabar Amber: This is as close to a pop song that The Fireman comes on this album. A funky drum beat and an electric guitar riff play over lots of percussion, and another guitar comes in playing the same riff that was used extensively on "Fluid." More spoken words run in and out of the mix, mostly from the woman who told her story in the previous track. At the very end, the piano returns, playing a slightly different passage.

Bison: A mishmash of synths and treble-y drums dominate the mix, with some discordant notes played over the basic track. More than any other of the tracks on "Rushes," this sounds like it was ad-libbed.

7 **A.M.:** Over the same musical theme, some strings play a brief melody in a minor key. This continues until halfway through, when a persistent tapping and some backwards recordings give the track some extra color. Every once in a while, there is a spoken phrase.

Watercolour Rush: This track reprises the musical theme of the opening track, with some strings added.

Liverpool Sound Collage

Released August 21, 2000
Hydra (U.K.) 724352881727; Capitol (U.S.) CDP724352881727
Highest chart position: Did not chart
Producer: Paul McCartney
Musicians: Paul McCartney: various voices and sound effects; The Beatles: studio chatter; Super Furry Animals: various instruments; Youth: various instruments

Liverpool Sound Collage is an ambient/trance album consisting of various beats, minced and diced percussion and synthesizers, with lots of studio chatter, sound effects and repetition galore.

McCartney took studio chatter from his former bandmates and superimposed it in places over the hypnotic basic tracks. On two tracks he's assisted by the Welsh group Super Furry Animals, and his sometime The Fireman partner Youth contributed another track.

This is an interesting historical artifact in that the listener gets to hear snippets of Beatles studio chatter, most of which hadn't surfaced. Other than that, it's not that interesting and doesn't stand up well against the similar albums McCartney made as The Fireman.

The CD was released on vinyl and CD. The album was nominated for a Grammy in 2001 in the Best Alternative Music Album category.

Plastic Beetle: Over a hypnotic trance groove, snippets of Beatles studio chatter can be heard, with all four accounted for. Most interesting are the last two minutes of the track, when lots of chatter can be heard clearly, although some of it is treated with echo and reverb.

Peter Blake 2000: This piece was created to accompany an artwork exhibit by Peter Blake, designer of the *Sgt. Pepper* album cover. This track includes a snippet of George Harrison saying "do what you want to do" repeatedly and manipulated with certain effects and speed variations. It also includes McCartney singing, over a beefy drum part, the "gotta get free" mantra that was released on the 2017 release of *Sgt. Pepper* as part of one of the early run-throughs of the title track. Toward the end are bits of McCartney's 1991 classical work *Liverpool Oratorio.*

Real Gone Dub Made in Manifest in the Vortex of the Eternal Now: More snippets from *Liverpool Oratorio* and some wobbling video game sound effects pepper the basic drum track. Lots more studio chatter from the Fabs, most of which can be heard in the other tracks on this album. McCartney can also be heard doing "street interviews" with Liverpudlians. The net effect is that this track sounds like "Revolution 9" on methamphetamines.

Made Up: More street interviews, complete with street sounds, in which McCartney asks the locals what they think of Liverpool and the Beatles and includes a quick swing by the Cavern Club prior to McCartney's 1999 gig there.

Free Now: Still more Beatles studio chatter laid over a bed of funky drums and percussion.

Twin Freaks

Released June 13, 2005 (U.K. only)
Parlophone 094631130014
Highest chart position: Did not chart
Producers: Paul McCartney and Freelance Hellraiser (Roy Kerr)

Twin Freaks is a collaboration between Paul McCartney and Roy Kerr, better known as Freelance Hellraiser. McCartney asked Freelance Hellraiser to open his 2004 live gigs with mash-ups of various McCartney songs and liked the results so much that he suggested an album of mash-ups. This should appeal mostly to McCartney completists and trance fans.

Really Love You: This tune from *Flaming Pie* takes the original vocal and distorts it and treats it with heavy echo. The heavy persistent beat gives it a hypnotic twist. There is a break in the middle where the vocals drop out and a synthesized bass part plays over the percussion and lots of frenetic tambourine. It fades slowly from there, just after some brief studio chatter.

Long Haired Lady: The worst song on Ram gets a funky remake. Over the main track, a slightly speeded up guitar riff from "Oo You" from *McCartney* plays over and over again. It isn't until 2:29 that the vocals from "Long Haired Lady" emerge. There's a nice break where you can hear the harmonies sung by Paul and Linda isolated over some basic percussion. The whole thing melts into a wild chant of the song's closing chorus.

Rinse the Raindrops: This underrated song from *Driving Rain* uses the original vocal and underscores it with a wild drum beat and a distorted electric guitar riff. Lots of syncopated moments that turn the song into a fun but careening ride.

Darkroom: This obscure song from *McCartney II* is cast as a funky jam that combines the original vocals and synthesizers over a persistent beat punctuated by heavy bass and a swirl of sound effects.

Live and Let Die: This starts out with echo-y testimonials from McCartney fans talking about why McCartney matters to them over the first line of "Live and Let Die," played over and over. Some guitar figures from "Goodnight Tonight" show up in various spots for good measure.

Temporary Secretary: This starts with a heavily gated acoustic guitar from the original playing the two chords from the chorus over and over until McCartney's untreated vocal from the original song gets supplemented by a big, bruising drum part. The break in the middle has lots of handclaps, sound effects and a heavily distorted electric guitar.

What's That You're Doing: This begins with a jazz bass part and some trebly percussion, before Stevie Wonder's vocal from the original comes in. McCartney's vocal is enhanced by reverb and sounds funkier than the original mix. Some of the harmonies from the original are superimposed over the mash-up toward the end of this fun romp.

Oh Woman, Oh Why: A reporter recalls seeing Wings take the stage for one of their *Wings Over* America concerts as "Venus and Mars" begins to play. Then you hear McCartney talking and some studio chatter from an unidentified woman. One of the guitar riffs from "Band on the Run" is laid over the basic track and then the vocals from "Oh Woman, Oh Why" appear over the incessant drums.

Mumbo: A fast Latin beat with some guitar plays under the speeded-up vocals from "Mumbo." The vocals are soaked in reverb. The beat gets wilder as the song goes on. This is the most repetitive track on this album.

Lalula: More frantic drums and lots of additional percussion under a foreboding synthesizer part, and lots of crunchy electric guitars, adorn this two-chord workout. Guitar riffs from "Old Siam, Sir" and "Oh Woman, Oh Why" appear during the middle.

Coming Up: Some fret dancing on an electric guitar opens this track while the chords to "Morse Moose and the Grey Goose" start playing over a different drum track from the original. Then McCartney's vocal from "Coming Up" plays over the minor key chords, which makes for an interesting sound since "Coming Up" is in a major key. Then it all stops and handclaps and a tambourine usher in a snaky bass part and more vocals.

Maybe I'm Amazed: A sped up version of "Maybe I'm Amazed" opens this track, with a new and much busier drum part. During the guitar solo break, the secondary guitar part that plays the chords appears, but not the solo guitar part. Then some studio trickery rearranges McCartney's vocal over drums, bass and guitar. The long fade-out is a wild mélange of McCartney's vocals from all parts of the original song. Nothing in this mash-up diminishes the pure artistry of "Maybe I'm Amazed."

Electric Arguments

Released: November 25, 2008 (U.S.); November 24, 2008 (U.K.)
One Little Indian OLI04033 (U.K.); ATO ATOPR029 (U.S.)
Highest chart position: 67 (U.S.); 79 (U.K.)
All songs performed and composed by Paul McCartney
Produced by The Fireman

The third of McCartney's collaborations with Youth is by far the most listenable and pop-oriented of the three efforts. In fact, this ranks as one of McCartney's hidden gems and certainly one of his finest albums since the turn of the century.

Filled with shimmery guitars, in your face vocals and pop hooks galore, the album is strong from start to finish. McCartney plays all the instruments, and Youth gives sympathetic pop production to the proceedings. The songs were recorded in 13 days over the course of a full year.

For the most part, gone are the trance and ambient textures of the first two albums. When they appear at all, it's typically at the very end of a song, when the ambient sensibilities form a musical eddy that spins the track out. In their place is a smooth and sure-handed rendering of some carefully crafted songs. McCartney seems to have taken the palette that Youth provided and painted onto it some vocals that did nothing but improve the overall feel and accessibility of the music. Moreover, a certain sunny optimism pervades most of the songs.

Nothing Too Much Out of Sight: A bluesy harmonica starts off this bashing rocker, which is very reminiscent of "Helter Skelter." It's loud, brash and the singer pretty much shouts the lyrics throughout. It even has the same kind of guitar frenzy ending that distinguishes "Helter Skelter." The plodding drums are treated with a tincture of echo, and several guitars play the repetitive riff. A perfect album opener.

Two Magpies: A nice little country ballad based around two acoustic guitars and McCartney's double-tracked vocals. The drums are played with brushes, given the song an almost lo-fi sound.

Sing the Changes: An anthemic pop song based on four chords with McCartney in fine voice. Several vocals were recorded and the lead vocal is awash in echo. The guitars and solid drum part drive the song along. McCartney added this to his live set in 2008–09.

Travelling Light: This song kicks off with an ominous sounding synth, piano and guitar mix. McCartney sings it with something just barely over a whisper, which gives it a certain dramatic effect. Later in the track, he switches to a higher register singing the same melody. At 3:38, the tempo, chords and melody morph into almost a waltz-like ballad. There is a certain hypnotic vibe to this track.

Highway: Another song from the album that McCartney added to his live act, "Highway" is a fun little rocker with an infectious hook. It sounds like 1970s-era Steve Miller. The multilayered vocals toward the end of the song give it an almost live feel.

Light from Your Lighthouse: A great combination of highest register

McCartney with a booming bass voice. The chorus sounds right out of the American south, with its faux country-gospel propulsion and its call and response. There's a nice acoustic guitar solo right in the middle.

Sun Is Shining: Beautiful acoustic guitars limn this song throughout, along with some friendly nature sounds and aquamarine keyboards. The lyrics are hopeful, optimistic and downright celebratory. The drums have a definite Ringo Starr sound to them. The catchy nonsense syllables sung after the middle eight have a certain joyful quality.

Dance 'Til We're High: The introduction is right out of the Phil Specter songbook, with bells, prominent percussion and a certain tasty overproduction. Think "River Deep, Mountain High." Once again, McCartney twins his high tenor with a deep bass on the double-tracked vocals. The transcendent lyrics are backed by synth strings and various keyboards.

Lifelong Passion: Harmonica and keyboards lead this track off, along with some synthesizers. The melody is tricky and complicated. Some Indian-inflected percussion supports the whole thing. Like so many of McCartney's songs, love is the theme.

Is This Love?: This is the most New Age-y sounding track on the album, with a plaintive woodwind kicking the whole thing off. Add to that the complex percussion and a chiming keyboard, and you get the idea. The vocal sounds as if it was shouted down from a mountaintop, with an ethereal, faraway effect. The ending features an overmodulated bass part and some nonsense words from the singer.

Lovers in a Dream: Some synth strings and wispy percussion give this track a creepy start. It sounds like something you might hear in a haunted house on Halloween. Once the beat is established the track starts to gallop. Some simple lyrics are almost chanted over the backing track. This track could easily find a comfortable place on a soundtrack album for a David Lynch film. Without the vocal track, this could have just as easily fit on the two previous efforts by the Fireman. It's trance at its finest.

Universal Here, Everlasting Now: A beautiful piano part opens this track. What sounds like a barking dog interrupts the proceedings, along with lots of synthesizers. A female voice whispers over the track. At 1:50, a drum part is added, along with some electric guitar, and this gives the track some much-needed lift. Some echo-y nonsense singing by McCartney is superimposed until the lovely piano melody makes its reappearance and takes the song to its haunting conclusion.

Don't Stop Running: A wash of synthesizers and loud guitars announce the final track. A simple half-step downward chord progression provides the foundation for this track. McCartney sings in his highest, non-falsetto register, and once again welds his multitracked vocals, each sung in a different register, in a cohesive fashion. The drums are expertly played, and the bass part is as prominent as on any song on the album. "Don't Stop Running" ends at 5:54, after which there is 2:03 of silence, before the surprise bonus track—"Road Trip"—starts at 7:57. The track is not listed on the album. A fusillade of machine gun sounds and loud synth effects announces the bonus track. There are no lyrics and no vocals (except for a couple of backward spoken words at the very end) and it slowly fades into an inauspicious ending.

Electric Arguments has been released in a variety of packages. There was a digital only release of the album; a CD and digital package; a vinyl, CD and digital package; and a deluxe edition released in 2009 that featured two vinyl LPs, two CDs, two DVDs and a digital download. The second CD features seven bonus tracks that include alternate versions and mixes of some of the songs on the original album.

Classical and Orchestral

The Family Way

Released January 6, 1967 (U.K.); June 12, 1967 (U.S.)
Decca LK 4847 (U.K.); London MS 82007 (U.S.)
Highest chart position: Did not chart
Produced by George Martin
Musicians: Neville Marriner and Raymond Keenlyside: violins; John Underwood: viola; Joy Hall: cello; the Tudor Minstrels, plus session musicians on tuba, organ and assorted brass instruments.

The Family Way was a movie starring Hayley Mills and directed by Ray Boulting. Paul McCartney composed two brief snippets for the film, upon which George Martin elaborated and eventually created 24 minutes of soundtrack music. McCartney is credited as the sole composer, chiefly because his was one of the biggest names in the world at the time.

"Love in the Open Air" was part of the soundtrack and contains many of McCartney's signature touches: acoustic guitar in a minor key supplemented by a lovely string and horn arrangement by Martin. It's definitely a musical descendent of "Yesterday" and "Eleanor Rigby." It appears in different variations throughout the soundtrack, including a James Bond theme/Monkees hybrid section, complete with electric guitar and thrashing drums.

The soundtrack was recorded in CTS Studios in London in December 1966. It is unknown if McCartney attended the sessions. It was originally released on CD in 2003, when only a mono version was made available. In 2011, a remastered version was released on CD. The original release named both sides of the LP "The Family Way." The CD version listed tracks in a number-letter-number format (2M1 and 6M4, for example), except for "Love in the Open Air" and "Theme from the Family Way."

It's an interesting artifact in the McCartney oeuvre, but is far from essential listening. However, it did presage his forays into classical music in the 1990s and 2000s, by which time his composing abilities had ripened considerably.

Thrillington

Released: April 29, 1977 (UK); May 17, 1977 (U.S.)
Regal Zonophone EMC 3175, 0C 062-987 45 (U.K.); Capitol ST-11642 (U.S.)
Highest Chart Position: Didn't chart
Produced by Percy "Thrills" Thrillington
Musicians: Richard Hewson: conductor; Vic Flick: guitars; Herbie Flowers: bass guitar; Steve Gray: piano; Clem Cattini: drums; Jim Lawless: percussion; Chris Karan: cuica; the Swingle Singers and the Mike Sammes Singers: backing vocals

Too Many People/3 Legs/Ram On/Dear Boy/Uncle Albert/Admiral Halsey/Smile Away/Heart of the Country/Monkberry Moon Delight/Eat at Home/Long-Haired Lady/Back Seat of My Car

Percy "Thrills" Thrillington was the cover that McCartney used for this over the top, blowsy orchestral version of *Ram*. It was recorded in June 1971, just after the release of the original album, but was not released until 1977 (on vinyl only).

Several notices in the society pages of the *London Times* and the *Evening Standard* mentioned the peculiar comings and goings of Thrillington, in the process building up a certain curiosity about the enigmatic band leader.

The album itself is quite enjoyable. It features the typical orchestral treatments that all band leaders applied to their covers in those days. Loud, brassy, percussive and swinging, each rendition of the songs on *Ram* has something to recommend it. It's a lark, of course, but that's okay. Now if Percy would just get his baton out of storage, perhaps he could give the same treatment to *Venus and Mars* and *Speed of Sound*.

Thrillington (CD only) was re-released in 1995 and again in 2004. A CD of the album was included in the *Paul McCartney Archive* release of *Ram* in 2012, and on CD, vinyl and a special edition color vinyl on May 18, 2018.

Liverpool Oratorio

Released: October 7, 1991 (U.K.); October 22, 1991 (U.S.)
EMI Classics CDS 7 54371 2
Highest chart position: 177 in the U.S. and 36 in the U.K.
Produced by John Fraser
Musicians: Royal Liverpool Philharmonic Orchestra and Royal Liverpool Philharmonic Choir; Liverpool Cathedral Choristers; Carl Davis: conductor; Ian Tracey: conductor; Kiri Te Kanawa: soprano; Jerry Hadley: tenor; Sally Burgess: mezzo soprano; Willard White: bass

War: Andante/Non Nobis Solum/The Air Raid Siren Slices Through/Oh Will It All End Here?/Mother and Father Holding Their Child

School: We're Here in School Today to Get a Perfect Education/ Walk in Single File Out of the Classroom/Settle Down/Kept in Confusion/I'll Always Be Here/Boys, This Is Your Teacher/Tres Conejos/ Not for Ourselves

Crypt: And So It Was That I Had Grown/Dance/I Used to Come Here When This Place Was a Crypt/Here Now/I'll Always Be Here/ Now's the Time to Tell Him

Father: Andante Lamentoso/O Father, You Have Given/(Ah)/Hey, Wait a Minute/Father, Father, Father

Wedding: Andante Amoroso—I Know I Should Be Glad of This/ Father, Hear Our Humble Voices/Hosanna, Hosanna

Work: Allegro Energico/Working Women at the Top/Violin Solo/ Did I Sign the Letter/Tempo/When You Ask a Working Man/Let's Find Ourselves a Little Hostelry

Crises: Allegro Molto/The World You're Coming Into/Tempo I/ Where's My Dinner?/Let's Not Argue/I'm Not a Slave/Right! That's It!/Stop. Wait/Do You Know Who You Are/Ghosts of the Past Left Behind/Do We Live in a World

Peace: And So It Was That You Were Born/God Is Good/What People Want Is a Family Life/Dad's in the Garden/So On and On the Story Goes

Liverpool Oratorio is Paul McCartney's first attempt at writing classical and symphonic music. It loosely tells the story of his life, from coming into the world during a World War, school days, marriage and fatherhood, work and every other life experience.

Composer Carl Davis collaborated with McCartney on the music. Davis was instrumental in producing the work, as McCartney was (and still is) unable to read or write music notation on staff paper. Davis, who looks a little like Beethoven himself, acted as "translator" of the musical ideas and passage that McCartney hummed or played for him. Nearly three years in the making, the work premiered at Liverpool Cathedral, with Paul and Linda McCartney in attendance. The oratorio also commemorated the 150th anniversary of the Royal Liverpool Philharmonic Orchestra, which provided the music for the work. The vocal performances were delivered by four well-known classical singers, as well as some 200 choristers from the Royal Liverpool Philharmonic Choir and the Liverpool Cathedral Choristers.

Recorded on June 28 and 29, 1991, the recording reached the top of the classical charts, and later had premieres in New York and London, with subsequent performances taking place around the world. The album was released on CD, vinyl and cassette. The Liverpool performance was filmed and released on video. A documentary about the making of *Liverpool Oratorio* was shown on the BBC.

At first, the pop critic cognoscenti seemed mildly bemused at the prospect of Paul McCartney writing such a highbrow and complicated work. But most agreed that it was actually a fine piece of work.

The *Liverpool Oratorio* is heavy with obvious McCartney influences, from the strong melodies to the homespun folksiness of the narrative. As in most of his work, family, love, and peace play paramount roles. There are also moments of genuine whimsy and good humor. Many of the movements are in minor keys (as you might expect given some of the tragic circumstances depicted in the story) but those passages in major keys are often sunny and optimistic. And breathtakingly beautiful.

His appetite for symphonic and orchestral music whetted, he would produce four more works in this genre during the subsequent 10 years.

Standing Stone

Released September 25, 1997 (U.S.); September 29, 1997 (U.K.)
EMI Classics 7243 5 56484 1 9 (U.K.); 7243 5 56848 2 6 (U.S.)
Highest chart position: 194 (U.S.)
Produced by John Fraser
Musicians: London Symphony Orchestra and Chorus

Movement I: Fire/Rain/Cell Growth/"Human Theme"
Movement II: Meditation/Crystal/Ship/Sea Voyage/Lost at Sea/Release
Movement III: Safe Haven/Standing Stone/Peaceful Moment/Messenger/Lament/Trance/Eclipse
Movement IV: Glory Tales/Fugal Celebration/Rustic Dance/Love Duet/Celebration

Standing Stone was Paul McCartney's second original classical music work and was based on a long poem McCartney wrote. The London Symphony Orchestra conducted by Lawrence Foster provided the instrumentation and a choir—without soloists—sang the vocal parts.

The album was recorded over three days (April 30 to May 2, 1997) at Abbey Road studios. The world premiere of the piece took place on October 14, 1997, at the Royal Albert Hall. A month later, a video of the performance was released. In 1999, a DVD of the same performance with a special feature on the creation of the piece was released. The album cover photo was taken by Linda McCartney in 1969. This is the last album McCartney released before Linda's death in April 1998.

According to the booklet included in the album packaging, the piece tells the story of "the way Celtic man might have wondered about the origins of life and the mystery of existence." The work itself is alternately moody and melodramatic, sad and mournful, and in the end, celebratory and uplifting.

Most of the movements have signature McCartney melodic flourishes, and it's easy to discern that a master of the pop music genre might be behind the composition of *Standing Stone.* Therein lies the essential flaw. It's not so much a classical piece based on a poem, but a distillation of pop music conventions and sensibilities scored for orchestra and choir, and it sounds precisely like what it is. The album received lukewarm reviews, mostly because the classical music world still couldn't completely get their arms around the fact that the greatest pop music writer in history could effortlessly switch gears and write a classic piece of music in a completely different genre.

It's a problem that comes with the territory. None of the five classical albums McCartney eventually released were met with unanimous approbation, and only *Ecce Cor Meum* held up to the lens of critical scrutiny applied by the classical music press. But the fact that he produced memorable music in the classical genre is in itself quite an accomplishment.

Working Classical

Released October 18, 1999 (U.K.); November 1, 1999 (U.S.)
EMI Classics 7243 5 56897 2 6
Highest chart position: Did not make the pop charts, but reached 1 in the U.S. and 2 in the U. K. on the classical charts
Produced by John Fraser
Musicians: The London Symphony Orchestra and Loma Mar Quartet

Working Classical is a more pop oriented work than the other classical music albums Paul McCartney recorded, due in part to the fact that he gave some of his own pop songs the classical treatment. There are also five songs he composed especially for this album.

The album is a love letter to Linda McCartney, gone slightly more than a year by the time the album was recorded. Each of the McCartney songs remade were written for Linda, and the classical treatment gives them an aching poignancy and underscores further the grief and anguish McCartney endured in that first lonely year after her death.

What comes across throughout *Working Classical* is the facility McCartney has for weaving indelibly catchy melodies, and most translate comfortably into a new musical form.

Standouts include the exquisite "Warm and Beautiful," a haunting take on "Junk," the playful "She's My Baby," the transcendent "Calico Skies" and, of course, the declarative devotion of "The Lovely Linda."

Junk/A Leaf/Haymakers/Midwife/Spiral/Warm and Beautiful/ My Love/Maybe I'm Amazed/Calico Skies/Golden Earth Girl/Somedays/Tuesday/She's My Baby/The Lovely Linda

A Leaf: This beautiful mediation moves between minor and major keys and has a sense of longing and discovery throughout. It's filled with interesting dynamics, easily moving from frenetic urgency to peaceful contemplation, and back again. At 11:08, it's the second longest track on the album.

Haymakers: This track features an interesting melody built over a chord sequence that could easily be the foundation for hundreds of pop songs. The string quartet that plays the melody recalls the elegant simplicity of "Eleanor Rigby."

Midwife: A fun, joyful romp bolstered by skillful pizzicato adding a percussive backdrop to the melody. It's wandering melody makes the listener eager to go along for the aural ride.

Spiral: A mountain of orchestral instruments create a tension under the simple melody played by violins and cello. The melodic theme keeps reappearing just when you least expect, like a question you just don't have an answer for. The piece ends on the quietest of notes.

Tuesday: Soothing music tailor-made for a Sunday morning, or a Tuesday, for that matter. There are some dramatic flourishes throughout, of course, but the main melody will soothe your meditative soul.

Ecce Cor Meum

Released September 25, 2006, in the U.K. and September 26, 2006, in the U.S.
EMI Classics 3704242/0946370424 2 7(U.K.); 0946370424 2 7 (U.S.)
Highest chart position: Did not make the pop charts
Produced by John Fraser
Performers: London Voices; Academy of St. Martin in the Fields; Boys of Magdalen College Choir; Boys of King's County Choir; Colm Carey, organ; Mark Law, Ppiccolo trumpet; Kate Royal, soprano.

Spiritus
Gratia

Interlude (Lament)
Musica
Ecce Cor Meum

Ecce Cor Meum is an oratorio in four movements and was specifically commissioned from Magdalen College. Its debut performance was to be on the evening of the grand opening of a new concert hall at the college, but in the interim, Linda McCartney died and the performance was delayed. The premier was delayed until 2001, and the recording of the performance occurred five years later. This recording took place March 13 to March 17 at Abbey Road Studios in London.

Its American premiere was on November 14, 2006, at Carnegie Hall in New York City and was simulcast over New York public radio station WNYC-FM.

The album reached number 2 in the U.S. classical albums and was McCartney's only orchestral recording not made available on vinyl.

This is arguably McCartney's most listenable and accessible orchestral work, and the flow from movement to movement is coherent and lovely. The orchestra and choirs are at the top of their games, and the oratorio holds the listener's attention for the entire 56:50 running time.

The English rendering of *Ecce Cor Meum* is "behold my heart." It's not difficult to imagine that this oratorio was inspired by Linda's death. It's sad and solemn, for the most part, and the whole thing is swathed in a sort of musical melancholy not found in abundance on McCartney's other forays into classical music. The first movement especially, has a tragic and foreboding theme of operatic sweep, made even more emphatic by the Latin rendering.

The second movement is softer and more playful and has a jaunty bounce to it reminiscent of McCartney's pop music tendencies. The interplay between the women's and men's vocal performances is effective and inventive. The last two minutes of this movement sound as if it could be an orchestral arrangement of one of McCartney's pop hits.

The "Interlude (Lament)" is a touching slice of mournful orchestration and could easily be McCartney's tribute to his recently deceased wife. One can imagine this piece filling your head and the space around you at the saddest moment of your life. Voices and piccolo trumpet provide the spare arrangement.

The third movement is confident and brimming with musical bravado. The fourth and final movement is the briefest of the four and features soprano Kate Royal voicing a melody so overwhelmingly majestic and beautiful that it nearly overwhelms the rest of the oratorio. In all, a scintillating finish to a tremendous work.

Ocean's Kingdom

Released October 3, 2011, in the U.K. and October 4, 2011, in the U.S.
Decca (U.K.) 723 3251; Hear Music (U.S.) HRM-33250-02
Highest chart position: 143 in the U.S.
Produced by John Fraser
Performed by the London Symphony Orchestra and conducted by John Wilson

Movement 1: Ocean's Kingdom
Movement 2: Hall of Dance
Movement 3: Imprisonment
Movement 4: Moonrise

Ocean's Kingdom is a symphonic soundtrack of a ballet commissioned by the New York City Ballet. It depicts a love story told in two earthly realms: The planet Earth and the ocean. One critic lamented that the story was "a kind of watery *Romeo and Juliet*."

The problem was that for the first time, McCartney was trying to tackle a major symphonic work with long movements and complicated musical themes. Out of all five of his classical compositions and releases, this is the one on which McCartney struggles to deliver a passable result when composing outside of his usual realm of pop music.

The album was released on vinyl and CD, and an iTunes only bonus track edition that added a version of the entire work performed live by the New York City Ballet Orchestra on September 21, 2011.

The first movement sets the tone with an overly dramatic and bombastic melodic theme in a minor key. It settles into a melancholic meander halfway through, before returning with a robust rendering of the original melody.

The second movement is emboldened by a jauntier melody and a more positive vibe, with some somber interludes so typical of symphonic works. About nine minutes in to the movement, a reflective and tender melody, so reminiscent of McCartney's pop songwriting, softens the entire affair, before going out in a frenetic blaze of orchestral chutzpah.

The third movement starts off with more McCartney-esque minor key variations that amble lazily throughout the movement before giving way to a brass and kettle drum-heavy instrumental interlocution. Ten minutes in, a sad and lonely cello part introduces the last section of the movement.

The fourth and final movement recalls the musical motifs throughout, with dramatic and exciting interludes that could easily be used to score a chase scene in a Hollywood movie. It ends with a clear-eyed and happy upbeat musical exclamation mark.

The Singles

Another Day/Oh Woman, Oh Why
Released: February 22, 1971 (U.S.); February 19, 1971 (U.K.)
Apple Records 1829 U.S.; R 5889 U.K.
Highest Chart Position: 5 in the U.S. and 2 in the U.K.
Produced by Paul McCartney

"Another Day" is a great debut single from Paul McCartney, act two. Lots of inventive guitar play—acoustic and electric—and swirling signature changes keep the listener interested. This could be a prequel to "Eleanor Rigby," with its theme of loneliness and being alone in life. It also hints at the superb harmonies Paul and Linda would soon augment with Wings. "Oh Woman, Oh Why" seems like it was made up on the spot in the studio. It does have some great wailing vocals.

Uncle Albert/Admiral Halsey/ Too Many People
Released August 2, 1971 (U.S. only)
Apple Records 1837
Highest Chart Position: 1
Produced by Paul and Linda McCartney

A surprise hit in the U.S., "Uncle Albert/Admiral Halsey" has enough Beatle-like musical flourishes to make the listening public think this was a leftover from *The White Album*. Stops and starts, funny voices and sound effects, and McCartney's usual quality vocals make this a winner. Pair it with the superb "Too Many People" as the B-side, and this ends up as one of McCartney's best singles ever. The wild guitar solo in "Too Many People" is worth the price of admission, and so is McCartney's snarly vocal.

The Back Seat of My Car/Heart of the Country
Released: August 13, 1971 (U.K. only)
Apple Records R 5914

Highest Chart Position: 39
Produced by Paul and Linda McCartney

Apparently, McCartney thought "Back Seat of My Car" was a better choice as a single in England, although it didn't fare nearly as well as "Uncle Albert" did in the U.S. It's a fantastic song and a perfect album closer. It's safe money that Springsteen took lots of notes the first time he heard it. "Heart of the Country" is chock full of Scottish farm charm.

Give Ireland Back to the Irish/Give Ireland Back to the Irish (instrumental version) (Wings)
Released: February 25, 1972
Apple Records 1847 (U.S.); R 5936 (UK)
Highest Chart Position: 21 in the U.S. and 16 in the U.K.
Produced by Paul and Linda McCartney

Wings' first single pushed some boundaries McCartney had never tested. Certainly as an Englishman with Irish lineage he had every right to single out the British government for misdeeds in this conflict, but it seems "Give Ireland Back to the Irish" had very little effect on either side, other than to have the BBC ban the record. It was received indifferently on both sides of the Atlantic, although it's raucous guitar-heavy fun, with a memorable chorus. The B-side is an instrumental version of the song, played at a slower pace and featuring some fine electric guitar work and an Irish pennywhistle.

Mary Had a Little Lamb/Little Woman Love
Released: May 29, 1972, in the U.S. and May 12, 1972, in the U.K.
Apple Records 1851 (U.S.); R 5949 (U.K.)
Highest Chart Position: 28 in the U.S. and 9 in the U.K.
Produced by Paul and Linda McCartney

Try banning this one, BBC. Why is it that when McCartney is writing meaningless songs about animals (see "Ode to a Koala Bear"), the song turns out to be very tuneful and almost overproduced? That's the case with the nursery rhyme "Mary Had a Little Lamb," which is perhaps the hokiest musical idea McCartney ever had yet sounds great as a song. Dramatic segues from verse to verse, an infectious chorus (complete with children's voices) and even a key modulation. That's a lot of work to devote to such a lightweight subject. "Little Woman Love" is a fun piano-based song, with interesting acoustic guitar licks overlaid throughout.

Hi Hi Hi/C Moon
Released: December 4, 1972, in the U.S. and December 1, 1972, in the U.K.
Apple Records 1857 (U.S.); R 5973 (U.K.)
Highest Chart Positions: 10 in the U.S. and 5 in the U.K.
Produced by Paul McCartney

One of the best authentic chunks of rock 'n' roll McCartney ever wrote and recorded, "Hi Hi Hi" was a concert staple in the band's 1970s repertoire, and he even resurrected it for some of the concerts he gave in 2015–16. Tawdry, snarly and lewd, the song rolls along relentlessly with heavily distorted guitars and a rollicking bass line. The echo on the vocal track is a perfect match for the sexually tinged lyrics, and the cold ending puts an emphatic exclamation mark on the song. A Rastafarian piano workout with simplistic and almost child-like lyrics, but clever and catchy instrumentation, "C Moon" stands as a quality B-side. After "Hi Hi Hi" was banned in the United Kingdom, the DJs flipped the single over and started playing "C Moon," which scored as a minor hit in England.

My Love/The Mess
Released: April 9, 1973, in the U.S. and March 23, 1973, in the U.K.
Apple Records 1861 (U.S.); R 5985 (U.K.)
Highest Chart Position: 1 in the U.S. and 9 in the U.K.
Produced by Paul McCartney

"My Love" was blaring out of transistor radios all over the U.S. in the summer of 1973. It has a stateliness to it and its sung beautifully. "The Mess" is a fun little rocker that showed Wings developing their chops as a live unit.

Live and Let Die/I Lie Around
Released: June 18, 1973, in the U.S. and June 1, 1973, in the U.K.
Apple Records 1863 (U.S.); R 5987 (U.K.)
Highest Chart Position: 2 in the U.S. and 9 in the U.K.
Produced by George Martin

McCartney teamed with George Martin for the first time since 1969 to create this wildly produced barn-burner of a James Bond film theme song. Discordant instrumentation between verses, supplemented by a brace of flutes (hardly the instrument that leaps to mind when you think of James Bond theme songs) and timpani lies in stark contrast to the standard 4/4 time of the simple piano ballad verses. This is among the top three Bond themes ever written and has been a staple of McCartney live shows on every tour starting in 1975 to the present day. "I Lie Around" is a goofy, "let's frolic in the swimming hole" kind of song destined to be a B-side. Despite this, McCartney gave it the full-on production treatment, with lots of guitars, double-tracked piano and a horn chart. Denny Laine is the main singer on this one, with McCartney jumping in here and there. It was recorded during the *Ram* sessions and Dave Spinozza plays some of the guitar parts.

Helen Wheels/Country Dreamer
Released: October 26, 1973
Apple Records PRO-6787 (U.S.); R 5993 (U.K.)
Highest Chart Position: 10 in the U.S. and 12 in the U.K.
Produced by Paul McCartney

The perfect bridge between *Red Rose Speedway* and *Band on the Run.* "Helen Wheels" is a rocking English travelogue based on just two chords: A and E minor. "Helen Wheels" was left off the British version of *Band on the Run* but added to the American release. "Country Dreamer," a sweet little acoustic guitar meditation, was recorded in September 1972 and resurrected for the B-side.

Jet/Let Me Roll It (U.K. and second pressings in the U.S.); Mamunia (U.S. first pressing only)
Released: January 28, 1974, in the U.S. and February 15, 1974, in the U.K.
Apple Records 1871 (U.S.); R 5996 (U.K.)
Highest Chart Positions 7 in the U.S. and U.K.
Produced by Paul McCartney

The most obvious choice for the first single off Band on the Run, "Jet" jumps out of the speakers with radio-friendly assurance. "Let Me Roll It" is probably the best B-side of any McCartney single. The initial pressings of the "Jet" single in the U.S. featured "Mamunia," but was quickly replaced by "Let Me Roll It" three weeks later.

Band on the Run/Zoo Gang (U.K.); Nineteen Hundred and Eighty-Five (U.S.)
Released: April 8, 1974, in the U.S. and June 28, 1974, in the U.K.

Apple Records 8XZ-3415 (U.S.); 8X-PAS 10007 (U.K.)
Highest Chart Position: 1 in the U.S. and 3 in the U.K.
Produced by Paul McCartney

The title track of Wings' new album resonated with fans on both sides of the Atlantic, but especially in America, where it quickly went to number one. McCartney won a Grammy for best pop vocal performance for "Band on the Run." "Zoo Gang" was a theme song that McCartney wrote for a British television show and features the first time that future Wings member Jimmy McCulloch played with the group. It's an electric guitar-based instrumental with way too much reliance on an overbearing synthesizer. As mentioned previously, McCartney seemed to be infatuated with the synthesizer during the recording of *Band on the Run*. It's prominent on the title track, "Jet" and "Mamunia." The problem is McCartney uses it as a primary instrument, when it's more sonically prudent to use it as a secondary instrument to add color to a recording. Otherwise, when it's out of vogue (like it is now), songs that feature the synthesizer as a primary instrument sound dated. "Nineteen Hundred and Eighty-Five" was a safer bet as the B-side for the American release.

Walking in the Park with Eloise/Bridge Over the River Suite (as The Country Hams)
Released: October 18, 1974, in the U.K. and December 2, 1974, in the U.S.
Label: Capitol/EMI P-3977 (U.S.) Parlophone/EMI EMI 2220 (U.K.)
Highest Chart Positions: Did not chart
Produced by Paul McCartney

A group of Nashville musicians, including Chet Atkins and Floyd Cramer, recorded this instrumental written by McCartney's dad, Jim. It's brass heavy and features some fine picking by Atkins and the unmistakable piano stylings of Cramer. "Bridge Over the River Suite" is a loping instrumental featuring some understated electric guitar vamping and a busy horn chart.

Junior's Farm/Sally G
Released: October 25, 1974, in the U.K. and November 4, 1974, in the U.S.
Apple Records 1875 (U.S.); R 5999 (U.K.)
Highest Chart Positions: 3 in the U.S. and 16 in the U.K.
Produced by Paul McCartney

It's interesting that McCartney namechecks Jimmy McCulloch just before his electric guitar solo in "Junior's Farm," as if he were announcing part of the new Wings line-up. The song has a harder sound to it that the songs on *Band on the Run*, and the band as a whole sounds tougher and more self-assured. "Sally G" resulted from a trip to Nashville where the new configuration of Wings got to know each other better and hung out with the elders of the Nashville country music scene. Oddly, McCartney decided to re-release the single with the sides flipped making "Sally G" the A-side, and it was released that way on December 24, 1974, in the U.S. and February 7, 1975, in the U.K. The thinking was that country music was much more popular in America, but the "new" single failed to chart.

Listen to What the Man Said/Love in Song
Released: May 16, 1975
Capitol 4091 (U.S.); R 6006 (U.K.)
Highest Chart Position: 1 in the U.S. and 6 in the U.K.
Produced by Paul McCartney

One of McCartney's finest singles featured two of the best songs off the forthcoming "Venus and Mars," released exactly two weeks later. "Listen to What the Man Said" is the perfect summertime pop confection, with the saxophone ringing out of car radios heading down the highway all around the United States. "Love in Song" is the perfect meditative antidote to the breezy whimsy of the A-side.

Letting Go/You Gave Me the Answer
Released: October 4, 1975, in the U.S. and October 18, 1975, in the U.K.
Capitol 4145 (U.S.); R 6008 (U.K.)
Highest Chart Position: 39 in the U.S. and 41 in the U.K.
Produced by Paul McCartney

A dismal chart performance from this single belied the fact that the A-side is one of the strongest tracks from "Venus and Mars." A DJ edit to make "Letting Go" shorter to better accommodate tight radio programming took some of the air out of the song. The B-side probably just didn't belong on a single in the first place.

Venus and Mars/Rock Show/Magneto and Titanium Man
Released: October 27, 1975, in the U.S. and November 28, 1975, in the U.K.

Capitol P-4175 (U.S.); R 6010 (U.K.)
Highest Chart Position: 12 in the U.S.; failed to chart in the U.K.
Produced by Paul McCartney

After three singles issued in five months—all with album tracks on both sides—the "Venus and Mars" train started grounding to a bit of a halt. Still, the A-side was destined to be the concert opener on the *Wings Over America* tour and the B-side was one of the big crowd-pleasers on the same live set list.

Silly Love Songs/Cook of the House
Released: April 1, 1976, in the U.S. and April 30, 1976, in the U.K.
Capitol 4256 (U.S.); Parlophone R 6014 (U.K.)
Highest Chart Position: 1 in the U.S. and 2 in the U.K.
Produced by Paul McCartney

"Silly Love Songs," with its infectious bass line and Stax-flavored horn charts, became the fourth straight Wings single to hit No. 1 in the United States. This is the apex of Wings' popularity in America, which was also bolstered by the *Wings Over America* tour. The wife takes over the kitchen duties on the B-side.

Let 'Em In/Beware My Love
Released: June 28 in the U.S. and July 23, 1976, in the U.K.
Capitol 4293 (U.S.); Parlophone R 6015 (UK.)
Highest Chart Position: 3 in the U.S. and 2 in the U.K.
Produced by Paul McCartney

One last gasp of rarified air near (but not at) the top of the pop charts, "Let 'Em In" rose to third and second on the U.S. and British pop charts, respectively. The B-side is the better song.

Maybe I'm Amazed/Soily
Released: February 4, 1977
Label: Capitol PRO-8574 (U.S.); Parlophone R 6017 (U.K.)
Highest Chart Position: 10 in the U.S. and 28 in the U.K.
Produced by Paul McCartney

Arguably the best vocal performance of Paul McCartney's solo career, this slow-moving but scorching live version of one of his best songs features vocal calisthenics of epic proportions, complete with blistering electric guitar solos and solid back-up from Linda and Denny Laine. It's possible that in retrospect, McCartney regretted not releasing "Maybe I'm Amazed" as a single when *McCartney* came out in 1970, but this version proves it was worth the wait. "Soily" was a song that had been hanging around since 1972. It's a powerful rocker, but it seemed like a weird choice to make it the closing number on the *Wings Over America* set list since no one stateside had ever heard the song.

Seaside Woman/B-Side to Seaside (as Suzy and the Red Stripes)
Released: May 31, 1977, in the U.S. and August 10, 1979, in the U.K.
Epic ASF 361 (U.S.); A&M AMSP 7548 (U.K.)
Highest Chart Position: 59 in the U.S.
Produced by Paul McCartney

A novelty record made by Suzy and the Red Stripes (Linda McCartney and Wings). "Seaside Woman" has that reggae vibe to it and for some reason hung around in the can for years. "B-Side to Seaside" is a total goof of made up words, loud guitars and is totally bereft of any meaning whatsoever.

Mull of Kintyre/Girls' School
Released: November 14, 1977, in the U.S. and November 11, 1977, in the U.K.
Capitol 4504 (U.S.); R 6018 (U.K.)
Highest Chart Position: 33 in the U.S. and 1 in the U.K.
Produced by Paul McCartney

"Mull of Kintyre" was Wings' most successful single, not only in the U.K. but in several other countries as well. The quaintness of the bagpipes/acoustic guitar combo is overcome by a strong melody, great lyrics and a really fine vocal performance by McCartney. In America, however, DJs scratched their heads and asked, "What's a Kintyre?" They quickly flipped the single and starting playing "Girls School," which they soon tired of, probably because of its semi-naughty theme, which was a recitation of a bunch of porn film titles. A monstrously successful single ... just not in the United States.

With a Little Luck/Backwards Traveller/Cuff-Link
Released: March 20, 1978, in the U.S. and March 23, 1978, in the U.K.
Capitol SPRO-8812 (U.S.); Parlophone R 6019 (U.K.)

Highest Chart Position: 1 in the U.S. and 5 in the U.K.
Produced by Paul McCartney

That "With a Little Luck" made it to No. 1 in the U.S. is a testament to Wings' popularity with American pop fans, and not the quality of the song. It was the most insipid, languid and porous single McCartney had released to date. Fake instruments, a stilted, predictable melody and silly lyrics doom this as a credible piece of music. It's long, too; so long that radio stations created an edited version for airplay that improbably made the song even more unlistenable. "Backwards Traveller/Cuff Link" are smug excursions into short and dull little ditties, neither of which makes up for the sting of having wasted good money on a two-sided dud.

I've Had Enough/Deliver Your Children
Released: June 16, 1978, in the U.K. and June 5, 1978, in the U.S.
Capitol 4594 (U.S.); Parlophone R 6020 (U.K.)
Highest Chart Positions: 35 in the U.S. and 42 in the U.K.
Produced by Paul McCartney

The problem with the *London Town* album is that it doesn't contain an obvious single. All of the songs seem like deep album cuts. A handful are decent, but not nearly as commercial as one would hope in the singles market. "I've Had Enough" is an atypical McCartney harangue against everyday nits (he pulled this off more believably on *Press to Play*'s "Angry" in 1986). For a guitar-based rock song, it's surprisingly flaccid and almost tinny sounding. "Deliver Your Children" is a story song based on an acoustic guitar chord progression in a minor key. Again, not much to write home about.

London Town/I'm Carrying
Released: August 26, 1978, in the U.S. and August 11 in the UK
Capitol 4625 (U.S.); Parlophone R 6021 (U.K.)
Highest Chart Position: 39 in the U.S. and 60 in the U.K.
Produced by Paul McCartney

Each of the three singles released off *London Town* performed worse than the previous one. This in itself isn't that surprising, but it does make one wonder when you consider that this single contains two of the finest songs from the album, both far and away better than the songs on the previous two singles.

Goodnight Tonight/Daytime Nighttime Suffering
Released: March 23, 1979
Columbia 23-10940 (U.S.); Parlophone R 6023 (U.K.)
Highest Chart Position: 5 in both the U.S. and the U.K.
Produced by Paul McCartney

This is one of McCartney's best—and most unusual—singles, with both sides delivering powerful performances and a multitude of musical surprises. "Goodnight Tonight" is pseudo-disco, with its bouncing bass line, weird sound effects and catchy chorus. "Daytime Nighttime Suffering" is a pro-woman manifesto with a great vocal, quirky chord changes and a fantastic ending. It's pretty much the opposite of the Rolling Stones' *Some Girls,* an astonishing study in the cruel subjugation and objectification of women, released less than a year earlier.

Old Siam, Sir/Spin It On
Released: June 1, 1979 (U.K. only)
Parlophone R 6026
Highest Chart Position: 35
Produced by Paul McCartney and Chris Thomas

The two punkiest songs from *Back to the Egg* really did nothing in the British album charts. Listeners were mildly surprised that McCartney was issuing a single with two heavy rock songs, especially after such recent pap as "With a Little Luck" made it onto a 45 rpm record, but it didn't hold their attention for long.

Getting Closer/Baby's Request (U.K.)—Spin It On (U.S.)
Released: June 5, 1979, in the U.S. and August 16, 1979, in the U.K.
Columbia 3-11020 (U.S.); Parlophone R 6027 (U.K.)
Highest Chart Position: 20 in the U.S. and 60 in the U.K.
Produced by Paul McCartney and Chris Thomas

"Getting Closer" sounded a little more like Paul McCartney to U.S. fans so it hovered in the top 10 for a short while. Paired with "Spin It On," it made for a spirited two sides at the beginning of the summer. The British version had "Baby's Request" as the B-side, which just isn't chart-worthy material.

Arrow Through Me/Old Siam, Sir
Released: August 14, 1979 (U.S. only)

Columbia 1-11070
Highest Chart Position: 29
Produced by Paul McCartney and Chris Thomas

Perhaps the most commercial song on *Back to the Egg*, "Arrow Through Me" barely cracked the top 30 in the U.S. Billboard charts. It capped a generally dismal showing in the charts for both the album and the singles that came from the album.

Wonderful Christmastime/Rudolph the Red-Nosed Reggae
Released: November 26, 1979, in the U.S. and November 16, 1979, in the U.K.
Label: Columbia 1-11162 (U.S.); Parlophone R 6029 (U.K.)
Highest Chart Position: 6 in the U.K. and 47 in the U.S.
Produced by Paul McCartney

Pop and rock stars have a long history of recording Christmas songs, both traditional and original. There are few worse than Paul McCartney's "Wonderful Christmastime." McCartney plays all the instruments and this is his first single since 1971 to have only his name on it. The instrumentation is amateurish and banal, the words are embarrassing, and one wonders upon first listen what—besides the title—does this song have to do with Christmas? Just sticking a children's chorus and some holiday bells on the track doesn't automatically make it a valid Christmas song. Still, it receives heavy airplay during the holidays to this day, and McCartney will occasionally play it live if he's on tour near the holiday season. The B-side is as bad; a straight rendering of the traditional song, with the melody played on a violin. The word "reggae" in its title is misleading as there is nothing even remotely reggae-like about this abomination. This is the worst two-sided single of McCartney's career.

Coming Up/Coming Up (Live at Glasgow)/Lunchbox/Odd Sox
Released: April 11, 1980
Label: Columbia AE7 1204 (U.S.); Parlophone R 6035 (U.K.)
Highest Chart Position: 1 in the U.S. and 2 in the U.K.
Produced by Paul McCartney

The second phase of McCartney's solo career started, ironically, with this hopped up little nugget of funky drums, trebly guitars, lots of synths and a speeded-up lead vocal. In the United States, the live version, performed by the final incarnation of Wings in Scotland in 1979, received most of the airplay. "Lunchbox/Odd Sox" is a Wings leftover from the *Venus and Mars* sessions and features the kind of piano playing McCartney excels in: think "Lady Madonna" and "Nineteen Hundred and Eighty-Five." Only the studio version of "Coming Up" is truly solo McCartney. The single did well on both sides of the Atlantic and allowed McCartney to repair his reputation after his January 1980 arrest (and subsequent jail time) for smuggling marijuana into Japan. "Coming Up" is one of McCartney's finer singles and the song goes down extremely well on the occasions when he plays it live. One question about the live version of the song: The crowd sounds are exceedingly appreciative and enthusiastic—more than one would expect for a song they most likely had never heard before. Any chance the crowd sounds were doctored in the studio during the final mixing process? Just asking.

Waterfalls/Check My Machine
Released: June 13, 1980
Label: Columbia 1-11335 (U.S.); Parlophone R 6037 (U.K.)
Highest Chart Position: 106 in the U.S. and 9 in the U.K.
Produced by Paul McCartney

It's interesting that there was such a huge difference between the U.S. and British chart performances of "Waterfalls." It's McCartney's first solo single not to at least crack the U.S. Hot 100 Billboard chart, and yet it was a top 10 hit in England. It's a simple recording of Fender Rhodes, synthesizer and a snippet of acoustic guitar, and it's sung well. One problem is that it just goes on too long and becomes repetitive after a while. "Check My Machine" is just McCartney having fun fooling around in the studio and repeating the title ad nauseum. In some ways, it's not even a good enough song for a B-side. For completists only.

Temporary Secretary/Secret Friend
Released: September 15, 1980 (U.K. only)
Parlophone 6039
Highest Chart Positions: Did not chart
Produced by Paul McCartney

Released only in the U.K. as a 12-inch single, "Temporary Secretary" failed to chart, mainly because only 25,000 copies were pressed. It ranks as one of McCartney's weirdest songs, a piece of faux electropop infused with a creepy vibe and a totally catchy groove. It wasn't until 2015, when

McCartney added it to his live show set, that people started to really appreciate its weirdness. "Secret Friend" is more aimless vamping with electronics in the studio, although this one at least had some interesting percussion and vocal flourishes. But at 10:41 is just too long to hold one's interest.

Ebony and Ivory/Rainclouds
Released: March 26, 1982, in the U.S. and March 29, 1982, in the U.K.
Columbia 44-02878 (U.S.); Parlophone R 6054 (U.K.)
Highest Chart Position: 1 in the U.S. and U.K.
Produced by George Martin

"Ebony and Ivory" stands as one of the greatest musical enigmas of McCartney's solo career. Widely popular in the U.S. and U.K., it also was derided for the triteness of its sentiment and the implied presumption by Messrs. McCartney and Wonder that if we could just get along like the keys on a piano, we could eliminate racial disharmony around the world. You can't blame them for trying. It's difficult to cure all the world's social ills in 3:41 of a catchy pop song. The best part of the song is the vocal interplay between McCartney and Wonder, two of the best pop vocalists of the 20th century. "Rainclouds" is surprisingly effective. Built over two acoustic guitars playing very simple chords, the vocal arrangements stand out for their inventiveness and for how they augment the rather stilted lyrics.

Take It Away/I'll Give You a Ring
Released: June 21, 1982, in the U.S. and July 5, 1982 (12-inch single) in the U.S. and U.K.
Label: Columbia 44-03019 (U.S.); Parlophone R 6056 (U.K.)
Highest Chart Position: 10 in the U.S. and 15 in the U.K.
Produced by George Martin

McCartney's reunion with long-time producer George Martin sounds as Beatles-like as any of his solo songs, with a storyline narrative and beefy horns. Ringo Starr's along for the ride, too. "I'll Give You a Ring" is an ornate pop song, with lots of production values, an affected lead vocal, and a middle eight that just takes the song to a new level. The lyrics make it sound like the writer/singer just discovered this little contraption called a telephone.

Tug of War/Get It
Released: September 6, 1982

Columbia 38-03235 (U.S.); Parlophone R 6057 (U.K.)
Highest Chart Position: 53 in the U.S. and U.K.
Produced by George Martin

"Tug of War" seems to make a less subtle plea for harmony than "Ebony and Ivory," and it's certainly a better song, yet it was pretty much a flop as a single. "Get It" has the homespun magic provided by country gentleman Carl Perkins. As an aside, it's interesting that during this period McCartney would tend to release three singles from the same album. It's fair to wonder whether he just figured his name would be enough to propel such prodigious product up the charts, or whether he was late in reading the tea leaves in terms of where the recording industry was headed.

Say Say Say/Ode to a Koala Bear
Released: October 3, 1983
Columbia 44-04169 (U.S.); Parlophone R 6062 (U.K.)
Highest Chart Position: 1 in the U.S. and 2 in the U.K.
Produced by George Martin

There's no question that "Say Say Say" was a massive international hit song, but the oddest thing about it is that the song bears such little resemblance to the typical McCartney or Jackson song brand. It's a hybrid anomaly. That's okay: My advice is just to flip this single and revel in the majestic beauty of "Ode to a Koala Bear," a song that might have been a hit if only the subject matter had been about peace, love and understanding, rather than an unnamed Australian marsupial. The beautiful pairing of the guitars and piano, the striking choppiness of the verses, and the magnificent, over-the-top vocal performance that McCartney delivers makes this a deeply buried gem. Seek it out and try to forget it's about ... ahem ... a koala bear.

Pipes of Peace/So Bad (U.K. only)
So Bad/Pipes of Peace (U.S. only)
Released: December 5, 1983
Columbia 38-04296 (U.S.); Parlophone R 6064 (U.K.)
Highest Chart Position: 23 in the U.S. and 1 in the U.K.
Produced by George Martin

"Pipes of Peace" was a major hit in Britain, but McCartney must have felt that "So Bad" would be more to the taste of Americans (despite the terrible grammatical errors in its lyrics). In fact, "So Bad" is the better, more commercial song of the two

No More Lonely Nights/No More Lonely Nights (playout version on original 7-inch release); No More Lonely Nights (special dance mix second 7-inch single)
Released: September 24, 1984
Label: Columbia 44-05077 (U.S.); Parlophone R 6080 (U.K.)
Highest Chart Position: 6 in the U.S. and 2 in the U.K.
Produced by George Martin

The ballad version of "No More Lonely Nights" is a fine McCartney song and made for a successful single. The "playout version" and the dance mix are exercises in lack of self-control and an inflated view of the legs of the song once transposed into different rhythm schemes. They are generally unlistenable and just detract from the simple beauty of the ballad version. The 12-inch picture discs released on October 8, 1984, just prolong the misery into eight minutes and 10 seconds of aural assault.

We All Stand Together/We All Stand Together (humming version)
Released: November 12, 1984 (U.K. only)
Label: Parlophone R 6086
Highest Chart Positions: 3
Produced by George Martin

There are so many hallmarks of McCartney's writing contained in "We All Stand Together" that's it's difficult to count them all. Most notable is the beautiful melody, which takes twists and turns that remind one that no matter what the topic, McCartney brings the same tunefulness most every time. The musical flourishes, undoubtedly augmented by the genius of George Martin, make this one of McCartney's most beautiful melodies. The short film that it was written for is worth a viewing, too.

Spies Like Us/My Carnival
Released: November 18, 1985
Label: Capitol SPRO-9556 (U.S.); Parlophone R 6118 (U.K.)
Highest Chart Positions: 7 in the U.S. and 13 in the U.K.
Produced by Paul McCartney, Hugh Padgham, Phil Ramone

When you produce a bad movie with atrocious acting, it would be hard to save it with a theme song. No exception here, as "Spies Like Us" is one of McCartney's worst songs ever and would have only been improved by remaining on the cutting room floor. To make matters even worse, a 12-inch single was released that featured a "party" mix, an alternative mix and a DJ version, each outdoing the other in blandness and lack of humor. Do yourself a favor and flip this single over to the B-side; at least "My Carnival" sounds as if it was fun to make.

Press/It's Not True
Released: July 14, 1986
Capitol SPRO-9763 (U.S.); Parlophone R 6133 (U.K.)
Highest Chart Position: 21 in the U.S. and 25 in the U.K.
Produced by Paul McCartney and Hugh Padgham

It's clear McCartney had high hopes for *Press to Play*, and he certainly picked the most commercial song on it to release as the first single. "Press" is infectious and fun, and although it relies too heavily on the synthesizers du jour, it's still pretty catchy. "It's Not True" is a hidden treasure, in which a song with a slow, loping tempo turns into a screaming match, replete with loud drums and lots of echo. Still, the single's performance in the charts was tepid. On second pressings of the U.K. single a third track—"Hanglide"—was included. It's nothing more than five minutes of energetic bass, noodling synths and an insistent beat.

Pretty Little Head/Write Away (7-inch and 12-inch)
Released: October 27, 1986
Capitol SPRO-9928 (U.S.); Parlophone R 6145 (U.K.)
Highest Chart Position: Did not chart
Produced by Paul McCartney and Hugh Padgham

Even in 1986, this single had no chance of becoming a hit. It's not at all radio-friendly and didn't make a dent in the charts. The B-side at least has a melodic structure to it.

Stranglehold/Angry
Released: October 29, 1986 (U.S. only)
Capitol SPRO-9860
Highest Chart Position: 81
Produced by Paul McCartney and Hugh Padgham

"Stranglehold" was one of the more commercial songs on *Press to Play* and probably would have scored bigger as a second single from the album. Or better still, make "Angry" the A-side and give a pissed off McCartney song a shot at climbing the charts.

Only Love Remains/Tough on a Tightrope
Released: December 1, 1986
Capitol B-5672 (U.S.); Parlophone R 6148 (U.K.)
Highest Chart Positions: 34 (U.K.); Did not chart in the U.S.
Produced by Hugh Padgham

Press to Play had been out for exactly three months when this single was released, and during that time McCartney issued four singles from the album. Clearly there wasn't a hit song in the bunch, but he remained steadfast in trying to wring whatever remaining juice might be left. "Only Love Remains" is a quality McCartney ballad, but charts dominated by Lionel Ritchie, Peter Cetera, Whitney Houston and Billy Ocean couldn't find room for it.

Once Upon a Long Ago/Back on My Feet
Released: November 16, 1987 (7-inch and CD single); November 23, 1987 (12-inch single) in the U.K.
Parlophone R 6170
Highest Chart Position: 10
Produced by Phil Ramone

This is one of the oddest singles in McCartney's career, but also a very important one. The A-side was a hit in England and the B-side was his first released collaboration with Elvis Costello, representing a sign of things to come. The single brought McCartney back to the mainstream pop fold after stumbling through the years 1983–86. Both songs were produced by Phil Ramone, and included session musicians Tim Renwick, Nick Glennie-Smith, Charlie Morgan, Louis Jardim, Nigel Kennedy, Stan Salzman and Henry Spinetti. Both songs featured that sort of slow rock ballad vibe that was so popular in the 1980s, and there was the obligatory sax solo in "Once Upon a Long Ago." Two 12-inch releases included songs from the *Choba B CCCP* sessions: "Midnight Special," "Don't Get Around Much Anymore," "Lawdy Miss Clawdy" and "Kansas City."

My Brave Face/Flying to My Home
Released: May 27, 1989, in the U.S. and May 8, 1989, in the U.K.
Capitol B-44367 (U.S.); Parlophone R 6213 (U.K.)

Highest Chart Position: 25 in the U.S. and 18 in the U.K.
Produced by Paul McCartney, Mitchell Froom and Neil Dorfsman

The catchiest and most commercial song on *Flowers in the Dirt* is paired with one of McCartney's best B-sides, the astounding "Flying to My Home." Girded by a big drum sound and lots of guitars, the melody is simple but engaging. Listen for the Elvis-style vocals during the second middle eight. For the 12-inch and CD singles, McCartney added two more songs from the *Choba B CCCP* sessions, "I'm Gonna be a Wheel Someday" and "Ain't That a Shame."

This One/The First Stone
Released: July 17, 1989
Capitol 7PRO-79700 (U.S.); Parlophone RX 6223 (U.K.)
Highest Chart Position: 94 in the U.S. and 18 in the U.K.
Produced by Paul McCartney

The second single from *Flowers in the Dirt* featured another outstanding A-side and a forgettable B-side. "The First Stone" tries to turn a biblical parable into a pop song, and just doesn't work. Added to the 12-inch and CD singles of the U.K. release were a bland reworking of "The Long and Winding Road," a bluesy shouter called "I Wanna Cry," still another leftover from *the Choba B CCCP* sessions "I'm in Love Again" and the incredible funky "Good Sign," which featured a signature McCartney bass part, and lots of beats.

Figure of Eight/Où Est Le Soleil?
Released: November 13, 1989
Capitol 4JM-44489 (U.S.); Parlophone CDR 6235 (U.K.)
Highest Chart Position: 92 in the U.S. and 42 in the U.K.
Produced by Paul McCartney, Chris Hughes and Ross Cullum

"Figure of Eight" is an outstanding rocker but just never found its niche on the charts. The B-side is a bunch of trance-y nonsense, repeated over and over again.

Put It There/Mama's Little Girl/Same Time Next Year
Released: February 5, 1990
Label: Capitol 4JM-44570 (U.S.); Parlophone R 6246 (U.K.)
Highest Chart Position: 32 in the U.K.; did not chart in the U.S.
Produced by Paul McCartney

"Put It There" is a fine acoustic guitar song, but just not even close to what would appeal to the mass pop music market at the time. The B-sides include two Wings songs; the first from 1973 and the second from 1978. It's little wonder this single did not chart in the U.S.

Birthday/Good Day Sunshine
Released: October 16, 1990, in the U.S. and October 8, 1990, in the U.K.
Capitol 4JM-44645 (U.S.); Parlophone R 6271 (U.K.)
Highest Chart Position: 29 in the U.K.; did not chart in the U.S.
Produced by Paul McCartney

Both songs come from the 1989–90 world tour set list. This spirited version of "Birthday" appeared on the *Tripping the Live Fantastic* album, but "Good Day Sunshine" was the only song in the set list not to appear on the album (it got cut in deference to the handful of jams and sound check outtakes included on the album). The U.K. 12-inch and CD single versions added live renderings of "P.S. Love Me Do" and "Let 'Em In," neither of which were part of the regular set list for the tour.

All My Trials/C Moon
Released: November 26, 1990 (U.K. only)
Parlophone R 6278
Highest Chart Position: 35
Produced by Paul McCartney

An oddly arcane single, "All My Trials" was only performed six times during the 1989–90 tour and the version of "C Moon" does not sound live at all. There are no crowd sounds or ambience. The 12-inch and CD singles included live recordings of "Mull of Kintyre" (Scotland) and "Put It There" (Germany). Another CD single came out a week later and replaced "Mull of Kintyre" and "Put It There" with a strange but clearly heartfelt medley of three of John Lennon's best-known songs: "Strawberry Fields Forever," "Help" and "Give Peace a Chance." The song was first performed in Liverpool, naturally. McCartney muffs some of the words of "Strawberry Fields Forever" and lets out an audible little screech in response to the gaffe.

Hope of Deliverance/Long Leather Coat/Big Boys Bickering/Kicked Around No More

Released: January 12, 1993, in the U.S. and December 28, 1992, in the U.K.
Capitol S7-56946 (U.S.); Parlophone R 6330 (U.K.)
Highest Chart Position: 83 in the U.S. and 18 in the U.K.
Produced by Paul McCartney and Julian Mendelsohn

"Hope of Deliverance" was easily the best song on "Off the Ground" so it seemed like an obvious choice for the first single. The other three songs alternately tackle animal rights, the benefits of a meat-free diet and the total futility of trying to get politicians to effectively address environmental issues (especially in the early 1990s). "Long Leather Coat" is a punchy rocker and "Kicked Around No More" is an underrated McCartney keyboard ballad. "Big Boys Bickering" is mostly notable for the inclusion of the word "fucking" twice, a very un–McCartney like move.

C'Mon People/I Can't Imagine/Keep Coming Back to Love/Down to the River
Released: February 22, 1993
Label: Capitol S7-17489 (U.S.); Parlophone CDRS 6338 (U.K.)
Highest Chart Position: 41 in the U.K.; did not chart in the U.S.
Produced by Paul McCartney

Despite its lofty aspirations to be a crowd-pleasing anthem for peace, "C'Mon People" is weak tea and its chart performance confirmed that. "I Can't Imagine" is a catchy midtempo song. "Keep Coming Back to Love" features intricate harmonies and some innovative instrumentation. As noted previously, "Down to the River" sounds like McCartney's tribute to Creedence Clearwater Revival.

C'mon People/Deliverance/Deliverance [dub mix]
Released: February 22, 1993
Label: Parlophone CDR 6338 (U.K.)
Highest Chart Position: 41 in the U.K.; did not chart in the U.S.
Produced by Paul McCartney and Julian Mendelsohn

"C'mon People" is the album version and the other two songs are billed as "the Steve Anderson mixes" of "Hope of Deliverance."

Off the Ground/Cosmically Conscious
Released: April 19, 1993

Label: Capitol DPRO-79792 (U.S.)
Highest Chart Position: Did not chart
Produced by Paul McCartney and Julian Mendelsohn

A bland single that was nowhere near what FM radio was playing in 1993, or what listeners were sending up the charts. Three weeks after its release, a new single was released that added "Style Style," "Sweet Sweet Memories" and "Soggy Noodle," three of the songs recorded during the very productive *Off the Ground* sessions. Only "Style Style" among them is the least bit listenable.

Biker Like an Icon/Things We Said Today
Released: April 6, 1993, in the U.S. and April 26, 1993, in the U.K.
Capitol S7-17319; Parlophone CDRDJ 6347
Highest Chart Position: Did not chart
Produced by Paul McCartney

One of McCartney's worst songs as the A-side, backed with the hot little live version of "Things We Said Today" from the 1991 MTV *Unplugged* performance (but not included on the *Unplugged* album). Other releases of this single (there were three altogether) added a live version of the A-side and a live version of "Midnight Special," also recorded during the *Unplugged* performance but not included on that album.

Young Boy/Looking for You/Oobu Joobu Part One (CD 1)/Broomstick/Oobu Joobu Part Two (CD 2)
Released: April 28, 1997 (U.K. only)
Parlophone CDRS 6462
Highest Chart Position: 19
Produced by Paul McCartney

The first single from *Flaming Pie* was the very Beatle-esque "Young Boy." Lots of chiming acoustic guitars and harmonies make this choice a winner. The B-sides were two songs that were left off the album. They are similar in style; one is a bluesy rocker with lots of crunchy electric guitars and the other is more acoustic based and is more of a straight 12-bar jam. *Oobu Joobu Part One* and *Oobu Joobu Part Two* were included in two different releases. *Part One* features McCartney talking about "Young Boy" and also playing for the first time "I Love This House." *Part Two* features the debut of unreleased track "Atlantic Ocean" and several variations of the *Oobu Joobu* theme song.

The World Tonight/Used to Be Bad
Released: April 17, 1997, in the U.S. and July 7, 1997, in the U.K.
Label: Capitol C2 7243 8 58650 2 2; Parlophone 7243 8 84298 7 0
Highest Chart Position: 64 in the U.S. and 23 in the U.K.
Produced by Paul McCartney and Jeff Lynne

One of the best songs on the album and one of McCartney's finest solo rockers was issued as the second single from *Flaming Pie*. The B-side is a generic guitar, bass and drums rocker that sounds as if it was made up on the spot.

Beautiful Night/Love Come Tumbling Down/Oobu Joobu Part Five (CD 1)/Same Love/Oobu Joobu Part Six (CD Two)
Released: December 15, 1997 (U.K. only)
Parlophone RP 6489, 7243 8 84970 7 7
Highest Chart Position: 25
Produced by Paul McCartney and Jeff Lynne

The final single from *Flaming Pie* was the cheery "Beautiful Night," with big assists from Ringo Starr, Jeff Lynne and George Martin. "Love Come Tumbling Down" and "Same Love" are McCartney piano ballads cut from the same musical cloth. *Oobu Joobu Part Five* features a chat with McCartney and Starr about the making of "Beautiful Night" and *Part Six* features McCartney talking about Abbey Road and the debut of the unreleased track "Love Mix."

No Other Baby/Brown Eyed Handsome Man/Fabulous
Released: October 24, 1999
Capitol DPRO 7087 6 13851 2 0 Parlophone R 6527
Highest Chart Position: 42 in the U.K.; did not chart in the U.S.
Produced by Paul McCartney

The stark beauty of "No Other Baby," when viewed through the prism of Linda McCartney's death the previous year, makes this a real tear-jerker and an apt choice for the first single from *Run Devil Run*. He leavened the sadness with the jaunty B-side, which he delivers with just the right amount of unironic stoicism. "Fabulous" was written by Charlie Gracie in 1957 and is almost a complete rewrite of Elvis Presley's "Don't Be Cruel."

From a Lover to a Friend/Riding into Jaipur
Released: October 29, 2001

Capitol DPRO 7087 6 15992 2 0; Parlophone R 6567
Highest Chart Positions: 45 in the U.K.; did not chart in the U.S.
Produced by David Kahne

Perhaps the most melancholic song ever sung by McCartney, "From a Lover to a Friend" ushers in a new period of introspection on the part of the artist. It defies easy description in terms of musical form; it's all over the place. A remix of "From a Lover to a Friend" was included on the cassette and CD single releases. David Kahne's remix turned it into a mystical, haunting take on what was already a pretty dark song. The B-side is basically a throwaway track about a trip he made to India.

Freedom/From a Lover to a Friend
Released: November 5, 2001
Capitol DPRO 7087 6 16903 2 3; Parlophone 7243 5 50288 2 2
Highest Chart Positions: 97 in the U.S.; did not chart in the U.K.
Produced by David Kahne

"Freedom" is just too pat as a reaction to the tragedies of 9/11. It lacks depth and meaning and seems almost too retaliatory to be credible. It's simple and not very melodic. It's possible McCartney just thought that since he was going on tour, he should have a musical reaction to the tragedies, but sometimes it's okay not to chime in on these incomprehensible events that affect so many lives. None of us were looking to McCartney for leadership during that awful time, but since he has the forum, it's his decision to make. That said, his organization of *The Concert for New York* made a much bolder impact, with much more tangible results.

Tropic Island Hum/We All Stand Together
September 20, 2004 (U.K. only)
Parlophone R 6649
Highest Chart Position: 21
Produced by Paul McCartney

"Tropic Island Hum" is the theme song from McCartney's second animated short film. It features a sort of calypso vibe, with dutifully playoff lyrics and all sorts of interesting voices. "We All Stand Together" was a fitting choice for the B-side. It nearly cracked the top 20 on the U.K. charts.

Fine Line/Growing Up Falling Down/Comfort of Love (CD single)
Released: August 29, 2005

Capitol 0946 3 34259 2 7; Parlophone R 6673
Highest Chart Positions: 20 in the U.K.; did not chart in the U.S.
Produced by Nigel Godrich

A great first single from McCartney's best album of the 2000s and a tempting taste of the theme of the that album, *Chaos and Creation in the Back Yard*. "Growing Up Falling Down" is a spacy, psychedelic tune shifting easily from major to minor keys. "Comfort of Love" is very similar to "Fine Line" in compositional structure. Another song from the album—"This Never Happened Before"—was released in 2006 as a promotional CD single.

Jenny Wren/Summer of '59 (7-inch single)/I Want You to Fly/This Loving Game (CD only)
Released: November 21, 2005 (U.S. & UK)
Capitol DPRO 0946 3 49375 2 8; Parlophone CDR 6678
Highest Chart Positions: 22 in the U.K.; did not chart in the U.S.
Produced by Nigel Godrich

This is a phenomenal single, and all four songs made available in different formats are interesting on their own. "Jenny Wren" is a beautiful composition, with the acoustic guitar panned way up high in the mix. Unfortunately, an edited version was played by most DJs, taking the song's 3:47 running time and quashing it into two minutes and nine seconds. "Summer of '59" is a marvel of economy, with McCartney's voices triple-tracked and a very subdued electric guitar playing the spare chords. "I Want You to Fly" seems to be McCartney urging then wife Heather Mills to strive to succeed at whatever she does. "This Loving Game" also seems to be directed toward Mills. This song especially sounds very much stylistically like the other songs on the album.

Ever Present Past/House of Wax (7-inch only)/Only Mama Knows/Dance Tonight (CD only)
Released: May 15, 2007, in the U.S. and November 5, 2007, in the U.K.
Hear Music 0888072306219 (7-inch); CD single 72306202
Highest Chart Position: 110 in the U.S. and 85 in the U.K.
Produced by David Kahne

The jangly, upbeat "Ever Present Past" was an obvious pick as a single off *Memory Almost Full*. The 7-inch single had the live version of "House of Wax" taken from the Amoeba Records gig as its B-side; the CD single featured "Only Mama Knows" and "Dance Tonight" as the extras, both taken from the Amoeba Records gig. An iTunes download featured "Ever Present Past," "Only Mama Knows" and "That Was Me," with the latter two taken from the Amoeba Records show.

Dance Tonight/Dance Tonight/Nod Your Head
Released June 18, 2007
Hear Music PRO-HM-0184; MPL Communications 72 30384
Highest Chart Position: 69 in the U.S. and 26 in the U.K.
Produced by David Kahne

A digital download with two versions of "Dance Tonight" was released on McCartney's sixth-fifth birthday and slowly moved up the U.K. charts. In the U.S., "Nod Your Head" was the B-side. Although it really didn't do anything in the U.S. charts it received a 2008 Grammy nomination for best male pop vocal performance. "Nod Your Head" was also later released as a free iTunes download.

iTunes Festival EP
Recorded at the London Institute of Performing Arts on July 5, 2007
Released by the iTunes store on August 21, 2007
Coming Up/Only Mama Knows/That Was Me/Jet/Nod Your Head/ House of Wax

This six-song sampler EP was from a full concert of 25 songs, most of which were mainstays in McCartney's live shows during this period. This is a surprisingly loose but competently executed collection.

Sing the Changes
Released: December 16, 2008 (U.S. & UK)
ATO Records (U.S.) and One Little Indian (U.K.) MPL1006-CDPROMO
Highest Chart Position: Did not chart
Produced by The Fireman

This was released as a promo CD to tease the release of the *Electric Arguments* album.

(I Want to) Come Home
Released: As a digital download in the U.K. on March 1, 2010, and in the U.S. in 2009

Hollywood Records, MPL BVPR002552 (U.S.)
Highest Chart Position: Did not chart

The perfect McCartney piano ballad: A great melody, a tasty string arrangement, horns and a fine vocal. This was written for the film *Everybody's Fine,* starring Robert DeNiro and directed by Kirk Jones. The song did get a Golden Globe nomination and McCartney even occasionally included it in his touring set list.

My Valentine/Only Our Hearts
Released: January 9, 2012 (U.S.)
Hear Music PRO-HM-0487
Highest chart position: 20
Produced by Tommy LiPuma

McCartney released the two original songs from *Kisses on the Bottom* as a single in plenty of time to get airplay before Valentine's Day 2012. "My Valentine" has been a staple of his live shows since 2012.

NEW
Released: Released August 28, 2012, as a digital download on iTunes; September 2, 2012, as a digital download available exclusively at amazon.com
Highest chart position: 18
Produced by Mark Ronson

The upbeat title song of the *NEW* album enjoyed broad currency digitally and while McCartney was performing it live on the talk show circuit.

Queenie Eye
Released October 24, 2013, as a digital download
Highest Chart Position: 27 in the U.S.
Produced by Paul McCartney and Paul Epworth

Probably the least interesting song on *NEW,* but McCartney seems to love it. He included it in his touring sets lists from 2013 on, and even retained it on the set list of the tour to promote *Egypt Station,* an unusual move for him.

Save Us
Released March 31, 2014, as a digital download

Highest Chart Position: Did not chart
Produced by Paul McCartney and Paul Epworth

Another rather bland single from the *NEW* album. The songs were there, but McCartney released a couple of clunkers instead.

Appreciate
Released May 16, 2014, by digital download
Highest chart position: Did not chart
Produced by Giles Martin

This one of the best songs on *NEW* and has a certain soulfulness to it that gives it some oomph. This would have been a great addition to his live set, but he's never played it on tour.

Early Days
Released July 7, 2014, by digital download
Highest Chart Position; Did not chart
Produced by Ethan Johns

The story of the early days of Lennon and McCartney, as told by McCartney. He turns this into a bit of a complaint about how so many people misappropriate the Beatles story and he's definitely not wrong about that.

Hope for the Future
Released December 8, 2014, as a digital download and on January 13, 2015, as a 12-inch single
Hear Music
Highest Chart Position: Did not chart
Produced by Giles Martin

"Hope for the Future" was written for the very popular video game Destiny and plays over the credits that air at the end of each game. It contains the usual McCartney optimism about the planet's future. It's an excellent song; majestic and brimming with good feeling. It did not make a dent in the charts, however. The single release is backed by four alternate mixes titled "Thrash," "Beatsession Mix," "Jaded Mix" and "Mirwais Mix."

I Don't Know/Come on to Me
Released: June 20, 2018
Capitol B002879821 (U.S.); 00602567545026 (U.K.)

Highest Chart Position: 58 in the U.K. and 39 in the U.S.
Produced by Greg Kurstin

This double A-side single announced unabashedly that Paul McCartney was back after a five-year studio album hiatus. Despite the obvious septuagenarian libido-driven force of "Come On to Me" the real treasure here is "I Don't Care," a beautiful ballad in the pure McCartney tradition. He sounds vulnerable and sad, two emotions he hasn't plumbed much in his career.

Fuh You
Released August 15, 2018, via streaming services
Capitol
Highest Chart Position: Did not chart
Produced by Paul McCartney and Ryan Tedder

This song is overproduced and perhaps the worst song on *Egypt Station.* I understand trying to push the limits of lyrical decorum, but this seems like a deliberate attempt on McCartney's part to inflame. And it worked.

Who Cares
Released December 17, 2018, by digital download
Capitol
Highest Chart Position: Did not chart
Produced by Paul McCartney and Greg Kurstin

This punchy single is McCartney's anti-bullying anthem. His entire touring band is in fine form on this one, with especially raunchy electric guitars leading the way.

Get Enough
Released January 1, 2019, by digital download
Capitol
Produced by Paul McCartney, Ryan Tedder and Zach Skelton

The main controversy about this song is McCartney's first ever use of Auto-Tune. I'm not surprised he tried Auto-Tune. It's totally in keeping with the old Beatles studio mantra to try any technology available to manipulate the sound. This is actually a pleasant enough piano ballad, with some cool twists and turns.

In a Hurry/Home Tonight

Released November 22, 2019 as a digital download; November 29, 2019 as an extended disc to celebrate Record Store Day. Recorded during the original sessions for *Egypt Station.*

In a Hurry: This has a certain Beach Boys vibe. Lots of keyboards, prominent bass guitar, surprise key changes, and mellifluous backing vocals. Many time signature shifts make this an interesting listen. The false ending is fun.

Home Tonight: This has a decidedly old school feel, with an insistent drum part, galloping bass line, and horns to round out the sound. This could have easily fit in on *Wings at the Speed of Sound* or *London Town.*

Selected Bootlegs

There are literally thousands of McCartney bootlegs, almost all of which you can listen to on YouTube. For our purposes, I've chosen a handful of the most widely circulated and those with the best sonic quality. Bootlegs that include live performances often are taken right from the sound board and are usually not properly mixed and mastered.

Almost every one of McCartney's solo albums (with and without Wings) has a bootleg of session tapes that consist of working versions of the album's songs or songs that went unreleased in the end. McCartney and his team have done an outstanding job of curating this material and including it on expanded re-releases of original albums. The *Paul McCartney Archive Collection* pays special attention to unreleased recordings and mostly renders "session" bootlegs redundant (which, of course, is probably one of the goals of the *Archive Collection*).

Cold Cuts
Club Sandwich SP-II
Never released
Recorded from 1970 through 1987
Various musicians

Cold Cuts is the only bootleg that was nearly officially released by McCartney. He had planned to release it as a curio filled with B-sides and unreleased songs; of course, this is frequently done today but considered a major career misstep in the 1970s and early 1980s. Even an artist of McCartney's stature would have trouble convincing a record label to release an album full of filler.

After many false starts, McCartney abandoned the idea for good in 1987, chiefly because it had already been widely bootlegged. A version was released in 1987 on vinyl, and in 1996 it received its first CD release (Pegboy 1002). It was released on CD in Russia only in 2013 (TOCP-98615).

It's been rumored for years that the original album was to contain twice as many songs, and much speculation has been bandied about concerning what those songs were. An Australian bootleg surfaced in 1989 (Condor 1963) that purported to be the full *Hot Hits—Cold Cuts* (sometimes spelled Kold Kutz) double album. Additional songs include "I Would Only Smile," "Oriental Nightfish," "Lunchbox/Odd Sox," "Send Me the Heart," "Wild Prairie," "Tomorrow" and "Proud Mum." For the most part, *Cold Cuts* is fun to listen to, but it does not hold together as a cohesive work. Nor was it ever meant to. A discerning McCartney fan could peg almost every song to the year of its recording. Most of these tracks are discussed elsewhere in this book.

A Love for You/My Carnival/Waterspout/Momma's Little Girl/Night Out/Robber's Ball/Cage/Did We Meet Somewhere Before?/Hey Diddle/Tragedy/Best Friend/Same Time Next Year

"Waterspout" is from the *London Town* sessions, and chugs along with a faux Caribbean beat and a nice chord sequence. As usual, the melody is strong, and the vocals are recorded with precision. "Robber's Ball" is a manic novelty song that was recorded in 1978 during the *Back to the Egg* sessions. "Cage" was also recorded during those sessions and is probably the best song on *Cold Cuts*. It features two distinct song fragments; the first a fast-moving rave-up (beautifully sung with the obligatory rock 'n' roll strain in his voice), and the second a slow ballad dominated by piano that morphs into a synth-laden carnival-like instrumental interlude, before returning to the original melody. There is also an abrupt cold ending. "Same Time Next Year" was recorded in May 1978 and was originally slated to be the theme song of the movie by the same name, starring Ellen Burstyn and Alan Alda, but was never used. It has a certain majestic quality to it just made for the big screen. It attempts to summarize the plot of the movie in 3:08, compete with strings. "Twice in a Lifetime" has a 1980s feel, complete with a "soft jazz" saxophone intro. This song played over the credits at the end of the movie of the same name, which starred Gene Hackman and Ann-Margret.

Return to Pepperland
Recorded in 1986–87
Released 2000 (Japan only)
Sergeant M Records SM 0001
Produced by Paul McCartney and Phil Ramone

Lindiana/I Love This House/We Got Married/Beautiful Night/Loveliest Thing/Squid/Big Day/This One/Love Come Tumbling Down/Christian Bop/Atlantic Ocean//Love Mix/Return to Pepperland/P.S. Love Me Do/Same Love/Don't Break the Promise

This is mostly a hash of alternate versions of songs that finally showed up on official releases, B-sides, demos, and two songs ("Lindiana" and "Return to Pepperland") that remain unreleased. "We Got Married," "This One" and "Loveliest Thing" are demo versions of songs that eventually ended up on *Flowers in the Dirt*. "Atlantic Ocean," "Love Come Tumbling Down," "Same Love," "Beautiful Night" and "Love Mix" were coproduced by Phil Ramone.

For years, there have been persistent rumors that McCartney and Ramone (best known for his work with Billy Joel) were making an album together in the mid–1980s. It's true that Ramone produced or co-produced several tracks for McCartney in New York, but there was never any talk of making an entire album together.

Avoid the two Beatle references on this album. "P.S. Love Me Do," is an embarrassing mashup of two of the earliest Beatles songs with fake drums and lots of synths; you know, the anti–Beatle instrumental track. McCartney even played it a couple of times during the 1989–90 tour until he noticed everyone going to the concessions stand for a drink every time he played it.

"Return to Pepperland" is just another chunk-o'-junk with bouncy piano and the singer telling banal stories of "everyday people." It bears no resemblance at all to anything remotely related to *Sgt. Pepper*, except for a brief snippet of backwards guitar at the end.

By far, the best two songs are "I Love This House," which McCartney originally dropped on an episode of *Oobu Joobu* and features scorching guitar played by David Gilmour, and "Don't Break the Promise," co-written with Eric Stewart. This version is a chunky reggae-inflected track with McCartney singing in falsetto.

Another popular bootleg is called *Pizza and Fairy Tales*, and features the same tracks as *Return to Pepperland*, but adds working versions of many of the songs from *Press to Play*, and also includes the studio versions of "Once Upon a Long Ago" and "Peacocks."

But the real revelation is the inclusion of the beautiful "Yvonne," co-written with Eric Stewart. A simple guitar song with a simple chord sequence, the melody is sweet and soft. It's difficult to understand why this song was not included on *Press to Play*, an album desperately in need of some tunefulness. It meanders a bit but is saved by the melody as sung by McCartney. Stewart re-recorded it as "Yvonne's the One" for the 10cc 1995 album *Mirror, Mirror.*

Unless you are a fan of soundcheck recordings or alternative versions of album tracks, Paul McCartney bootlegs, for the most part, are now a bit redundant. There are many out there that consist of a mishmash of McCartney songs from various eras that are somehow slightly different than the officially released version. As mentioned previously, the *Paul McCartney Archive Collection* so far has almost completely depleted the supply of recordings that haven't been heard before.

Oobu Joobu

Oobu Joobu was a proto-podcast that Paul McCartney hosted on the Westwood One Radio Network. Fifteen episodes were produced and aired during the summer of 1995. McCartney referred to the program as "wide screen radio," a sneakily prescient term in those days before media devices could all but fold your laundry for you.

The episodes featured rehearsals, demos, outtakes, live performances, soundchecks, unreleased recordings and other audio ephemera from the vault. McCartney seemed very at ease in this format and it would have been interesting to see how the show would have evolved had he kept doing it. He was a genial host who somehow, despite his stature, seemed to affect a sort of "Gee whiz, how did I get so lucky to be able to do this" attitude about the whole affair.

Of most interest are the numerous unreleased songs he recorded and the stories behind them. For example, he plays a snippet of a song he and Eric Stewart co-wrote called "Don't Break the Promise." The song never appeared on a McCartney album but Stewart recorded for his own album and McCartney graciously plays Stewart's version on the show. He also unveils "I Love This House," "Squid" and "Love Mix," among dozens of other unreleased songs he recorded.

But McCartney is truly at his best when he's playing songs from his vast roster of musical influences. James Brown, Eddie Cochran, Carl Perkins, Little Richard, Bill Haley, Marvin Gaye, Fats Domino, Elvis and dozens of other rock pioneers all get their turn on McCartney's turntable, with accompanying exposition on how and why they influenced McCartney.

He also shines when he has a guest. It's not so much an interview, but a conversation, and the listener gets a sort of fly-on-the-wall feeling when listening to McCartney and his guests chat.

Most episodes featured the show's theme song, played in many musical styles by its host, who also wrote the simple song. There was often a segment called "Cook of the House" in which Linda McCartney offered several of her favorite vegetarian recipes.

Because it was chock full of pretty obscure material, *Oobu Joobu* was heavily bootlegged. Segments from the first six episodes were released as B-sides of three singles off the *Flaming Pie* album. For a further discussion of these segments, see the singles chapter.

In 1997, a limited edition promotional CD called *Oobu Joobu—Ecology* was released. It consists of nine songs, most of which have pro-ecology themes: "Oobu Joobu Theme"; "Looking for Changes"; "Peace in the Neighborhood"; "Wildlife"; "Mother Nature's Son"; "Cow"; "How Many People" and "We All Stand Together." "Cow" was written by Linda and Paul McCartney and their friend Carla Lane and is a rather stark description of what becomes of most cows.

Oobu Joobu was a really fine radio program—if you were a fan of McCartney—and was ahead of its time in terms of presaging the whole podcast concept. It's a shame it couldn't have continued.

The Videos and DVDs

Let's take a brief look at the various videos and DVDs McCartney has released. We'll look at those that were not included in a *Paul McCartney Archive Collection* release that are tied to specific albums. A few of these are now out of print.

Rockshow
Released November 26, 1980

This is a concert film of the highly successful *Wings Over America* tour. This followed a documentary called *Wings Over the World* that was originally broadcast on the BBC in 1979. A remastered version of this rarely seen TV special was included as part of the 2013 rerelease of the *Wings Over America* album. While this is a must see for Wings fans, the video version of *Rockshow,* while accurately capturing the excitement of the Wings tour in America, is grainy and at times poorly edited. Seek out the June 2013 remastered version on DVD. The quality is much improved.

Give My Regards to Broad Street
Released October 13, 1984

Don't bother. The movie is poorly written, the plot is predictable and the acting is amateurish. Combine that with banal remakes of Beatles classics that sound vacuous and uninspired, and you have a film that is wholly undeserving of the one hour and 49 minutes it'll take you to watch it.

The Paul McCartney Special
Released November 6, 1987 (U.S.) and November 27, 1987 (U.K.)

This is an hour-long video that featured an interview conducted by the BBC that included a long look at the making of the video for the song "Press," as well as lots of good discussions about Wings and the Beatles, and some promotional clips and concert footage. It was originally taped for television and appeared on BBC1 and BBC2 in late 1986. It appears that most of the motivation for this special was to promote the single "Press" and the album from which it came, *Press to Play*. It is out of print.

Put It There
Released September 1, 1989

This is a really enjoyable hour-long look at the making of the *Flowers in the Dirt* album. It includes studio performances of 20 songs, many of which were in the set list for the 1989–90 tour supporting the album. McCartney talks about the inspiration for many of the songs on the album. An expanded version was later released on DVD which included a photo gallery and some concert footage.

Get Back
Released October 25, 1991

This is a no-frills chronicle of the *Paul McCartney World Tour* of 1989–90 and includes performances of 23 songs from the tour set list. It was directed by Richard Lester, the man who directed the Beatles in *A Hard Day's Night* and *Help!*

Liverpool Oratorio
Released October 28, 1991 (DVD release in 2004)

This recording was filmed at the Liverpool Cathedral with Sir Paul in attendance. It was his first major classical work. The DVD has two exceptional added feature films: "Ghost of the Past," a deep dive into the making of *Liverpool Oratorio*, and "Echoes," in which McCartney visits his old school, by now called the Liverpool Institute for Performing Arts.

Movin' On
Released September 29, 1993

An unremarkable hour-long film of McCartney in the studio, working on the video for "C/mon People," some band rehearsal clips, a visit to Linda McCartney's Los Angeles photo exhibition, and McCartney working with an orchestra conducted by Angelo Badalamenti. The film was made to help promote the *Off the Ground* album and the upcoming tour to support it.

Paul Is Live
Released March 24, 1994

This is simply a concert performance film, featuring 21 songs from the "The New World" tour, the most uninspiring tour of his post–Wings career. It was released on VHS in 1994 and then on DVD in 2003, with a photo gallery and a biography as added bonus features.

In the World Tonight
Released October 6, 1997

An astonishing and overlooked documentary showing McCartney at home and in the studio, recording the *Flaming Pie* album. While it gets hokey at times, especially in the beginning when McCartney wields a chainsaw to fell some trees, then strums his acoustic guitar while sitting at a bonfire in the woods, it also includes an intimate, inside look at McCartney in the studio and at home, talking about his days with the Beatles, and demonstrating how he played the introduction to "Strawberry Fields Forever" on the Mellotron. McCartney is relaxed as he conducts business by phone with long-time PR man Geoff Baker, shows off the first amplifier he ever owned (an El Pico that did not have a dedicated guitar jack), and plays the upright bass owned by Elvis Presley's bass player Bill Black. Lots of great stuff, and worth a look if you can find it anywhere other than on YouTube.

Standing Stone
Released November 24, 1997 (rereleased on DVD in October 1999)

This is the full premiere performance of McCartney's symphonic poem *Standing Stone,* at London's Royal Albert Hall on October 14, 1997. The DVD also includes a documentary examining the creation of *Standing Stone,* and a photo gallery.

Wingspan: An Intimate Portrait
Released May 20, 2001

This beautifully produced history of Wings is essential viewing for any McCartney fan. Interviewed by his daughter Mary, McCartney recalls the trials and tribulations of trying to shed the overwhelming burden of being a Beatle, while at the same time attempting to keep the several incarnations of Wings together. It's an intimate look at 1970s vintage

McCartney, and the whole thing looks wildly fun. It bears mentioning again that this documentary would have been improved by interviews with former Wings members, but that just wasn't in the cards. Special features include promo videos of a few Wings songs and a gallery including many rarely seen photographs.

Live at the Cavern Club!
Released June 26, 2001

A fantastic document of McCartney's return to the famed Cavern Club in Liverpool. More than 300 lucky souls squeezed into the cramped club to watch McCartney tear through 12 songs, mostly culled from *Run Devil Run*, and a show-stopping finale of "I Saw Her Standing There." The bonus features include an interview and promotional videos of "Brown-Eyed Handsome Man" and "No Other Baby."

Back in the U.S.
Released November 26, 2002

This is concert film of McCartney's hugely successful 2002 American tour, and watching it as a film is the next best thing to being there live. The entire concert is here and the set list doesn't have one weak moment. The crowd is responsive and clearly ecstatic throughout. This DVD was released to support the double album of the same name, and both the album and the film went platinum in the U.S. and Canada.

Paul McCartney: The Music and Animation Collection
Released September 27, 2004

This is a 43-minute collection of three animated short films that McCartney wrote and scored: *Tropic Island Hum*, *Tuesday* and *Rupert and the Frog Song*. It's charming in an inoffensive way and is very kid-friendly. The animation is beautiful and the music has that McCartney melodic mystique firmly affixed. McCartney introduces each of the three films, and there are some behind-the-scene segments about the making of the films and an interview.

Paul McCartney in Red Square
Released June 14, 2005

A breathtaking film of McCartney and band playing two concerts in

Russia: one in Moscow's Red Square in 2003 and one in St. Petersburg's Palace Square in 2004. The crowds are massive and exhilarated and the band sounds as good as it ever has. This closed the final door on the Cold War, at least in terms of easy access to popular culture and the arts, and the entire film has a vibe of freedom. A couple of extra features examining the relationship of Russia and the Beatles and recalling memories from Red Square add a little punch to the package.

The Space Within Us
Released November 13, 2006

Arguably the best film McCartney ever released captures the incredible 2005 U.S. tour. Jam-packed with special features, the 115-minute film includes concert footage, soundcheck run-throughs, interviews with McCartney, his band and the tour crew (this is especially interesting), the film that was shown before every concert of the tour and lots of intimate and revealing clips.

The McCartney Years
Released November 12, 2007

This is an exhaustive set of 46 videos, several live performances, some talk show interviews and other things from McCartney's vault that tells the story of his solo career in almost too much detail. First, who knew that he produced videos for release of 46 of his solo and Wings songs? Songs like "I've Had Enough" and "Biker Like an Icon" don't seem to rise to the level of quality that would call for a video. Yet here they are. It makes for an interesting artifact. The first two CDs include the 46 videos, plus extras ranging from talk show appearances to alternate versions of videos. By far the shining jewel among the extras is the short film called *Creating Chaos at Abbey Road,* a tutorial given by McCartney on multitrack recording and some fine performances of several of his songs. The DVD is filled with live performances, including seven songs from *Rockshow,* four from *Unplugged,* and McCartney's entire set at the 2004 Glastonbury festival. Extras on the DVD include McCartney's solo performance of "Let It Be" at *Live Aid* (complete with malfunctioning microphone), and he and his band performing at halftime during Super Bowl XXXIX. All in all, a great package loaded with 6 hours and 25 minutes of goodies.

Ecce Cor Meum
Released February 4, 2008

This is a film of the London premiere of Paul McCartney's best classical composition. The DVD also includes a 50-minute documentary of behind-the-scenes footage and insights from McCartney about the work.

The Love We Make
Released November 28, 2011

This black and white film directed by Albert Maysles chronicles McCartney's travels as he makes his way around New York City not long after 9/11. It shows him hobnobbing with people on the street and also planning and preparing for the Concert for New York City, a star-studded extravaganza, which McCartney organized. There are some uncomfortable moments, to be sure, as McCartney seems to realize at one point that he is making himself too visible, and therefore, too vulnerable. At that point, he asks his driver to take him away. The best parts of this film are the performances, especially the nuanced and moving version of Paul Simon's "America" that David Bowie delivers.

Live Kisses
Released November 12, 2012

This is a film of the live in-studio concert McCartney did to promote his *Kisses on the Bottom* album of American standards. It includes 13 songs from the album, all performed live with Diana Krall at the piano and a cast of talented musicians. The album package has lots of extras besides the concert, including several versions of the video of "My Valentine," starring Johnny Depp and Natalie Portman, scenes from the album photo shoot, and an interview with McCartney and album producer Tommy LiPuma. A 40-page book filled with photos comes with the package as well. But the concert is the real draw. McCartney seems relaxed and gives the proper love and attention to some of the best songs ever written and recorded.

Afterword

The long journey from the germ of the idea to finishing this book was filled with surprises, twists and turns. I knew my subject well enough and was pretty sure I had a good handle on how to write this book and what should go into it.

The project that lay before me was daunting. The sheer volume of material—B-sides, digital downloads, bonus tracks—sometimes made me feel like I'd never make a dent in it. Sure enough, right about the time when I should have been wrapping this book up, McCartney released *Egypt Station.* Just as I was finishing writing about that album, he announced the forthcoming release of *Wild Life* and *Red Rose Speedway* in their new archival incarnations.

When I told a close friend that I was writing a complete discography of Paul McCartney's solo career, he said "I hope you don't run out of synonyms for 'mediocre.'" This friend is a long-time Beatles fan, but not so much a McCartney fan. He believes McCartney's tendency to control ruined the Beatles and really doesn't care for much of their post–*Revolver* music, which he regards as McCartney-dominated.

Still, I knew what he was saying. And there *is* a lot of mediocrity in the McCartney solo catalog. But how could there not be? The man's written just shy of 600 songs, not including the 193 songs he co-wrote during his time as a Beatle.

I can think of so few albums by rock and pop stars that have great songs from beginning to end. Even the best bands and solo artists record and release songs that are really bad. The difference with McCartney is the gulf is much wider between his best songs and his worst ones.

I was too young to have been a fan of the Beatles when they were together from 1962 to 1970. It was only after they broke up that I discovered their music. Consequently, I became huge fans of each ex–Beatle as solo artists and bought all their records and followed their careers as best as a boy could in those pre-internet days.

To my way of thinking they could do no wrong. I enthused over Ringo's new single, and George's *Extra Texture* album. I even tried to find something good to say about John's *Sometime in New York City.* Even more incredibly, I once wrote a review of McCartney's *Pipes of Peace* for a local newspaper that fairly gushed about how great that album was. It's not. The fact is, I was an intractable fan. I could find nothing wrong emanating from the ex–Beatle product machine.

Age, perspective and some accumulated wisdom (I hope) have proven the folly of my unconditional adoration. Lennon's first two albums are stellar, but the rest of his solo catalogue is pretty forgettable. Starr's music is of so little consequence (and gets such limited airing) that it's hard to take him seriously as an artist (although he is still a fabulous drummer). Harrison's first and final two solo albums are top-notch, but his music from 1972–85 is virtually unlistenable.

That leaves us with Paul McCartney. He, too, has made some regrettable music, but in his 50 years as a solo artist, he has made a lot of timeless, unforgettable music that people still love today. Perhaps Lennon and Harrison, if they hadn't died so early, would have gone on to do the same thing. Somehow, I doubt it. Simply put, McCartney knows how to put together a melody that sticks in your head better than anyone in the past 100 years.

I'm tempted to posit that without the juggernaut Beatles launching pad, Lennon, McCartney, Harrison and Starr would not have had successful solo careers, but I think that's wrong. All were supremely talented and would have found a path to success somehow. In some ways, McCartney's solo career has surpassed his career as a Beatle, certainly in terms of longevity, but also in terms of success.

How do we decide what sounds good? Musical tastes are subjective and difficult to pin down. This became even clearer to me as I listened to McCartney's classical albums, something I've only ever done once before. Not trained to recognize what gives classical music its unique qualities, I was nevertheless able to decide what sounded good to my ear and what didn't. In the case of McCartney's classical music, there was no tricky science involved in assessing it.

I really enjoyed the time I spent revisiting the Wings albums and singles, as they are especially evocative of a certain time in my life. In preparation for revisiting the Wings catalogue, I asked each of my four siblings to listen to two Wings albums (I actually assigned them two each), take some notes and report back to me their visceral reactions to the music.

I was not surprised to learn that each of my siblings liked what they had originally liked when the albums were new.

For the most part, the solo albums—that is, those albums made before and after the Wings era—were suffused with all the things that made Beatles songs so memorable: Great melodies, carefully recorded lead and backing vocals, and top-notch musicianship. Still, other than McCartney's 1970s albums, and a few 1980s hits, he has not scored a lot of chart success in terms of hit songs. You're still more likely to hear "Let 'Em In" on the radio today than you are "From a Lover to a Friend." Of course, a lot of that has to do with how we receive our music today.

I had not previously spent a lot of time listening to the three albums McCartney made as The Fireman, *Twin Freaks* or *Liverpool Sound Collage*. These were revelatory, and often as I was listening to them I marveled over how the man who had composed some of the most beautiful music ever could wander so far afield from his wheelhouse style. That he could pull this off with aplomb and taste is another thing that makes Paul McCartney a genius.

The Oxford Dictionary defines genius as "exceptional intellectual or creative power or other natural ability." This truncated definition certainly fits McCartney. But it also assumes that genius is natural, and not something that can be learned.

As is well known, McCartney grew up in a home with lots of music. His dad fronted a traditional jazz band, and the family weekend get-togethers around the upright piano would yield many beery renditions of the contents of the great American songbook. Surely, McCartney plugged into this at an early age and started learning about melody and chords. And what sounded good to his ear. For a man who has claimed that he wrote "When I'm Sixty Four" when he was 16 (at his father's piano), we have to assume that natural talent (the genius part of this equation) and the informal musical schooling he received combined to situate him above the crowd in terms of innate musical ability.

Now, of course, McCartney has earned just about every accolade that could be conferred upon a rock artist. A two-time inductee into the Rock and Roll Hall of Fame (as a Beatle and a solo artist), he's won 18 Grammys and one Academy Award, he's been knighted by Queen Elizabeth, he has been the recipient of the coveted Gershwin Award for his contributions to popular music, he's got an attic full of honorary doctorate degrees from some of the world's finest universities, and he probably still has that little MBE (Most Excellent Order of the British Empire) award that he and his fellow bandmates received, amid much outcry, way back in June 1965.

As he has aged, he seems to have attempted to close the unseen gap between Paul McCartney the international mega-superstar and the regular Joe he purports to aspire to be. He's a frequent guest on the late-night talk show circuit, regularly appearing in silly sketches, and he almost invariably brings someone from the audience up on stage at his concerts, something he would never have done even 20 years ago. He and his band often play unannounced intimate concerts in venues so cozy that the people in the front row can almost touch him. He's embraced social media and uses it smartly, carefully avoiding the embarrassing public gaffes that so many celebrities with a Twitter account have inflicted upon themselves (and their careers). He's been a leading curator of the Beatles catalogue and his own, most of which sells like hotcakes even at this late date. But most important of all, he's a leading and high-profile ambassador for world peace, vegetarianism, animal rights and sensible gun laws, among many other things. He's used his celebrity wisely and productively, and that's a big reason he's so universally loved.

So what if *Pipes of Peace* is not a good album (despite what I wrote about it back in the day)? Paul McCartney has given the world so much joy and happiness that today he seems almost universally loved and respected. I hope this book played a role in helping to understand why Paul McCartney still matters, and why he always will.

Appendix 1: Albums in Order of Release

The Family Way 1967
McCartney 1970
Ram 1971
Wings Wild Life 1971
Red Rose Speedway 1973
Band on the Run 1973
Venus and Mars 1975
Wings at the Speed of Sound 1976
Wings Over America 1976
Thrillington 1977
London Town 1978
Wings Greatest 1978
Back to the Egg 1979
McCartney II 1980
Tug of War 1982
Pipes of Peace 1983
Give My Regards to Broad Street 1984
Press to Play 1986
All the Best 1987
Choba B CCCP 1988
Flowers in the Dirt 1989
Tripping the Live Fantastic 1990
Tripping the Live Fantastic Highlights 1990
Unplugged: The Official Bootleg 1991
Liverpool Oratorio 1991
Off the Ground 1993
Paul Is Live 1993
Strawberries Oceans Ships Forest (The Fireman) 1993
Flaming Pie 1997
Standing Stone 1997
Rushes (The Fireman) 1998
Run Devil Run 1999
Working Classical 1999
Liverpool Sound Collage 2000
Wingspan: Hits and History 2001
Driving Rain 2001
Back in the U.S. 2002
Back in the World 2003
Twin Freaks (with Freelance Hellraiser) 2005
Chaos and Creation in the Backyard 2005
Ecce Cor Meum 2006
Memory Almost Full 2007
Electric Arguments (The Fireman) 2008
Good Evening New York City 2009
Ocean's Kingdom 2011
Kisses on the Bottom 2012
NEW 2013
Pure McCartney 2016
Egypt Station 2018
Amoeba Gig 2019

Appendix 2: Other Non–Solo Album Live Recordings

Concerts for the People of Kampuchea
Released March 30, 1981
Atlantic Records
Produced by Chris Thomas

The Concerts for the People of Kampuchea was a series of benefit concerts organized by Paul McCartney and then–Secretary General of the United Nations Kurt Waldheim to benefit the people of Kampuchea (Cambodia), who were suffering under the tyrannical leadership of Pol Pot.

McCartney and the *Back to the Egg* configuration of Wings performed "Got to Get You Into My Life," "Every Night" and "Coming Up" and then the Rockestra lineup, along with Wings, performed "Lucile," "Let It Be" and "Rockestra Theme." The concerts were held over four days at the end of December 1979 at London's Hammersmith Odeon.

McCartney's performance is spirited but ragged around the edges. His voice sounds like someone who indulges in too many scotches and cigarettes, especially on "Let It Be." A film of highlights from the show was released in August 1980.

All the Very Best Live—The Best of The Prince's Trust Concerts
Released in 1993 in the U.K. and Europe
Star Direct Limited

This is a compilation album of 49 tracks taken from several years of the Prince's Trust concerts, a charitable organization led by Prince Charles to help disadvantaged kids leaving care facilities to stabilize their lives. The cream of British rock royalty usually participates in the Prince's Trust concerts, and Paul McCartney made an appearance. He performed three songs ("I Saw Her Standing There," "Long Tall Sally" and "Get Back") at Wembley Stadium on June 20, 1986. What's most significant about his performance is that it reignited this desire to play live, something that he hadn't done since 1979. Although it would be another three years before he would take his band out on tour, McCartney has cited the 1986 Prince's Trust concert as the event that inspired him to decide to perform live again.

Music for Monserrat
Released January 9, 1998
Image Entertainment
Produced by George Martin

This is a concert by several rock 'n' roll superstars to benefit the island of Monserrat after it was partially destroyed by a volcanic eruption in early 1997. Monserrat is the island on which George Martin built his AIR Studios, and many of the artists who performed in this concert had recorded there in the past. McCartney performed "Yesterday," "Golden Slumbers/Carry That Weight/The End," "Hey Jude" and "Kansas City," ably backed by an all-star band that included Eric Clapton, Elton John, Phil Collins, Sting, Mark Knopfler and Carl Perkins, among others.

Concert for George
Released November 17, 2003
Warner Bros.
Produced by Jeff Lynne

The *Concert for George* was held at the Royal Albert Hall on November 29, 2002. It featured the usual musical friends of Harrison's, including Jeff Lynne, Eric Clapton, Tom Petty, Ringo Starr, Jim Keltner, Billy Preston and Ravi Shankar. Harrison's son, Dhani, is also prominently involved. McCartney sang four Harrison songs ("For You Blue," "Something," "All Things Must Pass" and "While My Guitar Gently Weeps," on which he sang harmony vocals to Clapton's lead vocals and played piano). The emotion in McCartney's voice as he introduces "Something" is clearly evident and provides just the right amount of drama to the proceedings.

Others

McCartney performed "Coming Up" and "Hey Jude" on *Knebworth: The Album* in 1990; performances of "All You Need Is Love" and "Hey

Jude" from a concert to celebrate Queen Elizabeth's Golden Jubilee appeared on the album *Party at the Palace* in 2002; and a performance of "Helter Skelter" was included on the 2012 album *12-12-12: The Concert for Sandy Relief.*

Appendix 3: Songs for Others

Let's Love
Appears on Peggy Lee's album of the same name released in 1974 on Atlantic Records

See discussion about this song written by Paul and Linda McCartney in the section on *Venus and Mars.*

Six O'clock
Appears on the 1973 Ringo Starr album *Ringo*

Paul and Linda McCartney wrote this catchy song and contributed very distinctive backing vocals. This appeared on Starr's very successful first ever solo pop album.

Mine for Me
Appears on Rod Stewart's 1974 album *Smiler* on Mercury Records

Paul and Linda McCartney wrote this one for their buddy Rod Stewart, who does his raspy best to deliver a soulful version of what essentially is a slow guitar ballad.

Pure Gold
Appears on Ringo Starr's 1976 solo album *Ringo's Rotogravure*

A beautiful piece from McCartney's song-writing treasure trove. Fully aware of his former bandmate's limited vocal range, he limits the intervals between notes in the melody and Ringo nails it. Paul and Linda McCartney recorded the backing track and added some very subtle backing vocals to this underrated piece of pure pop gold.

Appendix 3

All Those Years Ago
Appears on George Harrison's 1981 album *Somewhere in England*

An oddly uninspiring tribute song to John Lennon, who was murdered in December 1980. The McCartneys and Denny Laine added Wings-like backing vocals to the track. Ringo is on it, too.

Private Property
Attention
Both songs appeared on Ringo Starr's 1981 album *Stop and Smell the Roses*

"Private Property" is a driving rock song, with wailing saxes, bouncy piano and a hot little guitar solo, but because of the lyrics it's dated and inappropriate. People can't be private property. "Attention" sounds a lot more like a song Wings would have recorded, but there are too many tricky vocal intervals and Starr goes flat more than once during the song.

On the Wings of a Nightingale
Appears on the Everly Brothers' 1984 album *EB 84* on Mercury Records

McCartney, who grew up idolizing the Everly Brothers, wrote this great song with them in mind. It has all the conventions of a good Everlys song: chiming acoustic guitars, close harmonies, and rat-a-tat drums. The song did fairly well in three Billboard chart categories: number 50 in the Hot 100, number 49 in Hot Country Singles and number 9 on the Hot Adult Contemporary Singles chart. It was their most successful single since 1970 and was their last release to appear in Billboard's Top 100 chart.

If I Take You Home Tonight
Appears on Diana Krall's 2015 album *Wallflowers* on Verve Records

Originally, McCartney recorded a version of this song for inclusion on the *Kisses on the Bottom* album, but it didn't make the final cut. Krall, who played piano on that album, asked McCartney if she could record it for her next project. This is a beautifully haunting song played on the piano in a minor key, with many McCartney hallmarks in place, such as a lovely melody and a gripping string arrangement.

Songbird in a Cage
Appears on Charlotte Gainsbourg's 2017 album *Rest* on Because Music Records

Written by McCartney around 2007, he gifted this odd song to Gainsbourg, a British and French actress and indie singer. It's a rather spacey affair, with lots of instrumental and vocal effects. McCartney played piano and bass on it.

Appendix 4: Collaborations

With Steve Miller

My Dark Hour: McCartney sang backing vocals and played bass and drums on this song from Miller's 1970 album *Brave New World.*

With Carly Simon

Night Owl: Paul and Linda McCartney sang backing vocals on this James Taylor-penned song from Simon's 1972 album *No Secrets.*

With James Taylor

Rock and Roll Is Music Now: Paul and Linda McCartney provided backing vocals on this song from Taylor's 1974 album *Walking Man.*

With Mike McGear and the Scaffold

McCartney made many vocal and instrumental contributions to his brother's solo album *McGear* (1974) and McGear's band the Scaffold's 1975 album *Sold Out.*

With Denny Laine

McCartney made numerous vocal and instrumental contributions to Laine's *Holly Days* (1977) and *Japanese Tears* (1980) albums.

With Laurence Juber

Maisie: McCartney and Wings' recording of this song, which didn't make the cut for *Back to the Egg,* was included on Juber's 1982 album *Straight Time.*

With Carl Perkins

My Old Friend: Carl Perkins wrote this beautiful tribute to his friend McCartney and asked him to sing harmony on it. The song was written on the night before Perkins flew back to the States after spending eight days with McCartney in Monserrat helping with the recording of *Tug of War*.

With Michael Jackson

The Girl Is Mine: This piece of guileless smarm actually went to No. 2 on the Billboard charts in 1982. Many weren't sure McCartney could bounce back from this at the time.

With Johnny Cash

New Moon Over Jamaica: A piece of waltzy country music written by McCartney while visiting Johnny and June Cash at their house in Jamaica. It was recorded in 1988. McCartney plays bass and sings harmony.

With Elvis Costello

Veronica: A very catchy tune that is stylistic almost exactly like "My Brave Face." Lots of words fit into a very small space musical place. So like Costello. McCartney co-wrote the song and plays bass. It was released in 1989.

With Smokin' Mojo Filters

Come Together: McCartney appeared on this benefit album on the track "Come Together," along with Paul Weller and Noel Gallagher, among others. It's from a 1995 album called *Help*.

With Lindsay Pagano

So Bad: McCartney lends his voice to Pagano's version of "So Bad," included on her 2001 album *Love & Faith & Inspiration*.

With Lulu

Inside Thing (Let 'Em In): A weird mash-up of "Let 'Em In" with "Inside Thing," which appeared on Lulu's 2002 album *Together*, an LP of duets with a-list pop stars and C-list wannabes. She sings her song over the original basic track of "Let 'Em In," with a few new vocal interjections from McCartney.

With Dave Stewart

Whole Life: Written by McCartney and Stewart, this track was most likely recorded during the *Memory Almost Full* sessions as part of Nelson Mandela's AIDS awareness campaign. The song appeared on the charity album *One Year on 46664* in 2003.

With Brian Wilson

A Friend Like You: A plaintive ode to friendship, delivered by arguably the two greatest songwriters of the 20th century. This was released in 2004.

With Rusty Anderson

Hurt Myself: McCartney supplied backing vocals, electric guitar and bass on this song from his current bandmate's 2005 album *Undressing Underwater.*

With George Michael

Heal the Pain: A simple acoustic guitar-based song with a faux calypso beat. It was originally recorded and released in 1999, but Michael re-recorded a new version with McCartney in 2005. That version ended up on Michaels' greatest hits album *Twenty-Five,* released the following year.

With Tony Bennett

The Very Thought of You: A great rendering of this American standard, with Bennett and McCartney swapping lines. This song ended up on Bennett's *Duets* album in 2006, and neatly presaged McCartney's own "Kisses on the Bottom."

With George Benson and Al Jarreau

Bring It on Home to Me: A very spirited jazzy version of this R&B classic written by Sam Cooke in 1962. It sounds like everyone was having great fun in the studio. It evolves into a stomping gospel shout-out at the end. This was released by frequent collaborators Jarreau and Benson in 2006. McCartney adds an inspired lead vocal.

With Nitin Sawhney

My Soul: A collaboration with the British Indian multi-instrumentalist and mix master Nitin Sawhney, this song is simple and beautiful. The lyrics are much more reflective than McCartney is usually comfortable with. It was released in 2008.

With Ringo Starr

La De Da: McCartney plays bass and adds backing vocals on this song from Starr's 1998 album *Vertical Man.*

Walk with You: McCartney adds a second lead vocal to Starr's on this touching song about the durability of friendship. Appeared on Starr's 2010 album *Y Not.*

We're on the Road Again: McCartney plays bass and adds backing vocals on this song from Starr's 2017 album *Give More Love.*

Show Me the Way: McCartney plays bass on this song from *Give More Love.*

With Yusuf Islam

Boots and Sand: McCartney provided backing vocals to this 2009 song written by the artist formerly known as Cat Stevens.

With Dave Grohl, Krist Novoselic and Pat Smear

Cut Me Some Slack: McCartney gets his "Helter Skelter" on with the surviving members of Nirvana. He also plays a cigar box guitar on the track. This song appeared in Grohl's film *Sound City* in 2012. Any notion that McCartney could no longer muster the requisite hard rock vocals he'd perfected decades earlier fly out the window with one listen to this mostly improvised song.

The Justice Collective

He Ain't Heavy, He's My Brother: Paul McCartney contributed lead guitar and vocals to this remake of a Hollies song to benefit charities associated with the so-called Hillsborough disaster, in which 96 fatalities and 766 injuries occurred during a crowd crush at a soccer game in Sheffield in April 1989. Dozens of English musicians and singers chipped in, and it went to number one in the British charts at Christmastime 2012. While certainly well-intentioned, the song is marred by some Whitney Houston-esque oversinging.

With the Bloody Beetroots and Youth

Out of Sight: The Italian electronic dance group sampled snippets of "Nothing Too Much Out of Sight" off The Fireman's *Electric Arguments* album and darkened it up considerably. McCartney appears in the video of this song, which was released in 2013.

With Kanye West

Only One: This lovely ballad had McCartney's voice—significantly altered—in spots. Apparently, all you need to do to get a writing or performance credit on a Kanye song is just show up for the recording session. It was released on the last day of 2014.

All Day: This tough and profane hip hop song samples a bit of McCartney's unreleased "When the Wind Is Blowing," recorded in New York in October 1970 (see entry for the expanded *Wild Life*). McCartney also adds some vocals. This was released in 2015.

With Kanye West and Rihanna

FourFiveSeconds: This is a great tuneful song built around a common chord sequence played by McCartney on acoustic guitar. He thought so much of this song that he added it to his tour set list in 2015, the year it was released.

Hollywood Vampires

Come and Get It: The debut album by Alice Cooper, Johnny Depp and Joe Perry (the Hollywood Vampires) contains a cover version of "Come and Get It" with vocals by McCartney and Cooper.

Odds and Ends

Twice, McCartney has contributed songs to Elvis Presley projects. In 1991, he recorded "It's Now or Never" for the soundtrack to the film *The Last Temptation of Elvis*. In 2002, he contributed his version of "All Shook Up" for a tribute album called *A Tribute to the King*.

He contributed a cover of "I'm Partial to Your Abracadabra" for the Ian Dury tribute album *Brand News Boots and Panties* in 2001. In addition, McCartney contributed a raucous rendition of Buddy Holly's "Maybe Baby" to the soundtrack of a bad movie of the same name in 2000. In 2001, he contributed the title song to the Tom Cruise movie *Vanilla Sky*, which was nominated for an Oscar for best song. McCartney contributed a remake of Fats Domino's "I Want to Walk You Home" to the album *Going Home: A Tribute to Fats Domino* in 2007.

Bibliography and Suggested Reading

The albums that have so far been released as parts of the *Paul McCartney Archive Collection* contain valuable information that the author accessed throughout the writing of this book, mostly via the information in the elaborate tabletop books that come with each archived release. *McCartney, Ram, Wild Life, Red Rose Speedway, Band on the Run, Venus and Mars, Wings at the Speed of Sound, Wings Over America, McCartney II, Tug of War* and *Pipes of Peace* are all part of the collection so far, and it is expected that the rest will follow over time. In addition, the concert programs from McCartney's 1989–90, 1993, 2002 and 2004–05 tours contained a treasure trove of good information.

Books

Blaney, John. *Paul McCartney: The Songs He Was Singing.* Great Britain: Paper Jukebox, 2003.
Carlin, Peter Ames. *Paul McCartney: A Life.* New York: Touchstone, 2009.
Doyle, Tom. *Man on the Run: Paul McCartney in the 1970s.* New York: Ballantine, 2013.
Du Noyer, Paul. *Conversations with McCartney.* Great Britain: Hodder & Stoughton, 2015.
Each One Believing: Paul McCartney On Stage, Off Stage, and Backstage. San Francisco: Chronicle, 2004.
Gambaccini, Paul. *The McCartney Interviews: After the Break-up.* London: Omnibus, 1976.
Harry, Bill. *The Paul McCartney Encyclopedia.* London: Virgin, 2002.
Jasper, Tony. *Paul McCartney and Wings.* United States: Chartwell, 1977.
Lewisohn, Mark, ed. *Wingspan: Paul McCartney's Band on the Run.* London: Little, Brown, 2002.
McGee, Garry. *Band on the Run: A History of Paul McCartney and Wings.* New York: Taylor Trade, 2003.
Norman, Philip. *Paul McCartney: The Life.* New York: Little, Brown, 2016.
Peel, Ian. *The Unknown Paul McCartney: McCartney and the Avant-Garde.* London: Reynolds & Hearn, 2002.

Salewicz, Chris. *The Legend, The Man, McCartney.* New York: St. Martin's, 1986.
Sandford, Christopher. *McCartney.* New York: Carroll & Graf, 2006.
Welch, Chris. *Paul McCartney: The Definitive Biography.* New York: Proteus, 1984.

Magazines and Periodicals

Billboard Magazine
Club Sandwich (now defunct)
Fame (now defunct)
GQ
Guitar Player
MOJO
Musician
New Musical Express (NME)
Q
Rolling Stone
Uncut

Websites

allmusic.com
discogs.com
paulmccartney.com
rollingstone.com
themaccareport.com
the-paulmccartney-project.com
youtube.com/user/PAULMCCARTNEY

Index

Index